On Giving Advice To God

Devotions on the Wisdom of God and the Foolishness of Man

Part 1

DANIEL M. DEUTSCHLANDER

Art Director: Karen Knutson
Design Team: Diane Cook, Pamela Dunn

All Scripture quotations, unless otherwise indicated, are taken from the Holy Bible, New International Version®. NIV®. Copyright © 1973, 1978, 1984, 2011 by Biblica, Inc.™ Used by permission of Zondervan. All rights reserved worldwide. www.zondervan.com.

The "NIV" and "New International Version" are trademarks registered in the United States Patent and Trademark Office by Biblica, Inc.™

All hymns, unless otherwise indicated, are taken from *Christian Worship: A Lutheran Hymnal.* © 1993 by Northwestern Publishing House.

Scripture quotations marked "ESV" are taken from *ESV® Bible (The Holy Bible, English Standard Version®).* Copyright © 2001 by Crossway, a publishing ministry of Good News Publishers. Used by permission. All rights reserved.

All rights reserved. This publication may not be copied, photocopied, reproduced, translated, or converted to any electronic or machine-readable form in whole or in part except for brief quotations, without prior written approval from the publisher.

Northwestern Publishing House
1250 N. 113th St., Milwaukee, WI 53226-3284
www.nph.net
© 2017 Northwestern Publishing House
Published 2017
Printed in the United States of America
ISBN 978-0-8100-2874-6
ISBN 978-0-8100-2875-3 (e-book)

Preface

Already in the Garden of Eden, we see man's desire to know everything better than God does and the resulting need to give God advice. Satan tells Eve that she will become more God-like if she sins. He says, in effect, that God obviously has made a mistake and that perhaps it was even out of malice on his part. And so, Eve and her husband are only too happy to fix things by taking matters into their own hands: they sin and by implication, their advice to God is that he should accept their sin as an improvement on his own will and design.

And so begins the centuries-long and universal arrogance and foolishness of all their children, who imagine that God rarely gets things right. Luther once remarked that all the world thinks that God is the poorest and most dull-witted student there ever was. If he would just listen to us, then all would be well.

St. Paul, perhaps with tongue in cheek and a smirk on his face, takes this universal desire into account when he tells us that he too knows how to talk such foolishness (2 Corinthians 11). Some of the members of the congregation in Corinth, a congregation he had founded, looked down on the lowly apostle. They were more impressed with the superfine, outwardly more impressive pseudo-apostles who were misleading them. So Paul takes the matter in hand and speaks with the folly that they seem to like, the folly of following appearances instead of the will and Word of God.

In this work we will follow the example of St. Paul. We will boldly—no, foolishly—take in hand sections of the Bible and suggest to God how he could improve them. We will let him know how he could have behaved more wisely than he did, especially in the work of Jesus. Had God only asked us—if he had just been willing to be instructed by us—then everything in Jesus' life and in his Word in general would all have worked out so much better!

Then having given God our best advice, like Paul, we will take a closer look at what God says and what Jesus did. And lo and behold—maybe, just maybe—we will discover that God had it right all along. Indeed, had he followed our advice, everything would have been ruined; our salvation would have been lost; the vision of God in grace and glory would have been changed into a horrible raining down of death and destruction and eternal torment for us.

At the end of it all, we may learn a little better what it means when twice the Bible declares that "the fear of the LORD is the beginning of wisdom" (Psalm 111:10; Proverbs 9:10). Then just maybe we will see again that the beginning of such wisdom is in the prayer of all pious sons of the church: "Speak, LORD, for your servant is listening" (1 Samuel 3:9). It is in the sigh of all her devout daughters: "Behold, I am the servant of the Lord; let it be to me according to your word" (Luke 1:38 ESV). If we could just learn to listen to him and to take him at his Word, then maybe, just maybe, we would not be quite so quick to judge God and call him to account when things in our own lives do not go the way we think they should. Maybe, just maybe, we would get a little bit further down the road of rejoicing in all that he has become for us in the work of his Son—yes, even when he seems for a time to hide his kindness behind a cloud. For it is still true, that beautiful summary statement made about Jesus in the gospel of Mark: "People were overwhelmed with amazement. 'He has done everything well. . . . He even makes the deaf hear and the mute speak' " (7:37). People learned this and came to this conclusion only after they had suffered. They learned it only after there was no solution to their problems except to abandon themselves to the mercy and grace of Jesus. Often that too is the only way we learn to listen to him instead of being so quick to give him advice. To put it another way: How would we ever be amazed at him if he never permitted sorrow or suffering to come into our lives and then rescued us so that we might see how he turns everything to our good?

But let us not delay. What follows are devotions based on texts that the reader may know very well. But sometimes our very familiarity with a text or Bible story keeps us from being amazed at its beauty. We will look at such texts and Bible stories, imagining that we had never seen or heard them before in the hope that we may be reinvigorated by them as if it were the first time we looked. Yes, by taking another—perhaps a fresh—look at what we think we already know so well, we may regain our sense of surprise, of wonder, of awe at all that God has said and done in his Word, through Christ for us and for our salvation. Truly, it is always a surprise and astonishing, even more so the older we get and the more often we hear the story: God loved us, became man for us, gave himself for us—and in Word and sacraments still loves us, still gives himself to us, and still longs to have us with him in his glory forever.

Advent and Christmas

During Advent, Jesus prepares us for his coming. What better time than Advent for us to hear of John the Baptist, the one who proclaimed that the long-awaited time had finally come. Jesus had come. And so in these three devotions, we listen to what Jesus had to say about his own coming as had been proclaimed by John.

Three Meditations on Jesus and John the Baptist

I.

Luke 7:18-23 – John's disciples told him about all these things. Calling two of them, he sent them to the Lord to ask, "Are you the one who is to come, or should we expect someone else?" When the men came to Jesus, they said, "John the Baptist sent us to you to ask, 'Are you the one who was to come, or should we expect someone else?'" At that very time Jesus cured many who had diseases, sicknesses and evil spirits, and gave sight to many who were blind. So he replied to the messengers. "Go back and report to John what you have seen and heard. The blind receive sight, the lame walk, those who have leprosy are cleansed, the deaf hear, the dead are raised, and the good news is proclaimed to the poor. Blessed is anyone who does not stumble on account of me."

Poor John! Was ever a holy man treated as shabbily as he was? Even Jesus, in the verses following our reading, acknowledges that there has never been up until that time a man greater than John. But now he languishes in prison. And why? Because he told the truth. Because he sought the repentance of King Herod by rebuking his adultery. Yes, and even more important, John had always told the truth. He had always pointed away from himself to Jesus as the Lamb of God who was soon to begin his work: that all-important work of taking away the sin of the world—even the sin of Herod.

But still, what does John have to show for his faithfulness to the Word of God and his selfless service to his people? He has only shackles, chains, and a stinking prison. Herod listens to him from time to time but has not the least intention of repenting. Is that the reward of the faithful? Is that the wage of the holy? Is that what comes of true Advent preaching and teaching? It just doesn't seem right, does it?

In his imprisonment, John still had some limited contact with those who had been his disciples. Many of them had already gone to follow Jesus. But some held back. Some stayed with John. And now John sends these disciples to Jesus with such a sad question. Was the question one of doubt in his own mind? Or was it a question he wanted his remaining disciples to ask so that, hearing and even seeing Jesus' answer, they too would follow Jesus? Might it have been with both things in mind that he sent his question: "Are you the one who is to come?" That is, "Are you the one I myself pointed to as the promised Messiah and Savior?"

Maybe you have asked John's questions: At one moment my faith is strong and I am sure I will never fall or fail or even doubt. And then comes pain. Then comes loss. Then comes Alzheimer's disease in this loved one, cancer in another, the death of a child. Then comes a burning temptation so fast and furious that I didn't even have time to resist. What was it? Lust? Anger at someone who presumed to contradict me? Envy of someone faring better than I am and deserving it less?

And the question arises even as we prepare to celebrate his birth this Christmas: O Jesus, are you the Savior, or am I left to fend for myself—alone—in the prison of my doubts, shackled by the temptations from which I cannot find an escape? Yes, here, O Jesus, is my advice to you as well as my anguished plea: Rescue me before I perish in utter unbelief! Save me from my doubts and fears, lest I end up treating you as nothing more than a curiosity the way that Herod did. Rescue me lest, even worse, I give you no more credibility than the world gives to Santa Claus! Deliver me from John's prison cell!

Now consider Jesus' answer to the question posed by John and his two disciples. Jesus says not a word! Instead, he lets them stand there and watch as he fulfills one promise after another that God made in the Old Testament concerning the Messiah. The conclusion they are to come to and then take back to John should be inescapable and obvious: of course, this is the Savior and there is none other; we should neither want nor expect another. All of God's promises, he fulfills perfectly and to the letter.

But wait just a minute—the question still remains: If he has done all those things, couldn't he do this one other thing? Couldn't he get John out of prison? Yes, and even more important, couldn't he get me out of my cell of sorrow, my doubt, my pain? If John is so great, as Jesus will say in a moment, doesn't he deserve at least this consideration: that he be allowed to die and go to heaven in peace and with a measure of dignity? Why must he be subjected to this humiliation of imprisonment, a humiliation that will only get worse in the hour of his death? That would surely be my advice to God! Lord, show your might and your mercy to the righteous and just! Show it to me! For hasn't John and haven't I proven love and loyalty to you and to your Word often enough!

But that doesn't happen. St. Paul tells us why with such a beautiful summary of it all: *We live by faith and not by sight* (2 Corinthians 5:7). The report from John's disciples to their master reassured the greatest of the prophets, the one closest to Christmas. He could face unafraid the horrible and humiliating death that would soon be his; he could face it with courage and even with joy. And his disciples? They could weep at their teacher's disgraceful death and go on with joy to follow the One whose coming he had proclaimed. For that is the nature of faith: to cling to the promises of God even when all the evidence I can see seems to contradict those promises. And that Word itself creates and sustains such a trust that though I die a thousand deaths, his promise remains true that "in all these things we are more than conquerors through him who loved us" (Romans 8:37).

For us, as for St. John, the message of Advent will never be reduced to poinsettias and peppermint candy canes. Rather, we join John the Baptist in the day of doubt and in the hours when we stare down the abyss of despair. We join his disciples in looking for something solid, something sure. We look for the Jesus in Advent who will always keep his Word. He will never abandon his own. Yes, though we see the earth shake and the mountains fall into the sea (Psalm 46)—because he has said so in his Word—he remains faithful to his Word. For "heaven and earth will pass away," but his Word—never (Matthew 24:35)! John died before he saw the fulfillment of this promise; but see it he did. And so will we. Yes, if we think back on hours of doubt and anguish in the past, we have already seen it many times. If this time we must wait with John to the hour of death, it matters not. In heaven we will join with him in singing forever the praises of him who delivered us from our sins, our guilt, the consequences of our sins, and any future guilt. And we will sing thus to the Lamb of God to whom John pointed. And we will sing with him without a word of complaint over the things that so trouble us in the moment—we will give thanks for it all to the Lamb. For far greater is the joy and the glory awaiting us than any trouble or complaint that we might make now. St. Paul assures us, "I consider that our present sufferings are not worth comparing with the glory that will be revealed in us" (Romans 8:18).

> Even so, come, Lord Jesus! Come in the Christmas gospel! Come in every hour of anguish or doubt! Come in the hour of death and in the day of judgment! Come, O Savior of the world, my Savior. Amen.

II.

Luke 7:24-27 – After John's messengers left, Jesus began to speak to the crowd about John: "What did you go out into the wilderness to see? A reed swayed by the wind? If not, what did you go out to see? A man dressed in fine clothes? No, those who wear expensive clothes and indulge in luxury are in palaces. But what did you go out to see? A prophet? Yes, I tell you, and more than a prophet. This is the one about whom it is written: 'I will send my messenger ahead of you, who will prepare your way before you.' "

We often have occasion to note it: God marries so often, perhaps always, the high and the low; the higher the position and the greater the gifts, the more lowly the appearance and the greater the suffering. Few mirror that axiom better than John the Baptist. We have already noted his misery in prison. Still worse, humiliation awaits him in a death not of a great hero of faith but a death inspired by a bimbo and ordered by a drunk.

But listen in these verses to the great praise that Jesus has for John. However, Jesus says these things after John's disciples have left. We might be tempted here to give Jesus some advice: *Why didn't you say these things about John while his disciples were still there? Surely they would have been thrilled to hear these words about their beloved teacher and would likewise have been delighted to report them back to John.* But no, Jesus waits until they are gone. Hidden in the shrine of John's own heart is the awareness of his exalted position, a position that had been announced already before he was born. He had rejoiced in his Savior even in the womb of his mother (Luke 1:41-44). And now, in his suffering, he would cling to the joy that had been his the day he pointed his disciples to Jesus and declared, "Look, the Lamb of God, who takes away the sin of the world!" That message was the one John wanted his disciples to hear and remember, not praise about John himself. John showed it more than once: He had no interest in being praised; his all-consuming concern was to point to Jesus as the Savior, the only one really deserving of praise. So even John would not have wished his disciples to hear a message about John's greatness, lest their attention be diverted from Jesus to his forerunner (John 1:19-36; 3:22-36).

But we still need to listen to what Jesus says about John. Jesus could ask the same questions of us in church on Sunday morning that he asked of those who heard the sermons of St. John. When you went to hear John, when you came to hear your pastor, what were you looking for, hoping for, expecting? When you come to church during this Advent season, do you come for a reed blowing in the wind, for a messenger whose message changes with the latest fad? Do you come expecting the preacher to check out who is there to make sure the message floats easily over them, through their ears but past their hearts? If he sees members as self-righteous as the Pharisees, will he extol their piety as compared to the wickedness of the world? If he sees those who, like the Sadducees, are proud of how broad-minded and tolerant they can be of false doctrine and of their own sins and those of their relatives, will he praise them for being so understanding? If the poor and lowly are there, will he speak of the virtues of pious poverty? If the rich come, will he remind them that they are obviously the favored of the Lord? Or do you come expecting a fancy and entertaining preacher who certainly deserves wealth and fine clothing like those of princes among men? One who tickles our fancy, is always amusing, and never says anything that would leave us feeling bad? One who never reminds us of our total and desperate need for the Savior, never calls us to either sorrow over sin or turn away from it? If that's what you came for, or worse, if that's what you found in church, you're in the wrong place. For you have come to a reed blowing in the wind.

May it be that you come in Advent and find one who is a voice crying in the wilderness of our world. For truly our world is a wilderness. It is dead to shame. It boasts of its own imagined—but vain and empty—wisdom, while mocking both the fresh and life-giving truth of God's Word and the Savior who comes to us in that Word. In that wilderness, may you have a pastor like John the Baptist; may he with his preaching of the law pick the scabs off of your soul and open your heart to the truth of your desperate, oh, so desperate need for a Savior. May he hold you before the mirror of the law, so that you cry out with the tax collector in the temple, *God, be merciful to me, a sinner!* (Luke 18:13).

And then in that wilderness, may you find in your pastor one with the healing message of life and joy in Christ. May your pastor pour the oil of gladness into the mortal wounds in your conscience with this declaration: Behold the Lamb of God who takes away the sin of the world. The declaration may be from one as simple in appearance as John. It may be from one as obviously without eloquence like John, whose message was repeated over and over again in the simplest of terms: Repent! The axe is at the tree, and whoever does not bear fruit will be cut down and thrown into the fire (Matthew 3:10). Repent and believe the gospel of the Lamb who has come to redeem you by his sacrifice on that gruesome altar of the cross.

If you come to church and find one like John—not so glorious in appearance, not interested in flattering you or appealing to the mood of the moment—then give thanks to God for his gift of grace through the one he has sent to help you prepare for Christmas. Yes, and do all that you can to encourage and help such a pastor. For without pastors like John, the world (and we with it) will perish in the wilderness of unbelief. We will perish wallowing in filth, too surrounded and covered by it to recognize its horror.

That's what—in every age—follows the rejection of John's saving message about the Savior. That's what happened in Israel. That's what has happened in one place after another where the law was ignored and the gospel treated like a cheap cloak to cover up sins for which there was no repentance. God always takes his Word seriously, whether we do or not.

So then, let's get ready for Christmas! Let us hear the voice of John the Baptist crying out from amid all that is shiny and beautiful in this season but that is meaningless wilderness—dead as dust—without the vision of the Lamb of God coming in the manger. The decorated tree points us to the tree that one day will bear him. Its green reminds us of the life he brings by his coming. All of the decorations point us to the real decoration: a heart and soul that has cried out for pardon and then received the perfect and everlasting covering of pardon and peace from the Savior, who comes still and ever in his gospel.

> Even so, Lord Jesus, out of the abundance of your grace and mercy, look on us with pity, and send us faithful pastors and teachers who point us always to you. Bring us to a grateful appreciation for these your servants and to words and actions that support them in their all-important work of calling us to repentance and then pointing us to you, our God and only Savior. Amen.

III.

Luke 7:28 – "I tell you, among those born of women there is no one greater than John; yet the one who is least in the kingdom of God is greater than he."

Now here is surely an amazing thing! Jesus says that the least in the kingdom of God is greater than the greatest one born of women from the time of Adam and Eve to the time of Jesus' speaking. We have to ask: Who, then, is the least in the kingdom of God and thus greater than John the Baptist? Is it you? Is it me? Is it anyone we might know?

If we just focused on who is least, it wouldn't be so difficult to answer the question. Yes, I can see that you might be the least. You are not as famous as an apostle or prophet. I know some of your faults and have never understood how you could have them; they all seem so obviously foolish and easy enough to overcome. Why haven't you done that? To be sure, it's not difficult for me to see you as the least. But greater than John the Baptist? Could you be the least and at the same time greater than John the Baptist? That's a stretch indeed!

Or on further reflection, yes, I can see myself as the least—the least even compared to you and what I know about you. For I know myself much better. I have heard the call of John and repented. Oh, how often I have repented! Yes, and sometimes with tears—tears at least in my heart, if not in my eyes for all to see. But look at me now! I'm still a sinner. Have I learned nothing? Am I really so cold, so ungrateful for past pardon? Does the sight of the Lamb on the cross leave me with nothing but empty promises to improve, promises that too often have taken less time to disappear than they took to make? Look! One vice and temptation disappears only to be replaced by another. I used to be too passionate. Now I'm too cold. I used to be too eager for advancement. Now I resent the ones who got ahead of me, sometimes with less effort and less merit than I think I have. I used to . . . and now . . . The list could just go on and on. No, you are not the least in the kingdom; I am! But does that very unworthiness make me greater than John?

But wait! There is still one even less than you are and less than I am. Luther, perhaps with a smile on his face, suggests it: Who is least and then greatest? Why, it's Jesus! Don't you see him in the manger? He is stripped of all outward glory. He is poor compared to the poor. And then there's this: On the cross God will forsake him—oh, horror beyond horror! Who could sink lower than that? God never has forsaken you. He has never forsaken me either. But God will look at him and see all of my sin and shame—all of yours too (2 Corinthians 5:21). Yes, viewed from the manger to the cross, he is indeed least! In fact, that's what he even claimed for himself when he said that he came not to be served but to serve and give his life for our ransom (Mark 10:45).

And at the same time—and who would dare argue the point?—he is the greatest in the kingdom. He is the kingdom's all in all. He has the name above ever other, given him by God the Father as a reward for his becoming the least. For he and he alone has the name "Jesus," "Savior" (Philippians 2:9-11).

But then there is this (and in a way this is what Advent and Christmas are all about): With the recognition that it is Jesus who is both the least and the greatest, guess who gets to go along with Jesus into that category of the least and the greatest? Why, it's you! Why, it's me! For Jesus never leaves us behind. That's what makes us so full of joy at Christmas. He comes to join and be numbered with the lowliest of the low. And we get to bow low before him in worship and adoration, with thanksgiving overflowing that he did it all just for you—just for me. And then after he fulfills everything with his ultimate humiliation—with his becoming the least of the least on Good Friday—he will enter into glory on Easter Sunday with his resurrection and enthronement in heaven at his ascension. And are we left behind when he ascends into heaven? No, never that! The head has gone to be where he will one day take us, the members of his mystical body (Ephesians 1). That's what he promised. And his Word will remain forever true.

So then, there it is. Great John the Baptist proclaimed the coming of the one who was both greatest and least. Most gladly I confess it: *Because of everything in me, I too am the least. Because of everything, Lord Jesus, that you have come to win for me and give me, I too am the greatest in you, from you, and through you.*

So then, let us hear the call of John as Advent comes to a close. Let us bow low in the dust and ashes of repentance. In repentance we confess that we are indeed the least and we cry to him who became less than the least for us. And then with his manger in view, we lift up our heads in joy to him who for us became greater than the greatest and who takes us along with him into glory. All that is in us he forgives. And all that is in him he gives us in the reality that he has become the Savior-Lamb of God who takes away the sin of the world—your sin and mine too!

> Come, Jesus, come! I can hardly wait to hear again the message of the angels that you are the Savior of the world and therefore my Savior. I can hardly wait to run with the shepherds and to worship with wise men before your cradle so rude and bare. I can hardly wait to receive from you—in the Christmas gospel—the peace that the world cannot give but which God alone gives by his good pleasure and which you won for me by your forgiving work and grace. Yes, come, Jesus come! Amen.

Christmas

And here it is: the simple and sublime message of Jesus' coming. But right from the start it will not be difficult for us to suggest how God could have done it better. Indeed, through the whole account of Jesus' birth, there is one thing after another that just doesn't seem right. Consider this:

I.

Luke 2:1-3 – In those days Caesar Augustus issued a decree that a census should be taken of the entire Roman world. (This was the first census that took place while Quirinius was governor of Syria.) And everyone went to their own town to register.

Right from the start we have to say that this seems like the worst possible time for the Savior to be born. After all, just think of the turmoil that this census would cause throughout the Roman world. Everyone is packing up and moving long or short distances to their ancestral home. Everyone is upset and angry about it. Everybody is grumbling that the whole point of the census and the moving was to make sure a tax was paid. Even more than that, the unspoken point was that all should know who was in charge: it was Caesar and the Roman army that backed up his decree! What the locals might want was of no importance at all, and any resistance would be met with the pointed end of a spear.

And in Palestine this whole business would be even more disagreeable. The forced move would underscore the utter humiliation of the chosen people. They prided themselves in their heritage. But with this census, their subjugation to a heathen emperor and to his monster puppet, King Herod, would be seen as complete. Any notion that they were a free and special people would obviously be ridiculous.

And so the move begins. The roads are crowded with the jostling of rich and poor. The strong would push the weak. The "haves" would overcharge the "have-nots" for the necessities of life on the journey. And there would be thieves everywhere to take advantage whenever they could of the poor and powerless. It certainly doesn't seem like a good time for the most important event in all of human history to take place. Wouldn't it make more sense for Jesus to be born in a time of peace and quiet? Then the message of his birth could go out and people would be able to pay attention to it. But with his coming at this time, who will want to listen? Who will even be able to listen? No, it just won't do; it's the worst possible time for the birth of the Savior!

And yet, God rules over all of history—always for his own purposes and in the best interests of those he loves. There are considerations just beneath the surface that make this the best of times for the Savior's birth. There is the simple matter of Nazareth versus Bethlehem. For reasons of his own, Jesus chose to be born of a young girl living in Nazareth; but the prophet Micah (5:2) foretold that the Savior would be born in Bethlehem. Then there is the matter of Jesus' virgin birth. Mary is pregnant and engaged but not married yet. Joseph certainly was aware of the problem, both for himself and for Mary, if her pregnancy without the formal marriage ceremony would come to light. Then there is the whole larger business of mighty rulers thinking that they are in charge and really running things.

All of these problems are resolved by the Savior's birth at this time. Mary and Joseph will have to journey to Bethlehem because of the census. The matter of her pregnancy has ceased to be a problem for Joseph because of the message of the angel (Matthew 1:18-25); the general chaos of everyone moving and Joseph's care to take Mary perhaps sooner than he had planned as his wife removed the possibility of a humiliating scandal. And as for mighty Caesar, he does not at all realize that he is merely a pawn in God's great plan for our salvation. Caesar wants a census to count those subject to him for the purpose of taking a tax from them, but God, through this holy birth, wants to count us as his own. Caesar wants a tax; God wants to give us the gift of our Redeemer. Caesar wants to show everyone that he is in charge; God sits in heaven and laughs (Psalm 2) as he carries out his own plan for our eternal good.

And so the whole world is in tumult as God descends from his heavenly throne and home to the womb of the lowly virgin. And mighty Rome, horrible Herod, and thousands of people grumbling along the roads of the empire move in order that God's promise might be fulfilled. How rich in comfort that is for all of us who fear that perhaps God's promises to us might not be fulfilled because the powerful sin-filled world and my own wretched sinful flesh—yes, my own despairing conscience—obstruct his saving intent. No, that can never be! Let the devil, the whole world, and my own flesh be set in motion—be in turmoil—with their mighty running to and fro to distract and hinder and destroy. God brings his salvation. God keeps his Word. God fulfills his promise to each of his own, all unseen and unnoticed, but always true and certain. And he does it at just the right time: the time of his choosing and in circumstances altogether under his control (Galatians 4:4).

Just think of it: God ruled history in such a way that the Savior's birth would be at just the right time. What about your birth into his kingdom in the Sacrament of Baptism? He ruled over history to bring that about too! It was no accident, no mindless coincidence. It was all planned, all according to his good and gracious will and aimed at bringing you the benefit of this most holy birth in Bethlehem at just the right time!

> Lord Jesus, lift up my eyes to see the greatness of your love and grace for me in your coming. For behold, you have moved heaven and earth just to accomplish my salvation. All the raging of the foes against you—yes, even the foe inside of my own nature—could not prevent your coming, a coming just for me! To you all praise and glory be, now and in eternity! Amen.

II.

Luke 2:4-7 – Joseph also went up from the town of Nazareth in Galilee to Judea, to Bethlehem the town of David, because he belonged to the house and line of David. He went there to register with Mary, who was pledged to be married to him and was expecting a child. While they were there, the time came for the baby to be born, and she gave birth to her firstborn, a son. She wrapped him in cloths and

placed him in a manger, because there was no guest room available for them.

Does any of this seem at all right to you? From eternity to eternity, Jesus dwelt in the highest heavens. Before the world began, he lived in unity with the Father and the Holy Spirit absolutely independent, holy, and needing nothing and no one. The holy angels sang his praise endlessly. And now this? He is born of a lowly peasant girl from Nazareth, a backwater nothing of a town. And she goes to give birth in a town of no greater note. Oh, to be sure, she was descended from great King David; but so were thousands of others, and that descent had long ago become meaningless. Bethlehem had once been important as the hometown of David. But now it was just a nothing village a few miles removed from all-important Jerusalem. And as for Joseph, well, what can we say? He was just a carpenter. If God is going to become man, shouldn't it be from a woman of obvious noble birth and heritage and virtue? If he is going to have a foster father, shouldn't this father be an impressive figure of talent and wealth and power? Wouldn't that be more fitting?

And even the timing: it couldn't have been worse. Why not arrange it so that Mary is not so far along in the pregnancy? Why does she have to travel just days and hours before the birth of her child? How she must have suffered on that uncomfortable journey, even if she did have a donkey to ride—and the gospel record doesn't tell us that she did; she may have walked.

And what is this? God is born—for all practical purposes—outdoors, perhaps in a cave that is used as a barn for animals! How disgraceful! And there is no one except Joseph to assist at the birth? Couldn't just one pious man in Bethlehem be found to provide shelter for the hapless couple? Couldn't just one holy woman be on the scene to assist this young mother with the birth of her firstborn? And what of the angels? Soon we will hear of them. But they are not here, not now, not to assist with the birth, not even to sing his praises at his coming. Wouldn't their presence here have been much more useful than their appearance to shepherds? Indeed, would that not have been a great comfort, especially to Joseph, who had nothing but the appearance of an angel in a dream to assure him that this child was God's own Son?

To be sure, this child is the Son of God; God is his true Father. But doesn't a real and loving father want the best for his children? Shouldn't we expect that God the Father, who always expressed his love and his delight in this his only begotten Son (Matthew 3:17; Mark 9:7), would have provided better for his Son's birth? There should be noble attendants at the birthing. There should be soothing oils for his body and sweet incense to welcome him. But as it is, whether viewed from the standpoint of the chosen earthly parents or from the conditions of his birth, it is hard to imagine that things could have been more poorly planned and provided! Just a stable. Only a manger. Just this poor couple.

But behold! Jesus comes completely willing to empty himself of all the appearance of the almighty God that he is (Philippians 2:6-8). This is exactly what he wanted and how *he* arranged everything. He stoops to be born of a virgin. He comes into the world as the poorest of the poor. He makes his first home with smelly sheep and cattle. And that is just the beginning. Before it is all over, he will humble himself still more and more until he dies as an accursed criminal hanging on a tree.

Oh, grace and love beyond measure or compare! What if he had been born of the high and mighty, in comfort and ease in lordly castle and wrapped in silk and velvet? How could I ever imagine that he would understand me? How could I ever dream that he would want to be touched by my poverty, my shame, my sin, my disgrace? Yes, how could I ever even dream that he would welcome my embrace? But see, he embraces lowliness! He was wrapped in rags. Rags are what I wear on my best day because that is what my righteousness is: just rags (Isaiah 64:6). But wrapped in rags, I come to be wrapped by him in robes of white righteousness that he has come to give me. No incense do I bring. But he turns my prayers into sweet incense that is pleasing to his Father (Revelation 5:8). See how it is: He comes not to take but to give—to give himself to me, to one so lowly and so poor, so needy, and so like himself that first Christmas. But now in the Christmas gospel, he makes me rich and fills me up with praise and thanksgiving for his coming!

> Dearest Jesus, in your lowliness receive me in mine; in your poverty do not despise me in mine. Grant me the exaltation of being a child of your Father because of your lowliness; grant me the riches of your grace by forgiving me for the shame that I have brought on myself by my own sins. Then let me embrace you in Word and sacraments as you have embraced me in all that you have done to win my salvation. May I see you in your Word and sacraments and there find the only real glory—a glory you have earned for me by your lowly coming, by your suffering and death. Then let me imitate your humility: you gave your all to serve me in all lowliness. Grant me grace that I may learn from you how to serve those around me more and more as you have served me. Amen.

III.

Luke 2:8-12 (ESV) – In the same region there were shepherds out in the field, keeping watch over their flock by night. And an angel of the

Lord appeared to them, and the glory of the Lord shone around them, and they were filled with great fear. And the angel said to them, "Fear not, for behold, I bring you good news of great joy that will be for all the people. For unto you is born this day in the city of David a Savior, who is Christ the Lord. And this will be a sign for you: you will find a baby wrapped in swaddling cloths and lying in a manger."

Well, again, we just have to say it: It just isn't right. Oh, to be sure, the message of the Savior's birth needs to be announced. But to shepherds? They are the lowliest of the low. After all, how much intelligence and how much strength does it take to be a shepherd? But tending sheep is all these men are capable of. Shouldn't the birth of God's Son be announced in Rome, the seat of world power? Athens wouldn't be a bad choice for the proclamation; it was the seat of worldly wisdom. How about in Jerusalem, the throne city of God on earth, the city of the temple? Can't you just see it: Angels with trumpets mounted on the four corners of the temple singing a heavenly version of the "Hallelujah Chorus"! Or how about this: Have the angel choirs blasting their trumpets and singing in Rome, in Athens, and in Jerusalem all at the same time! Now that would be a fitting birth announcement for the Son of God and the Savior of the world! But to shepherds?! It just doesn't seem fitting. It just doesn't seem right.

But we have to say it again: How wonderful! How perfect! St. Paul echoes our joy when he reminds us that this is always going to be God's way: to choose the weak and the lowly as vessels of his power and glory (1 Corinthians 1:18-31). Indeed, is it not the case that when we think highly of ourselves we listen less to him? Is it not true that when we imagine ourselves better than the lowly shepherds, we lose our love and appreciation for the beauty of the gospel message of forgiveness for all and therefore also for ourselves? Do we recall the times when we were so important in our own eyes that we didn't have time to look up and listen to the joyful message of the angels: "Don't be afraid! I bring you good news! The Savior, your Savior, has come!"?

A vessel that is full wants nothing more. A vessel that is empty has no point or purpose until it is filled. And so at Christmas, no matter how precious the gifts we give or how expensive those are that we receive, we join the shepherd on the plains of Bethlehem. We have nothing. We are nothing. We merit nothing. But then comes the message: "Don't be afraid! Your nothingness matters not. Even your sins have not prevented it! Your Savior has come to you!" Now we have it all! Be grateful and enjoy the Christmas presents you get and give. Let them be reminders of the most precious gift of all and the One that makes all the others pleasant to us. Jesus has come! He has come even for me! Not life, not death, neither the past nor the future do I fear now. Oh, that I might be more like the blessed shepherds of Bethlehem! Oh, that I might join them on my knees in wonder and awe before the great message that the self-important, the wise in their own eyes, and those who consider themselves already good enough will miss! May I share with them in the fullness of this grace heaped upon grace that Jesus brings for the lowly, the guilty, and for those despairing of any virtue except that which Jesus brings as Savior!

> Lord Jesus, ever come to me, the lowliest of the low, the neediest of the needy. Come to me and take away all my fear, my self-loathing because of my sin, my poverty, and my need. Take it away by the glad tidings of the Christmas gospel proclaimed by your messengers and replace it all with boundless joy in their words: Fear not, the Savior is born! Amen.

IV.

Luke 2:13,14 – Suddenly a great company of the heavenly host appeared with the angel, praising God and saying, "Glory to God in the highest heaven, and on earth peace to those on whom his favor rests."

Now here is a wondrous and a curious thing. The angels sing! They are happy at Christmastime! Who would have thought it? Shouldn't they be sad and weeping? After all, they have known Jesus in heaven since the day of their creation. They have worshiped him and perfectly sung his praises there. Without any stain of sin or guilt, they have been able to love him perfectly and in every moment of their existence.

But look! Now this Jesus, whom they worship and adore, has come down from heaven. He has taken on a human nature. He has made himself capable of suffering and death in that nature. Even in his birth he suffers the indignity of being welcomed by no one but Mary and Joseph. He has to settle for birth in a barn! Yes, and the angels doubtless knew what kind of suffering and what kind of death he would endure. And for what? For fallen human beings who on this side of heaven will never fully grasp the depths of his humiliation. Even the best of those human beings will never succeed in loving him perfectly or always. And indeed, how few in number the best will be. Most will pass him by. Most will laugh at his Word. Most will think they have much better ways for passing their time than listening to him. And even most of those who do listen will pick and choose what they want to hear and dismiss the rest as unworthy of their attention.

But the angels are singing? Shouldn't they be crying out in protest? At the very least, shouldn't they object to having this mission of singing to these shepherds, or anyone else for that matter? Shouldn't they instead have gone to Bethlehem and sung to the holy infant if indeed they have to sing at all, given the gruesome mission that this child is on?

We pray in the Lord's Prayer, "Thy will be done on earth as it is in heaven." Nowhere is that petition seen in its fulfillment by created beings better than on Christmas Day in the joy and the song of the angels. How perfectly their will submits to the will of Jesus! He wants to redeem and save fallen mankind. The fact that fallen mankind deserves it not does not slow down the joy of the angels. If this is Jesus' will, then they can only rejoice and be glad. If Jesus chooses to suffer the humiliation of his lowly birth of the virgin and that in a barn, then they couldn't be happier; for that is his will, and his will can only be good, perfect, and filled with the glory of God on high and for us on earth.

And then listen to that song! Glory to God in the highest! And just what is God's glory in the highest? It is this: He has come down from the highest to be the lowliest. It is this: He chooses to become man while remaining fully and truly God. It is that as perfect God and perfect man he wills, he wants, and he longs for just one thing: to become and be our Savior! That's God's glory? Can you wrap your mind around it? We are so used to thinking of our own glory, a glory of our personal charm or beauty or accomplishments or virtues. But this is God's glory; he lowers himself so that he can give himself to us, for us, and for our salvation.

And that glory of God in giving brings peace on earth. No, not the peace of fools striving for dominance, not the peace for nations lusting and warring for their own advantage, not the peace of the mind-numbed drunkard or drug addict, not even the peace of the cemetery. This is the peace on earth, the only true peace possible, the only peace that matters: To us the Savior is born! God's wrath is stilled by his sacrifice. Death is conquered by his dying and rising. Hell's gaping jaws are slammed shut for those who have the peace of Christ by faith in his saving work. The devil's head is crushed, therefore, just as God promised (Genesis 3:15). And yes, it is the peace that stills even the sharpest accusations of my own conscience. For to and for me—even for me—the Savior is born! That is God's favor that rests on us and of which the angels sing. What a song that must have been! How wondrous its sound and, more important, how profound its effect. It worked faith and joy in the shepherds. It works the same in us. Yes, what a song!

What a lesson the angels teach us! In our deepest woe and on the darkest day, our will is like theirs when we join them to sing, "Glory to God in the highest!" For his will is always done. By his lowly birth, by his holy cross and passion he has saved me. By my own losses and lacks, by my own pain and sorrow, even by my remembrance of my sin and guilt, he draws me to himself; he brings me to find in him my deepest and my only lasting joy.

He teaches me to trust him when all the evidence is against it. And in it all, he does his will so that I might live forever.

> And so, Lord Jesus, your will be done on earth as it is in heaven. As the angels submit with joy and thanksgiving, so teach me also to submit and to trust that nothing could ever be better than your will because it always has your love for me at its center and my salvation as its goal. Therefore, glory to God on high and peace to those on whom his favor rests; such am I by virtue of your coming for me and for my salvation. Amen.

V.

Luke 2:15,16 – When the angels had left them and gone into heaven, the shepherds said to one another, "Let's go to Bethlehem and see this thing that has happened, which the Lord has told us about." So they hurried off and found Mary and Joseph, and the baby, who was lying in the manger.

Now is all of that really necessary? Don't the shepherds show us here how really dim they are? Wouldn't we have expected some discussion of the matter first? It could have gone something like this: "Well, what should we do now? It's the middle of the night, hardly a time to be running through fields and streets to Bethlehem. Let's wait until morning and then go to investigate. That will be time enough. Besides that, we have to decide which of us should go and who should stay with the sheep. After all, if we all go, who knows how many of them will wander off; and then we will have who knows how much work to round them all up again."

But the shepherds are no more interested in our advice on this holy night than God is. No discussion. No debate. No delay. They hasten in the middle of the night. They run as fast as they can to Bethlehem. They poke around—peering into stables and stalls, into caves and caverns—looking for a baby lying in a cattle trough and wrapped in rags. Just thinking about it makes us marvel at the faith of these lowly shepherds: a faith created and spurred on by the message of the Lord. (Did you notice that? They make reference not to angels but to the Lord who sent them!)

What great saints they are! How they put the imagined virtue and piety of most of us (most of the time) to shame! When I wake up in the morning, I may sometimes be just too busy to hasten to the manger. During the day I have such important stuff to attend to—it won't get done by itself—that there just isn't time to turn my attention to the child in the straw—he'll still be there tomorrow. And by day's end, well, I'm just too tired to attend to anything more important than the sports page and the television set. Tomorrow, later, when I'm old and retired—then I will think on these things. Maybe even on Sunday morning the enthusiasm of the shepherds sometimes flags a bit; it's too cold or too hot; I stayed up too late last night and I'm too tired; oh well, I'll go anyway, or maybe not.

But unto us a child is born; unto us a Son is given. It is the Savior, Christ the Lord. Let us hasten with the shepherds to see this wondrous thing that the Lord has made know to us.

Pastors have stood in for the angels and so too perhaps have our children in their yearly Christmas Service. They have brought glad tidings of great joy for all people, and yes, even for me. How my soul yearns and my heart longs to go and see him in his Word, in his Sacrament. Let us hasten then to our Bethlehem: to the place where he is to be found, where his Word and sacraments are. For there he is, in the company of sheep and goats and with lowly shepherds bowing low before him. There he wants to be found; it is where he has promised always to be, where his Word and sacraments are. Yes, and there he wants to find us, still wants to find us. Isn't it sad that so few found him that Christmas night so that they could be found by him in the message of the angels? Isn't it sad that so many—still after all these years—really just can't be bothered? Or worse, that at times even we find it all a bother?

But still, there he is in the manger, holding out his arms and awaiting our embrace of faith. Still, there he is, looking for the messy manger of our hearts. Still, there he is, longing not for our help but to be our helper, not so much to receive our gifts to him as to be God's gift to us for time and for eternity. There he is: our Jesus! Glory to God in the highest for the peace he is and the peace he has brought to me by his coming!

> With great joy, O Jesus, I come to adore you for the glory of God in heaven which you have now brought down to earth, even to me! Forever be for me the only glory I know, as you are my peace with God now and in eternity. Amen.

VI.

Luke 2:17,18,20 – When they had seen him, they spread the word concerning what had been told them about this child, and all who heard it were amazed at what the shepherds said to them. The shepherds returned, glorifying and praising God for all the things they had heard and seen, which were just as they had been told.

Again we have to say it: What great saints these shepherds are! They are not the least bit ashamed of what they find there in the manger. He is their Savior! That's what the Lord had told them in the message of the angels. And God does not lie or deceive. The lowliness of the God-man wrapped in rags does not cause them doubt or throw them into confusion. They simply rejoice to receive him in the Word of promise and then worship and adore him.

Note too how they show their joy and delight in the Savior who has come for them. They tell everyone they come across about the One they have seen in the manger. Again, we might be tempted to give them some advice: best you leave the telling to others; after all, you are just shepherds. No one is going to be interested in anything you have to say. And when they hear it from you—this message of God's birth in a barn—surely they will laugh at you for being so silly.

But the shepherds show no shame or hesitation. They tell everyone all about it. Even the response of the people they tell does not keep them quiet. Look at the response: People are amazed, but there is no record that anyone went to the manger to see for themselves, to receive the Christ Child for themselves, or to worship and adore him for themselves. One wonders of what their amazement consisted. Did they just marvel at the boldness of the shepherds? Did they just think the message too odd to be believed? Whatever the nature of their amazement, it did not stop the shepherds from sharing and continuing to share. Won't it be interesting to meet these shepherds in heaven and hear from them about how the rest of their lives went after the amazing events of this holy day?

Once we have heard from them in heaven how their lives went, we can share with them how our lives went because of the message concerning this holy child, which the Lord in this Christmas season has made known to us. May we say and confess it with the shepherds: I too told people about him; I told my spouse and my children; I did not keep it a secret from friends and coworkers and neighbors. I was not ashamed of the baby of Bethlehem, even though some who heard about him from me thought me a bit odd that I would still believe such things. I was not ashamed to be as silly as the shepherds seemed to the many who saw and heard them. For lowly though I am, not wise or eloquent, the message is high and holy; the message is the unerring wisdom of God that saves those who hear it and by its power, believe it.

So let the many in the world who are too high and mighty and too clever in their own eyes for this message say what they will; my joy in this holy child is too great to keep it a secret. Some—I don't know which ones—may hear it now or remember hearing it from me previously and come also to seek the holy child, their Savior. And then they too will yet find him in the manger of his Word, wrapped in the lowliness of the sacraments. It is good that heaven lasts forever; it will take that long to find all the reasons for rejoicing in him, and in the message of his coming we will rejoice with the shepherds and with those who heard of the Savior from someone like me!

Then think too what the shepherds themselves had to occupy their minds and attention for the rest of their lives. Could there be more tedious work than tending sheep? Could anything be more mind-numbing than doing the same thing over and over again, day in and day out, year after year? And for what? Crummy wages, smelly clothes, no appreciation, and even less respect! But then they could look up into the sky and see in their mind's eye again the angelic host. Over the racket made by the sheep, they could still hear the song of the angels. In the midst of whatever humdrum their lives had become, there was still this: They found Mary and Joseph and the baby. Ah, there he is: the reason for living, the cause of all real peace and true joy—the Savior, Christ the Lord!

A nice recipe for us, don't you think? Tomorrow, next week, next month, when the cold of winter depresses, when the noise of the house and of the world just annoy, when best efforts on my part are received with icy ingratitude, or when my own irritation with myself rises again, then there he is. Look up into the sky. Do you see the angels? Can you hear their song? Do you remember hastening with the shepherds to Bethlehem? There they were in the Christmas gospel. Yes, and there he still is—the Savior born just for you, Christ the Lord. And seeing him still there longing for your salvation and achieving it at so great a price, sing again with the holy angels: Glory to God in the highest! For unto us is born in Bethlehem, the Savior, our Savior, my very own and only Savior, Christ the Lord!

> Ah, dearest Jesus, holy child, you take away more than my sin and guilt by your coming. You take away even the crushing tedium of life that often seems to have no point or purpose or meaning apart from you and your coming to be my Savior. I worship and give you thanks and praise that you are pleased to give me the honor of serving you and delighting you as I serve those around me with my words about you and my work done as for you. Forgive me when I forget that, and plant deep in my heart the peace and joy of your coming to be my Savior and my Lord. Amen.

VII.

Luke 2:19 – But Mary treasured up all these things and pondered them in her heart.

Here we have just the smallest piece of advice to give to God. Wouldn't it have been better for Mary to have had more glorious things than the coming of the shepherds to treasure up and ponder in her heart? Wouldn't it have been nice if the angels would have come to Jesus, Mary, and Joseph to sing the praises of God and of the holy child? That would really have been something to treasure up and ponder! And that would be especially appropriate given the contradiction of her circumstances at the moment and the promise contained in this holy birth. This child is God's Son, yet here they are with nothing but a barn, an animal feeding trough, and rags to wrap him in. This child is the Savior of the world, but God his Father has saved him from nothing—not from need, not from the humiliation of his Christmas Day circumstances. Wouldn't the sight and song of the angels have been a pleasant corrective or at least provided some balance for the sorry plight of the holy family on Christmas Day?

But we hear no complaint from Mary. She hears about the angels' message and their hymn of praise. And she is content with that. No, more than content. It makes no difference to her who the messenger is; what matters is the message—the message about this holy child, her Savior. How she must have thrilled to see her son worshiped by the shepherds, who probably hadn't washed before they came and didn't even have decent clothes to wear to this greatest event in their lives. How filled with delight she must have been to hear that the Christmas gospel was not just for her and Joseph, but for all, for even the lowliest of the low. She treasured all these things; she locked them in her heart as in a bank vault, so heavily guarded that not the least thing contained therein could escape. She pondered all these things; she visited that bank vault and held those precious memories as though they were the finest pieces of gold or the most beautiful of diamonds. Given all that would happen in the coming years, those recollections would surely be a great comfort to her.

And so we bring our devotions on the Christmas gospel to a close. Soon we too will return to the business of living—a business so filled with distractions, with joys and sorrows great and small, with temptations, and with some triumphs too. But let us treasure all these things and ponder them in our hearts with Mary. Caught in traffic, let the heart revisit the bank vault where this gospel gem is stored: God has come down from heaven just for me. In a lonely night hour when sleep has not yet come, ponder anew the rest he has brought in the middle of the night to the shepherds, to Mary, and to you. It is rest in the protection of the holy angels; it is rest in the message of pardon and peace through him who despised no lack and no sorrow and not even the cross in order to win peace for you.

And all of it he did just so that you might see him, embrace him, and even spend eternity with him. In a fleeting second when the distractions of a busy life seem so important and all that needs to be done seems never-ending, take a moment to treasure and another second just to ponder: I bring you glad tidings of great joy; for you the Savior is born; he was not too busy in ruling over heaven and earth—over all of history—to think of you and bring this Christmas gospel to you. And he is not too busy for you now either; for you he remains the lowly Savior wrapped in his lowly Word, veiled in his humble sacraments. Yes, treasure; yes, ponder. The message is never old. The joy is never-ending.

> O Holy Child of Bethlehem, where will there be enough time to ponder all these things in my heart: You came from heaven for me! You humbled yourself by your lowly birth in a barn for me! You have even preserved this holy message of your coming for two thousand years just so that I also might hear and be saved by it! And you have done all this in spite of my unworthiness, in spite of all that continues to be wrong with me, in spite of my remaining failure to fully appreciate this gift of salvation purchased by you just for me and at so great a cost. So then where will there be enough time to keep and ponder all these things in my heart? Where else but in the heaven you have won for me by all that you have done for my salvation and all that you still do in the Word and sacraments to bring it to me? What else can I do but most gladly receive and receive again your pardon, your grace, your mercy, your promise—in sum, the blessings you give in your saving gospel? Amen.

The Circumcision and Naming of Jesus

Luke 2:21 – On the eighth day, when it was time to circumcise the child, he was named Jesus, the name the angel had given him before he had been conceived.

There are a number of beautiful but short verses in the Bible that sum everything up. This is one of the most sublime of those kinds of passages. We might wish that God had inspired a book-length commentary on it; so easy is it to miss even the most significant elements of this one short verse. But he didn't do that, so we will have to be content with just skimming over the top of it to ladle off the most obvious and what appear to us as the most important elements.

It is the eighth day and in accordance with the Law of Moses, every Hebrew male must be circumcised on this day to mark the child as a member of God's covenant people. Wonder of wonders: The Son of God joins himself to the people of God by this bloody act. On this day he begins the work of our redemption; a sinful human performs a ritual that makes the sinless Son of God cry in pain as for us he sheds blood for the first time—but not for the last time. We might be tempted to object to this first shedding of his blood. Why should the sinless Son of God need this ceremony that was intended for children conceived and born in sin? He doesn't need a ceremony to make him a member of God's people. He was already God's child. He was the whole point of Israel's existence as a people. But there he is, humbled and obedient to the law down to the smallest detail, not for himself but for us.

Later, he who cried out on the eighth day will replace for us the sacrament that called for the shedding of blood and called forth cries of pain with a sacrament of washing with water and the Word. Even the rite he institutes later for our entry into fellowship with him he makes gentle and soothing instead of painful and bloody. He wanted to bring an end to that earlier pain by his own pain and remove the necessity of shedding blood from us by taking it on himself.

And then, lest anyone miss the point: Just as we receive our name in Christ at our baptism, so he receives his at his circumcision. It is the name of his and his Father's own choosing. It is the name he wanted since the promise made in the Garden of Eden when Adam and Eve fell into sin. It is the name *Jesus*, the name that means "Savior." For that is what he has come to do: to save us. And how will he do it? By the shedding of his blood, which begins on this holy day.

And from what has he come to save us by the shedding of his blood? From the very curse that the law hangs around our necks when it declares us guilty of breaking it. He submits this day to the whole of the law, no part of which we could keep. He, who as God's own Son was above the law, keeps it perfectly, not for himself but for us. Then when the work of perfect submission begun on this bloody day has been finished, he will shed his blood again to finish the work promised by his name: the work of becoming our Savior. Bookends to his whole earthly life—that's what the shedding of his blood is for us and for our salvation.

There is yet another aspect of this verse that we don't want to miss. It has to do with the whole gospel point of the Old Testament sacrament of circumcision. By that sacred act, God made the child an heir of all of God's rich promises to his people. And those promises were rich indeed. They stretched all the way back to Genesis 3. He promised Adam and Eve a Savior who would crush the head of the serpent and thereby undo the curse of death and hell deserved by sin. He promised throughout the Old Testament that he would be with his people and bless them both spiritually and in earthly ways so long as they continued to trust in his Word. He promised that of all the people on earth, the descendants of Abraham would be the chosen bearers of the promised Redeemer. We could go on all day quoting promises of God in the Old Testament for his people—promises given to the individual child in circumcision.

But what promises did God have for this child, for his very own and only-begotten Son on this special occasion? After all, he was God's Son already from eternity, according to his divine nature. Were there any special promises that God had made in the Old Testament that could be seen as given and confirmed to his only-begotten Son on this special day?

Oh yes, many and rich were the promises that God made to his only-begotten Son in the Old Testament. In summary form they are recalled in the message of the angel to Mary and then to Joseph. They are sung with joyful voice in the greeting of Elizabeth and then in the hymn of Zechariah, even before Jesus' birth. They are quoted by the chief priests in answer to Herod's question about the birth place of the Savior. Again, just in sum: He would be *the* Savior so long awaited (Matthew 1:21); he would receive the throne of David and rule in his kingdom forever—a promise that stretched from the beginning of time to eternity, from earth to the highest heaven (Luke 1:32,33; Matthew 2:6); he would be the Lord clothed in human flesh from his mother (Luke 1:43); he would be the light of the Gentiles and the glory of Israel, yes, the fulfillment of all of God's promises (Luke 1:67-79).

Ah, but there were other promises too! God promised his Son pain already in the first promise in Genesis 3:15. Indeed, Jesus himself promised long before he was born that he would tread the winepress of God's wrath against all and every sin and would endure that anger all alone (Isaiah 63:1-6); in most graphic terms his anguish on the cross was promised to him (Psalm 22; Isaiah 53). Again, we can only sum up the matter: The promises of glory would only come after the promises of suffering—of the shedding of blood on the cross—had been fulfilled. His name *Jesus*, "Savior," would have to be earned!

Rich indeed are the special promises of God to his Son on this day when Jesus was made a child of promise, when he first shed his blood, and then when he received the name *Jesus*. And all of those promises were meant for his benefit? Oh, no! They were all for *our* benefit, both the promises and their fulfillment in all that Jesus did to accomplish our salvation.

There it is in this first summary of the life of Jesus: The recently sung, joyous song of the angels is tinged with his cries of pain and with the shedding of his blood. And so it will ever be in his earthly life—and in ours too, as we shall have occasion often to note in other meditations. But this is his feast day. So we will be content to bow low in adoration and in thanksgiving that today he began to shed his blood for us so that, for us, he might become what his name promised: our Jesus, our Savior. Yes, and we will give thanks as well that our entrance into his family so full of promises to us is accomplished not by our cries of pain in the shedding of our blood but by his washing us clean from our sins in the saving and gentle waters of Baptism.

> Dearest Jesus, so soon you shed your blood in obedience to the law and to fulfill everything needed for my salvation. So early on you deserved the name *Jesus.* From beginning to end, that's who you are: Jesus, my Jesus, Savior, my Savior! Oh, how great is my glory because of your lowliness, my holiness because of the holiness you give by the shedding of your blood to cover all my sins. Again I call it to mind: Heaven will have to last forever for there to be enough time for me to sing your praises for all that you have done for me and for my salvation as that was proclaimed already on this holy day! Amen.

The Presentation of Our Lord and the Purification of the Blessed Virgin Mary

I.

Luke 2:22-24 – When the time came for the purification rites required by the Law of Moses, Joseph and Mary took him to Jerusalem to present him to the Lord (as it is written in the Law of the Lord, "Every firstborn male is to be consecrated to the Lord"), and to offer a sacrifice in keeping with what is said in the Law of the Lord: "a pair of doves or two young pigeons."

As Jesus was brought to Jerusalem on the eighth day after his birth to be circumcised in obedience to the Law of Moses, so he is brought again on the 40th day in obedience to the Law. This time his legal parents, Mary his mother and Joseph his guardian and foster father, bring him to be presented to the Lord and redeemed. Every firstborn belonged in a special way to God as a remembrance of the slaying of the firstborn of the Egyptians, which had caused Pharaoh at long last to let the people of Israel go. But after the tribe of Levi was chosen to be the priestly tribe, the firstborn of every other tribe was released from the obligation of special priestly dedication to God—released only after a redemption price was paid and given to the Levites (Exodus 13:1,2,14,15).

Redeemed? The sinless Son of God and the Redeemer of the world has to be redeemed, bought back from special service to God? He alone in all the world would offer to God perfect service. How can it be that he must be redeemed? And his mother has to be purified in accordance with the law (Leviticus 12)? She has given birth to the only one ever born who was free from the stain of original sin. That she should be purified after such a birth just doesn't seem right. Wouldn't it have been better for them not to submit to the law in these points as a testimony to the sinless sonship of the only begotten and Son of the Father? Wouldn't it have made more sense for Mary to make no sacrifice for her purification? For though not sinless herself, certainly she was not made unclean by the birth of her sinless son.

And think of all the bother. They had to go to the temple in Jerusalem. Hadn't they had enough inconvenience already, what with the difficult journey to Bethlehem so close to the birth of the holy child? And what about the expense of the sacrifice? The wise men had not yet come from the east with their expensive gifts to relieve the poverty of the holy family. Whatever energy they might have had and whatever resources were left must have been pretty well spent by the 40th day. Why not skip it? Who would have better reason to omit the required redemption than the Redeemer? And who might more reasonably be excused the expense of the sacrifice for purification than she who gave birth to the One who could not possibly have made his mother unclean by his sinless birth?

But they came, the poor and the inconvenienced holy family. They came in all lowliness and humility. They came making no boasts, with not the least bit of pretension. They came almost unnoticed and in obedience to a law which in their case seems to make no sense and have no real purpose. There was no brass band. The choir of the holy angels did not sing at their approach to the house of God on earth. They were all but lost in the crowd of pilgrims and regular worshipers in the temple. They blended in, undistinguished with the throng of other parents who had come also to make the sacrifices of redemption and purification. Maybe they even had to wait their turn while more important people presented their richer offerings and sacrifices—a further humiliation!

It just doesn't seem right, does it? And yet—it is just as it should be! St. Paul sums up the explanation of it all in Galatians 4:4-7: "When the fullness of time had come, God sent forth his Son, born of woman, born under the law, to redeem those who were under the law, so that we might receive adoption as sons. And because you are sons, God has sent the Spirit of his Son into our hearts, crying, 'Abba! Father.' So you are no longer a slave, but a son, and if a son, then an heir through God" (ESV).

> Blessed Redeemer, you were brought to the temple to be redeemed! What an amazing thing that is to me. You were brought to become my Redeemer, the one who would—the only one who ever could—redeem me from the curse of the law. You have thereby won for me the matchless title of a child of God and have made me an heir of eternal life. And you

consider it the highest form of worship that I receive what you have inherited for me! You have heaped grace on grace: grace from your cradle to my grave, grace from there to heaven and eternal life! O blessed Redeemer, to you all thanks and praise now and forever. Amen.

II.

What an amazing thing! Jesus submits to the law. Jesus keeps it in all of its parts, including the ceremonial laws that we might have thought should not apply to him or even be all that important. He is redeemed; that is, he is bought back from God for his parents so that his obedience to the law would be perfect, accomplished for us in our place. Nothing is to be omitted, nothing left out or incomplete in that obedience. Too much is at stake for the slightest slipup.

And so already as an infant, he begins that work that is the whole reason for his coming: the work of *our* redemption; our purchase back from slavery to sin, death, hell, and the devil. That work of our redemption would of course cost much more than the sacrifices offered in the temple on that day of Jesus' redemption. It would cost the redeemed Redeemer everything. Our redemption will be accomplished in his total humiliation, a humiliation evident on this day of his redemption in the temple. It would be a humiliation not finished until it found its absolute depth on the altar of the cross. But because of it we are no longer slaves to death and hell, the just rewards of our sin-corrupted nature and impure lives from the moment of our conception to our last breath.

And so on the festival day of his presentation and his mother's purification, we sing with joy unbounded and unending: we are "sons," whether young or old, men or women, noble or ignoble, loaded with good works or crushed in conscience. We sing that we are now heirs of all the blessings that belonged by right to *the* Son. We sing of redemption and of the peace with God and even with our own conscience because of that redemption. We sing because the birthright that belonged to the only begotten Son is now our birthright too—heaven is ours, the loving protection and blessing of the Father are ours. We call out to him like little children in every need, "*Abba!* Father!" Father, dear Father, save us now and forever. The Redeemer has redeemed us so that for his sake, we are your dear sons and heirs of his birthright.

In the light of Jesus' submission to the entire Word of God in the Old Testament law—submission to its smallest parts no less than to the greatest—how silly and how shabby our excuses become when we seek to exempt ourselves from any part of God's Word. Just think of those parts of

God's Word that we so easily dismiss as of no importance. To mention just one example as typical of so many more that we might think of: The speed limit is 25 miles per hour and the Fourth Commandment says that I should obey the government. But that's such a trivial thing; who bothers with it? Even the police don't really care if I'm a few miles over. And besides that, I'm important; I'm in a hurry; I have more important and better things to do with the moments saved than whatever can be gained by . . . by what? By obedience even to the least of the things in the law!

And so, instead of behaving like a dear child whose whole pleasure is in pleasing the Father, I behave like an unwanted orphan who isn't really cared for and, as a result, doesn't much care what the Father wants either. The devil would dearly like us to behave like that—like uncared for orphans. If we are uncared-for orphans, then the Father probably doesn't notice us all that much and probably doesn't really care all that much about our attitude to him and to his Word. So if there is a doctrine that is difficult for us to accept, well, let's just not make too much of a fuss about that. If there is a commandment that just doesn't fit our preferred lifestyle at the moment—a traffic speed limit, a tax law—well, does it really matter all that much?

But we are sons! We are redeemed heirs of the inheritance to which Jesus alone was entitled. Therefore we listen with attentive, love-filled hearts to the voice of the Father and follow him. Is it difficult? Is it inconvenient? So much the better! Yes, St. Paul's admonition makes perfect sense: "I urge you, brothers and sisters, in view of God's mercy, to offer your bodies as a living sacrifice, holy and pleasing to God—this is your true and proper worship. Do not conform to the pattern of this world, but be transformed by the renewing of your mind" (Romans 12:1,2).

The Redeemer was redeemed. His mother was purified. And it happened as he submitted to the least part of the law, a law that really shouldn't even have applied to him. And now we, redeemed and purified by his blood, enjoy the honor of bringing to him sacrifices—not of doves in Jerusalem's temple but of loving submission and obedience.

> Blessed Redeemer, you redeemed me by your submission to all of God's Word. Kindle in me such a grateful love that I yearn for nothing more than to receive all that you have won for me. Then through the Word of your redeeming work on my behalf, grant me a devotion that holds to all of your Word and has no greater ambition than to submit to it in grateful thanksgiving. And then purify me still from anything in my thoughts, words, and deeds that rebels or ignores or somehow sets aside anything in your law and gospel. In all that I do, let me grow in happy obedience to you, my Redeemer. Amen.

III.

Luke 2:25-27 – There was a man in Jerusalem called Simeon, who was righteous and devout. He was waiting for the consolation of Israel, and the Holy Spirit was on him. It had been revealed to him by the Holy Spirit that he would not die before he had seen the Lord's Messiah. Moved by the Spirit, he went into the temple courts.

Let's tarry a while with Jesus, Mary, and Joseph on this solemn day of Jesus' redemption and his mother's purification. As we like to invite friends and relatives to those events in the lives of our children that are special and important, so it pleased God to invite a friend to celebrate this special day in the life of Jesus.

That friend is Simeon. He is an interesting man indeed. We might suggest to God that he should have invited a lot of others. We might advise him to at least invite people who are important and who will cause all others in the temple that day to stop and take note of the Christ Child. But as we saw throughout the Christmas story, that's not God's way.

And so who is this Simeon? Even here we might suggest to God that he give us a better description of the man. For, after all, when we are introduced or are introducing ourselves, invariably notable things about us are attached to the introduction: "Here is Fred; he works at . . ." "Meet Bertha; she is the one who won the prize for . . ." We identify ourselves—even define ourselves—by our most notable accomplishments, by things that we think make us worth meeting.

But here is Simeon. And what is his claim to fame? When God introduces him to us, what's the best, most important thing that he can say to us about Simeon? It's just this: To God he was special, that is, he was righteous and devout. And in what did his righteousness consist? Was it in some great works that he did? Did he make some great contribution to the life of the church or of his people? Was he a priest or a prophet? We don't know. Maybe he was important and maybe he did accomplish some really worthwhile things in his life. But this is his great work in God's eyes as he introduces Simeon to us: "He was waiting for the consolation of Israel." And the consolation of Israel was a person; that's what God himself had revealed to Simeon. And what a blessing: not that Simeon would be great, but that he would not die before he had seen the only one who is great, his Savior! And that was his righteousness: his Savior.

God blesses each of us with works that adorn our lives and make us important to at least some of those around us. He blesses us and gives us occasion at times to reflect on those things in our lives that make living worthwhile, not just for ourselves but for those whose lives have been blessed by our presence in their lives. In the world those things may be at times great or—most of the time—small and not likely to be long remembered. But when all is said and done, what's the best description we can give of ourselves? What sums you up and defines you? Indeed, how would you want God to describe you? God's description of Simeon was that he "was righteous and devout." Would that be God's happy description of you if he were to introduce you to the saints and angels? To be sure, we have an abundance of blessings in our lives that are part of our description of ourselves or of the way that others might introduce and describe us. You may want to think of what those things are and give thanks to God for them.

But as we consider God's description of Simeon, it would be well for us to ask: What *best* describes me? Today may it be or become this: I am one who waits with longing for the consolation of Israel; I am one to whom the Lord has revealed the only consolation that matters—has revealed Jesus and given him to me in his Word; I am one moved to come and worship him for the consolation he has brought to my soul now and for eternity by his coming!

> Lord Jesus, so rich are you in your gifts to me. Out of the abundance of your generosity, you have made me a parent/child, a worker with abilities for getting my job done, a friend to some and a helper to others. You have blessed me with certain talents and character traits that some will remember me for, even after I am gone. You have even given me such grace and such gifts that my life has become—at least for a few—a blessing for which they thank you. But above it all, there is this one description that I long for: Grant that my name ever be linked with yours! Grant that when I see myself and even when others see me, this first may come to mind: You are my greatest joy and consolation because you have become my Savior. That, after all is said and done, is what makes my life worthwhile to me and ultimately a blessing to those around me as I reflect your love in my words and actions. Forgive me when I fail in doing this and so prove yourself still to be my life, my light, my salvation, my all in all. Amen.

IV.

Luke 2:27-32 – When the parents brought in the child Jesus to do for him what the custom of the Law required, Simeon took him

in his arms and praised God, saying: "Sovereign Lord, as you have promised, you may now dismiss your servant in peace. For my eyes have seen your salvation, which you have prepared in the sight of all nations: a light for revelation to the Gentiles, and the glory of your people Israel."

Here is the high point of Simeon's life. How he must have thrilled at the moment! He got to hold Jesus in his arms! We don't know how old Simeon was when all this happened. And it doesn't matter. No matter how old he was, this is the crowning moment for one who was pious and devout, whose life was summed up by waiting for that One who would be the consolation of Israel. Let's listen in to his inspired song of thanksgiving and then join with him in singing it:

> "Sovereign Lord, as you have promised, you may now dismiss your servant in peace."

What a perfect line for anyone who has held Jesus in his arms! God has done what he promised. He has been faithful to his Word. How fitting that we sing this line and this song after we have held Jesus in our arms, in our souls by receiving his Word and in our bodies as well after we have received him in Holy Communion. O Lord, you promised to be here in Word and in bread and wine. And you have kept your promise. That's no surprise; for you always keep your word. But it thrills me nevertheless—thrills me every time I get to experience it in Word and the Sacrament. For by it I have peace: the peace of forgiveness full and free, the peace of rescue from death and hell, the peace of your constant companionship in good days and bad, the peace of knowing that all things work together for my good. For you have given yourself even for me, and you will never forget to keep your Word. And so most gladly I call myself your servant—a servant who serves you most importantly by receiving you and all you are and have given me in your Word. Most gladly I delight to then be your servant as well in singing your praises in words and deeds so that those around me may see me in your arms. I want them to know that you are my reason for living—indeed, the source of peace in my life. Oh, may my joy in receiving you and your peace draw them to desire the same for themselves!

> "For my eyes have seen your salvation, which you have prepared in the sight of all nations: a light for revelation to the Gentiles, and the glory of your people Israel."

Do you notice how Simeon looks at life and at history through the prism of God's Word? He ignores altogether what seems to be and instead focuses his attention on what actually is and how it is possible from God's standpoint. He has seen salvation! It certainly did not look that way on the outside; there was just this little nondescript baby, brought by parents of no note. Ah, but viewed from God standpoint—from the perspective of God's Word—there he is, the One who is salvation even if the world takes no note or just passes him by.

But wait a minute. That's exactly what the world does. How, then, can Simeon call this child the light of the Gentiles? The Gentiles, for the most part, close their eyes and shun the light. And how can he say that this child is the glory of Israel? Israel's chief priests and teachers of the law will call him a blasphemer and cry out, "Crucify him! Crucify him!"

Let the world look at him as it will. Let his own despise and reject him. The fact is that he is, nevertheless, the light—the only light possible for perishing Gentiles. The truth remains that he is indeed the only glory of Israel, the whole reason for its ancient history. If Gentiles pass him by, they do so in a darkness of their own choosing, a darkness in which they will stumble over the cliff into the abyss prepared for the devil and his angels. If Israel does not want Jesus, it will cast aside its only real glory and join the despised and despising Gentiles in their hellish fate.

But oh, may he ever be for us consolation and salvation. May he remain our light and our only glory. For in what sorrow is he not the consolation and our salvation? When we have fallen into the darkness of sin and guilt, he calls us to himself and shines upon us with the radiance of the gospel of forgiveness. When we experience suffering, pain, and loss, he brings light to our darkness of fear and doubt with the assurance of his Word: he is still in control and will bring everything to pass for our ultimate benefit and good. When we have days of gladness, he is the One to whom we give the glory with all our thanks and praise. When death draws near, still there is light at the end of day and glory in the darkest hour; he consoles us still with the assurance of eternal life with him in heaven. Yes indeed, we have seen his salvation every day and in every phase and experience of a lifetime! Therefore whether speaking of any part of our day, even of day's end or life's end, how blest we are that we can say with Simeon:

> Let me ever go in peace; for I have seen you, O Jesus, my light and my consolation, my only boast and glory! Amen.

V.

Luke 2:33-35 – The child's father and mother marveled at what was said about him. Then Simeon blessed them and said to Mary, his mother: "This child is destined to cause the falling and rising of many in Israel, and to be a sign that will be spoken against, so that the thoughts of many hearts will be revealed."

Here we really want to take God aside. It's really upsetting, isn't it? Why does Simeon have to go spoil such a beautiful song by ending it this way? And then even this: These final words of Simeon are called a blessing!

The day had been one of celebration, and God himself had invited Simeon to be a guest and so much more than that: He was a one-man choir who, by his inspired song, must have brought real joy to the hearts of Mary and Joseph when all around them were ignorant of how important this child and this day were. But now, as the beautiful and inspired work and words of Simeon draw to a close, he has to end it with a message of doom and gloom. So much for the tinsel and cheery Christmas tree lights! So much for "Ho, Ho, Ho!" Couldn't talk of pain and suffering have waited for another day? If God had asked us for our advice, surely that's what we would have suggested. After all, who comes to a family Christmas gathering or the celebration of a child's baptism and, after exchanging cheerful greetings, begins to talk about strife and suffering and death? It's just not the time!

But God, as usual, didn't ask for our opinion and isn't interested in our advice. As usual, it remains for us not to give him advice but to listen. And listen we will. For the whole section is fascinating.

To begin with, Mary and Joseph "marveled at what was said about him." Isn't that interesting? We might have expected Mary to say, "Well, of course, we know all of this already and don't need you, Simeon, to tell us. After all, the conception of this child was announced by an angel and took place miraculously. And an angel had made everything clear already to Joseph as well." But no, there is none of that. Mary and Joseph marvel at every revelation from God about the newborn Savior of the world, no matter how little or how much they may know about it already. They put to shame the mindless among us who can't be bothered with the Bible or with regular worship on Sunday morning because, "We know it all already and have heard it all before!" So amazing, so astounding, so blessed is it that Jesus has come for us—for me, even for me—that with Mary and Joseph, we marvel at the news, no matter how often we have heard it. For since the last time we heard it, we have given God still more reasons not to have sent us the Savior, and the Savior reasons aplenty for not coming. So with Mary and Joseph, we marvel at this good news and can never get enough of it.

Then there is this: The hearts of many will be revealed, and many will rise and fall on account of this child, his words, and his works. Remember that Simeon's definition of himself is one who waited and longed for redemption—for the appearance of the Christ Child. And now he declares it: The person, the words, and the works of this child will always be the defining moment, the ultimate event in the life of everyone who hears of it. Some will hear and turn away to things they think are more important; how

Advent and Christmas 33

tragic their fall will be when this child returns in judgment and they perish eternally because of their unbelief—because they thought something was more important than Jesus, his Word, his work for their salvation. And some will rise. Oh, what a rising that will be! They will hear of him, and by his Word, they will receive him. He will make his home—his shrine, his temple—in their hearts and souls and minds and lives. And they will, just as he promised, never die! Even though their bodies waste away and decay, it is only for a moment. They will rise when he calls them from the grave, just as they rose from spiritual death to spiritual life when he called them through the gospel message to trust in him alone for their salvation. And what a rising that second rising will be! They will rise to live with him as he has lived with them; they will live with him forever in the glory of the paradise he came to win for them. No, that message never gets old and its richness is never exhausted.

Still others—sadly, tragically—will see in this Jesus "a sign that will be spoken against." For all that he is and all that he does for us and for our salvation, they will have much more than ingratitude and unbelief. They will see in his message of salvation something that makes them angry. "What? You call me a sinner! What? You dare to say that all the best in me helps nothing toward my salvation! What? You dare to declare that full and complete salvation is to be found in you and in your work alone and you even warn that if I and mine reject you, we'll all go to hell! How dare you! Away with him! Crucify him! Rid the earth of his Book and those who teach such an insulting message!"

So the cross is promised to Mary and to the church in every age as well. Some will just reject him in unbelief. Some will persecute the Redeemer and seek to destroy his Word, either with violence or with gospel-denying false doctrine. And some, like Mary and Joseph and Simeon, will rise by the beauty and power of the Savior's Word and work. Oh, may each of us be in their number and with Mary rejoice to treasure all these things in our hearts throughout all of our days!

> Lord Jesus, I have heard the message of your Word so often that the devil tempts me to take it for granted. Oh, may it never be that I cease to be amazed by all that you are and all that you have done for one such as me. So many fall and perish in unbelief at your Word. But out of your unspeakable grace, you have kindled in my heart trust in your Word and saving work. Nothing could ever be as surprising or as amazing that even for me, you came and come still in your Word and sacraments. Save me still through your gospel message from the perverse wickedness of thoughtless ingratitude that ends up in careless

unbelief and then even in perverse opposition to you and your gospel message. Amen.

VI.

Luke 2:35 – "A sword will pierce your own soul too."

There is still one more thing to consider out of all the amazing things on this special day. Simeon prophesies that a sword will pierce the heart of Mary! Not the heart of Joseph? The cross is never far away, is it?! It is twofold here. Mary will suffer as with a sword through her heart when she sees her divine Son despised and rejected, ridiculed, spat upon, and then crucified. But Joseph will not be there to comfort her or to share her sorrow. He will already have died. We hear nothing about him after that one event when Jesus was 12 years old and went with both Joseph and Mary to the temple. By the time Jesus began his earthly ministry, Joseph had disappeared from the scene.

How sad! If Mary thought about the lack of any reference to Joseph in these words, which all by themselves already had enough of pain and suffering in them, then she would have felt the sword already. Her earthly protector and the guardian of both her and the child, who was not his, would be gone. She would be a widow long before her time.

It's hard to stifle the temptation to criticize God here: couldn't the holy family be spared at least this—the loss of the husband of Mary and the foster father of Jesus? But no; the path of the holy family will not be strewn with rose petals and cushioned with soft pillows. A sword will pierce the soul of the mother of God, and she will not be shielded from the pain of becoming a widow before that ultimate sorrow on Good Friday.

What will be her comfort and strength when all these things come to pass? It will be the same as the comfort and strength God gives to us when the tinsel and the laughter of Christmas Day give way to pain and loss. For to none of us is there the promise given that we shall escape sorrow and suffering because we have seen the Christ Child, our Savior, or because we have received him in his Word and by faith, have held him in our arms. With Mary and Joseph, we embrace him and hold him close to our hearts in his Word and sacraments. And then we await his blessing—a blessing like that spoken by Simeon. It is a blessing that promises times of loss; it is a blessing that promises times of rising again; it is a blessing whose entire content is in the person of this holy child who has come. He will be our Savior no matter how much he is spoken against. He will be the one who strengthens and keeps us in days of laughter and in days of weeping. And with Mary and Joseph we will marvel at how it all works out for us and for our salvation.

One last note that the mention of Joseph always brings to mind: All of the great saints in the Bible and in the history of the church are famous for what they did and often even more for what they said—all, that is, except Joseph. Not one word of his is recorded. Some of his thoughts are recorded. But he says nothing (Matthew 1:18-21; 2:13-23; Luke 2:39-52). His greatest work is that he listens to what God says. He doesn't argue with God. He doesn't doubt or question. He listens and then he obeys. What a great saint he is! What a model for all who think sometimes that they know better than God. St. Joseph hears the Word of God; St. Joseph believes that Word; and then St. Joseph carries the Christ Child in his arms with but one desire: the desire to serve his Savior in the role that the Savior has given him. May we ever strive to be like him!

One last little observation: We have to marvel again as so often in God's Word, God loves to marry the highest honor with the lowliest appearance—the higher the honor, the more humble the appearance. That is preeminently true in Jesus himself. And it is true in St. Joseph too. What a high, holy, unique, and unequaled honor he has: he is the earthly protector of God's own Son. And at the same time, he is so lowly that not one word that he ever spoke to his charge is recorded!

> Lord Jesus, you spared yourself no inconvenience, no suffering, and no loss in order to win my salvation. You did not even spare your mother and earthly father from loss and sorrow and pain. Yet that's what I want: always to be spared the least inconvenience. This day I give thanks that you have not granted that foolish desire. As you taught your mother and your earthly father by loss to rely on you alone from day to day to provide what was best and needed, so teach me to forsake the foolish notion that I should have a life of nothing but comfort and ease. Rather, bring me in every hour of need or pain to look to you to give whatever is best and necessary for my life here and for the ultimate goal of the life you died to win for me in heaven. Let me receive it all with trusting thanksgiving. Amen.

Epiphany

The Visit of the Wise Men

I.

Matthew 2:1,2 – After Jesus was born in Bethlehem in Judea, during the time of King Herod, Magi from the east came to Jerusalem and asked, "Where is the one who has been born king of the Jews? We saw his star when it rose and have come to worship him."

What a strange story and what a strange way of introducing it! It takes place some time after the night of the holy birth and after the two presentations of Jesus in the temple.

St. Matthew begins it by assuring us that this birth is not a myth or a fairy tale; the birth and everything following it that he records in his gospel is rooted in history: it all begins during the reign of King Herod. And what a king he was! He wasn't even Jewish. He was a monster with connections in Rome. His title and his lands were his only by a grant from the Roman emperor. His great contribution—what we would call these days his legacy—was the rebuilding of the temple in Jerusalem. But as beautiful and as magnificent as it truly was, there was nothing beautiful or magnificent about the man himself. He murdered most of his relatives and officials in his court out of fear that they might be plotting against him. At his death he ordered the murder of the rest so that there would be no one left to rejoice over his grave. *Peace* was not a word in his vocabulary. Nor did his heart cherish any love for God or his Word. He was no hypocrite: evil of every sort, violence, hatred, malice, greed, envy—all these he practiced openly and without any apparent tinge of regret. The contrast between King Herod and Jesus, the newborn King of the Jews, could not be more striking.

Accordingly, it is not difficult to imagine his rage, which was perhaps mixed with fear, when these sages come from the east seeking a new and different king of the Jews. Much of his life, after all, was devoted to the work of assuring himself and all around him that no other king was possible.

Then there are these Magi from the east. They were probably from present-day Iran or Iraq. They were among the most highly educated and highly placed men of their day. They were especially interested in the movements of the planets—in astronomy and astrology. And most surprising, they knew of the promised coming of the Savior as the real King of the Jews. How did they know about that? The best guess we can make is that the prophet Daniel had perhaps left behind promises of the Savior's birth in addition to those that are contained in his book in the Old Testament. Whether from the work of Daniel or from some special revelation that God gave them, they looked for the fulfillment of the promise, the promise of a King whose coming would be announced by the appearance of a star. And that star would lead them to the One promised. So this star is not just some natural phenomenon or constellation. It is *his* star.

How interesting! God brought a glimmer of light to the dark Gentile world first through a light in the sky. The darkness of the East was overwhelming. Idol worship was dominant. Few were there who knew of this promised star and fewer still who understood that it proclaimed the birth of God's Son. For there were only these few that come. But they come not just seeking an earthly king before whom they might bow in respect; they come looking for the child who is a king worthy of worship. And so eager are they to worship him that they spare no effort, no trouble, no inconvenience, and no danger to find him.

Yes, isn't it interesting?! They know so much and so little about him. They know that he is God and therefore worthy of worship. They know that he is therefore the almighty ruler of heaven and earth. They know that he was kind and gracious enough to come down from heaven and to reveal himself so that they might find and worship him. But what else do they know? Do they know of his lowliness? Probably not, for they seek him out in Jerusalem, the capital city and the city of God's temple—surely there is where he should be found. Do they know of his coming as the Suffering Servant of the Lord who came to redeem them by his sacrifice? We cannot say. But whatever else they may know, it is enough for them to sacrifice much of themselves to find and worship him. That they should seek and find him they know from God's promise connected to a star. That he should be found in Jerusalem they guess from reason.

What a lesson for us! What deep gratitude it should provoke in us who have the fullness of God's revelation of himself in the Word and the sacraments! And that revelation does not need guesses from our reason to tell us where we should find Jesus. No, his Word and sacraments tell us quite simply, quite fully, quite plainly where he is to be found, namely, exactly where his Word is purely preached and his sacraments rightly administered.

Oh, may our zeal to find the newborn King of the Jews not be less than that of these wise men from the east. Yes, and may we not become cold and indifferent to the bright light of his Word, which by day and by night leads us to him and brings him to us. For as much as we can know of God from nature or from reason and as wonderful, beautiful, and mighty as he appears there, only in his Word is his name—*Jesus*, our Savior—to be found.

> O Jesus, King most wonderful, shine ever in your Word and let its bright light ever bring me seeking you there where you have promised to be. Let that light of grace and truth, which reveals and gives you to me as King and Savior, inspire me more and more to treasure you and the bright light of your Word so that nothing may keep me from the worship of faith in you and life that grows in reflecting the bright star of your Word. Amen.

II.

Matthew 2:3-8 – When King Herod heard this he was disturbed, and all Jerusalem with him. When he had called together all the people's chief priests and teachers of the law, he asked them where the Messiah was to be born. "In Bethlehem in Judea," they replied, "for this is what the prophet has written: 'But you, Bethlehem, in the land of Judah, are by no means least among the rulers of Judah; for out of you will come a ruler who will shepherd my people Israel.'" Then Herod called the Magi secretly and found out from them the exact time the star had appeared. He sent them to Bethlehem and said, "Go and search carefully for the child. As soon as you find him, report to me, so that I too may go and worship him."

There is so much here to think about! Consider the contrast between Herod and the wise men. Herod knows the Scriptures; the wise men don't. Herod knows enough of God's Word to know that such a King was indeed promised in that Word, and he knows that the details of that King's coming could be found not in the stars and not in reason but only in that Word. The wise men know little of that. But Herod, for all that he knows of the facts and of the additional facts that the chief priests and teachers would tell him, sees that promised King not as a Savior but only as a threat. Again, how different from the wise men; they have only nature—what they know of the Savior is promised by a star; they have only reason—where else would reason suggest that they go to find a king but to the capital city? Neither of these was sufficient to bring them to the Savior-King or him to them.

And what about the chief priests and teachers of the law? They know why the wise men had come, namely, so that they might worship Jesus. And they know well the Scriptures' promises concerning the King those wise men were looking for. And so, when Herod calls these leaders of the church, who are so learned in his Word, they have no difficulty in giving Herod the information he sought from that Word.

But now what should we expect, if not from Herod then certainly from the teachers of God's Word? Shouldn't we expect that the priests and teachers would be the first to exclaim, *He's come! He's come! He's finally here, the fulfillment of all of God's promises! He's here at last, our King, our God-made-flesh, our Savior! Come, come, let us hasten to Bethlehem to find him and worship him!* That was the attitude of the lowly shepherds. How much more might we expect it from the priests and teachers of the law? But that's not what happened. Instead we are told that the news of the wise men was disturbing to them—not good news at all. Don't you just want to give them all a good kick and yell, *What's the matter with you people? Here is the solution to sin and death and hell! And all you can muster is annoyance that his coming poses a potential problem for you?!*

People and things in this world come and go, but at its core, the human race remains the same. The world is still full of people—yes, people who know God's Word—but many are people who find most of it more bothersome than it's worth. How the devil tempts us too to think of this Word as something to be learned but not so much lived. How quickly the sinful flesh urges that we take something of a smorgasbord approach to it: here there's something I like; however, there is something that is too difficult, too much of a bother—it is likely to cause people around me to think I'm silly for believing it and living according to it.

So then, when we think about the coming of the wise men from the east, who shall our models be today? The wise men hung on to what little they knew of God's Word and promise and dared to follow it. They did that not only at great risk, inconvenience, and expense; they did it when all of their friends and neighbors and fellow wise men stayed home and probably considered them rather foolish.

Or will we be like Herod? He knew the Bible. He knew where to go for answers to questions about the Savior. But the Book for him was no star of light shining in this dark world. Rather, it told him things he did not want to hear: things about One he hated and would soon seek to destroy. In the world there are still so many like Herod; they know about the Bible and the Savior revealed in it. But they think that the message has caused more trouble in the world than it has ever helped, and they would gladly be rid of both the message and its messengers.

Or will we be like the priests and teachers of the law? After all, like them, we know the Bible. We memorized parts of it and the catechism as well. But that's more than enough for us. Jesus said that we should let our light shine (Matthew 5:16) so that people would see our good works and come to glorify God. Yes, they would come to see Jesus, the Light of the world, because of his reflection in us. But that's a lot of bother and trouble. People more often than not won't come to Jesus but will just dismiss us as fools or hypocrites.

We might be tempted to give God advice concerning Herod and the chief priests and teachers of the law: *God, why didn't you just take your Word away from them altogether and let them rot in their deliberate despising of your Word and the newborn Savior?* But then we remember times when we were more like Herod or the priests and teachers of the law than like the Magi. And so instead, we would do better to marvel at the enormous grace and mercy of God. He didn't take his Word from them—astonishing as that is—at least not at that time. And he hasn't taken it from us either, at least not yet! Still he called to them from its sacred pages. And still he calls to us too.

Most of these priests and teachers perished in their persistent rejection of the Savior. Oh, may we not be in their number. Rather, may their example serve as a call to us: it is a call to marvel at God's continuing mercy in preserving his Word, even when we have been unfaithful. It is a call to repent of every sin—of despising that Word by indifference or disobedience in thought, word, or deed. It is a call to go there to that Word, his permanent star directing us to Christ. There again and always we find our King. There, in finding him, he gives us reason to rejoice that still we can receive him and then worship and adore him. For there he is with his matchless grace and mercy in the message of pardon and peace that is ours because he came and comes still in Word and in sacraments.

> Even so, Lord Jesus, ever come to me in grace and mercy, not in anger or in the judgment that I have deserved. For none other do I seek, none other do I long for than you, my only Savior, my God, my King. Amen.

III.

Matthew 2:9-12 – After they had heard the king, they went on their way, and the star they had seen when it rose went ahead of them until it stopped over the place where the child was. When they saw the star, they were overjoyed. On coming to the house, they saw the child with his mother Mary, and they bowed down and worshiped him. Then they opened their treasures and presented him with gifts of gold, frankincense and myrrh. And having been warned in a dream not to go back to Herod, they returned to their country by another route.

Epiphany

Can't you just see it? They are assured through God's Word that they have not been on a wild goose chase. Bethlehem—that's where they should go! But still, it is not until they see the star again that they are overjoyed. Was that perhaps because it seemed so strange to them that neither Herod nor the religious leaders were interested in going with them? Ah, but when they leave Herod, there it is again in the dark night sky: the star! And it was moving, leading them onward toward this strange little town. God has not forgotten them! God is still anxious for them to see his Son! God still would let nothing keep them away from the worship they had come to offer—no, not even the seeming indifference of those who should have rejoiced most at the promise fulfilled.

And so, overjoyed at the certainty of the Word and promise confirmed by the leading of the star, they quicken their pace. At last the star stops and shines over the place where God is! The Magi, perhaps with tears of joy in their eyes, lay aside their own dignity and glory to stoop and bow low before him.

And they have not come empty-handed. They have special gifts appropriate only for God-made-flesh. Those gifts suggest to us that they may indeed have known a great deal about this promised King who so ruled that he could use even a star to bring them before him. Their gifts? Gold! That's what's fitting for a king to whom tribute is due. Incense! That's what's used in worshiping God, used by a priest as a symbol of prayer. And myrrh! That's the most surprising gift of all. Myrrh was used in the temple, where it was mixed with incense. It was used as an ingredient in the oil of anointing for prophets and priests. And it was used in burial rituals. Jesus, the King has come as Prophet, Priest, and King—the One who would carry out his divine offices perfectly in his death! How much of that did these Magi understand? The more of it they understood, the more understandable it is that they went to such trouble to find Jesus and were overjoyed when they had found him.

But there is yet one more gift that they brought to Jesus that we don't want to miss. It was the most expensive gift of all. They brought him what we call the *sacrificium intellecti*—the sacrifice of their intellect and reason. St. Paul reminds us that not many of the wise in this world are willing to bring that sacrifice (1 Corinthians 1:26). St. Paul was one who did bring such a sacrifice, and so were these Magi from the east. Reason could have told them that going all this long way when no one else wanted to was probably silly. Reason could have suggested that there was something wrong with the promise when the king in Jerusalem and the learned scholars of the Bible weren't interested in finding the newborn King of the Jews. And yes, just coming into this backwater village of Bethlehem and being directed by the star to whatever lowly dwelling Mary and Joseph had found by that time—well, it just doesn't seem appropriate. Any intelligent person would have said, *This is the King long promised? Look at him! Look at his mother! They are poor, undistinguished, from the lower classes. There must be some mistake.*

But no such thoughts occur to them. They are overjoyed still and not the least bit disappointed. Even when God warns them in a dream to go home again and to avoid returning to Jerusalem to give Herod the location of the holy child, even then, they are not offended. They have found the Savior-King. They have worshiped him. At peace and without bothering themselves over all the objections of reason, they now obey without question and return home. How interesting it will be for us in heaven to ask them questions about all this and about their lives after they returned to the east.

But for now, let us rejoice with them and follow their blessed example. For the King has shown himself to us too. Yes, in the bright light of his Word and sacraments, he has drawn us to himself and given himself to us—he who is the center of the whole Bible, the reason for the world's existence and ours too. With joyful steps let us hasten to bow low to worship and adore. He is the King who has ruled over heaven and earth so that we would hear his Word and believe it. Who else then could be entitled to our tribute? He is the Prophet, the source of truth—yes, truth itself in the flesh. Let us then listen to him and trust his Word, even if all of the world turns aside and cannot be bothered with him. All wisdom, preeminently the wisdom that brings eternal life, is found in him alone. Let us then bring the sacrifice of our intellect too, which always wants to argue with God and contradict him. He is the sacrifice wrapped only for three days in myrrh; its sweet smell comes down to us not with the fear of death but with the assurance of our joy in his resurrection and ours too.

> Dear Lord Jesus, you came in such lowliness and revealed yourself to high and low, to rich and poor, to wise and ignorant alike. By your coming to me as God and Savior, grant me also this grace that whatever dignity or wealth or wisdom I have, I may lay it at your feet with joy. For whatever I have is only by your gift and kindness. And whatever good it is, it is good only when received as a gift and then given back to you again in service like yours. For to you belongs all wealth, all wisdom, all honor and glory now and for eternity. Amen.

The Flight of the Holy Family and the Slaughter of the Innocents

I.

Matthew 2:13-15 – When [the Magi] had gone, an angel of the Lord appeared to Joseph in a dream. "Get up," he said, "take the child and his mother and escape to Egypt. Stay there until I tell you, for Herod is going to search for the child to kill him." So he got up, took the child and his mother during the night and left for Egypt, where he stayed until the death of Herod. And so was fulfilled what the Lord had said through the prophet: "Out of Egypt I called my son."

We have just brought with the wise men the *sacrificium intellecti*, the sacrifice of our own wisdom and intellect and reason to the Christ Child. But now this happens! And we want to take the sacrifice back and give advice to God. For this just doesn't seem right, no matter how we look at it. Jesus is the Son of God, the King of the universe and the ruler over all of history. And now he and his family become refugees? How easy it should have been for God to prevent this from happening. All he had to do was kill Herod—something Herod richly deserved!—or just let Herod die even a natural death and none of this would have taken place. It's all so simple really.

But instead, just after such a wonderful confirmation of Jesus as deity has taken place with the coming of the Magi, this humiliation comes. The gold they brought—if not the incense and the myrrh, which could have been sold for a goodly price—could have provided for better housing and some decent clothes and food. But now it will have to be spent on the bare essentials during the journey and perhaps for an extended period of time before Joseph could earn a living in Egypt.

And what about the journey itself? Traveling over the hill country of Judea and then through the desert wilderness of the Sinai—probably on foot—would be no pleasure at all. It was a long trip and uncomfortable on every level. If they have to go to Egypt, why not have them transported miraculously, let us say, on angels' wings?

And then there is Egypt! Israel had been there before. And we know how well those four hundred years (many of them years of slavery) had passed! With signs and wonders God—yes, this same Jesus—had brought his people out of there. And now he has to go back, not as King and Lord but as a refugee from a petty and cruel tyrant? It just doesn't seem right at all. There was no welcome for him when he came to be born in Bethlehem. And, to say the least, he should expect no welcome in Egypt either.

But Joseph raises none of our objections. Again as before, he simply listens to God's Word and obeys. He does not wait until morning. In the middle of the night, he wakes up Mary and with the child, flees without the least visible sign of assistance from God. What a sight they must have been to anyone who might have seen them. How pathetic. How wretched. Who takes a woman and a baby in the middle of the night and scurries out of town as if being chased by demons? *Oh, God, it's just too much! This is no way for you to act, especially toward your only begotten Son and his family!*

But there it is, and we cannot change it. Nor should we want to, especially after having so recently offered up to the Christ Child with the Magi our own *sacrificium intellecti*. Jesus on his cross was willing to be abandoned by his Father for our sake. But not just on the cross was he willing to forego all his rights as God and God's Son. No, his whole earthly life was one of sacrificing his rights and his due—his giving up what was fair and his by merit—in order to accomplish our salvation. And so in his birth he comes in all lowliness. In his earliest days he is humiliated by this difficult flight into Egypt and his staying there until the death of that accursed nobody, Herod (so wrongly called Herod the Great!).

So then, we have a great Jesus who appears and suffers from the moment of his conception to the moment of his resurrection. And did you notice it? So often the shadow of the cross falls over his life just after a fleeting moment or glimpse of glory. It was so when Simeon sang his beautiful song in the temple; along with praises for the light who lightens the Gentiles and the glory of God's people, Israel, came the promise of the sword that would go through Mary's heart at the sight of her dying Son. And now here, the beautiful moment has passed when the few wise men, who were really wise, bowed down in worship and presented their so beautiful and meaningful gifts. After just a day or so the cross came, and the holy family began in the middle of the night its pathetic flight into Egypt.

And so it must ever be in the life of Jesus. And so it must be so often in our own lives too. Have you experienced it? Just when everything seems to be going so well, loss comes. A problem arises. A shadow of the cross falls as new temptations replace the ones you thought you had finally overcome. We follow Jesus and the holy family into our own Egypt of exile, of new insecurities, and of fears. God could have so easily prevented it and kept us on a path through a bed of roses. But no, we follow Jesus under the shadow of the cross.

Why did it have to be that way for Jesus—always the cross? Why does it have to be that way for us—so often the cross? In the flight of the holy family, we are reminded that we have no secure dwelling place here (Hebrews 13:14) any more than Jesus did. He came from his home, his eternal city in heaven, to be for us the only secure refuge and strength in this time of our pilgrimage. He came to lead us through all the insecurity of our lives here and to trust that in him, we are safe and secure on our way to his eternal home. He came to have always over him the shadow of the cross until his final victory on that cross so that we would have it imprinted deeply in our hearts and minds: *All that I endure here, he endured first and much more deeply; all that I endure here weans me away from a love devoted to the fleeting and brings me fleeing towards a fuller trust in him, my God and Savior.*

> Even so, Lord Jesus, I give you all thanks and praise that so often you have given me the gold of godly pleasure and the sweet incense of a peaceful conscience in my hours of prayer—gifts so far beyond anything that I deserve. And I give you thanks and praise that you mingle them often with myrrh when the shadow of the cross falls over my pathway; for then I learn to trust you and to love you more than the gifts that come and go. For only the gifts of your grace, of forgiveness, and of the promise of eternal life last forever; and these give joy in good days and sustain me in bad ones. To you, O pilgrim Christ Child, be all praise and glory now and forever. Amen.

II.

Matthew 2:16-18 – When Herod realized that he had been outwitted by the Magi, he was furious, and he gave orders to kill all the boys in Bethlehem and its vicinity who were two years old and under, in accordance with the time he had learned from the Magi. Then what was said through the prophet Jeremiah was fulfilled: "A voice is heard in Ramah, weeping and great mourning, Rachel weeping for her children and refusing to be comforted, because they are no more."

Oh, how horrible! Could anything be more monstrous? Herod reached a new low with the slaughter of the innocent children in Bethlehem. Is there a special place in hell for him and people like him: people entirely devoted to evil, devoid of compassion, predators preying on the weak and the helpless and even on little children?

But couldn't God have prevented it? To be sure, Matthew tells us that it had to happen in the fulfillment of a prophecy. But God didn't have to give that prophecy. How moved to tears we are at the sight of these women weeping for their children. It's bad enough that their children died; how incomparably worse for them to see them perish in such a gruesome manner. Does such suffering come to Bethlehem because its inhabitants had not listened to the preaching of the shepherds who had worshiped the Christ Child on Christmas night? Did it come because they did not follow the example of the Magi and bow low before the newborn King of the Jews? If these people deserved to be punished for that, why kill their infant sons?

Or, as difficult as that may be, are we to take the same long view of things that God takes of them? And just what is that long view? For all the anguish of their parents and for all the pain that the children suffered as they died, these children were spared the horrible example of their parents. As children made heirs of the kingdom of heaven through their circumcision, they came quickly to the crown of eternal life. For that Old Testament "sacrament" made them children of God and heirs of his kingdom, much as Baptism does for us today. In heaven, as we see from the pictures of heaven in the last book of the Bible, none of the saints or martyrs complain about what they endured on their way there. Rather, they join forever in thankful praise to the Lamb who was slain to win for them their place in glory.

That may well be threadbare comfort to those who suffer the loss of a child or of anyone else for that matter. The mothers of these children wept. And who wouldn't in such circumstances? But we are told they refused to be comforted. We weep with them and like them at the loss of a child, a parent, a sibling, a friend. But may it never be that we refuse to be comforted. Our tears are those of sorrow to be sure, sorrow at the loss of the love and companionship of the one who has died. But at the same time, may they be tears of gratitude as well to the Lord who gave us such people and the blessings that came to us because of them for the time that we had them. And then may our tears be tears of gratitude also for the promise that all who die with faith in the Savior do not die at all; they go home—to the home Jesus has won for us by his flight into Egypt, his exile there, and all that he did in his earthly life. The baby received into the arms of Jesus at Baptism or the aged warrior who longed to go to be with Jesus—both alike rejoice to be where they have gone. We struggle in our weakness to be happy for them as we grieve for our loss—until Jesus brings us to the army of the saints and angels where they have gone.

To be sure, at such times grateful joy over what we had and over what our Christian loved one now has in death may be a difficult, even a long and painful process for us. For relief we can fly to the arms of the Jesus who embraces them, to his arms in his gospel and in his sacraments. There he welcomes us as he has welcomed them. He greets them with a sight that in this life, they saw only with the eyes of faith. He greets us with the certainty that he always keeps his Word—even the gruesome words about the slaughter of the innocents in Bethlehem. He will not fail to keep his Word to be with us in our hours of lonely sorrow. Nor will he fail to dry our tears on the day when he brings us from faith to sight in our eternal home. So we close our eyes to everything merely temporal and fix them on Jesus, the beginning and the end of our faith. And we tune our ears to his words of grace and promise. Thus we join the weeping women of Bethlehem—and thus we leave them, not despairing but in the quiet comfort of Jesus' words and promise.

And therein is an important and so easily forgotten lesson for us in the here and now: We tend to judge everything in the short term—in the moment. If something is difficult for us to understand or accept in this moment, we assume that it will always be difficult to understand and forever unacceptable to us. But God looks at everything from the perspective of eternity; he knows how everything will turn out in the end, and he arranges history—the history of the world and our own history in it—so that it turns out as nothing but pure blessing for those who love his Son and trust in him for their salvation. And yes, he sees to it as well that things turn out in terror eternal for those who cast him and his so dearly bought salvation aside. The innocents whose martyrdom we remember now know that perfectly. And to his eternal shame, so does Herod! May we cling to Jesus: the refugee in Egypt, the crucified on the cross, the risen and ascended Lord who understands our confusion and brings our sorrows to a blessed end. That's what he promised, and he never lies to us or deceives us!

> Dearest Savior, when my eyes overflow, let me still see you in your grace and mercy. When my ears are plugged by the sounds of wailing, let me still hear your promise of rescue and relief. When my heart is aching, let it know that yours ached too and that you understand my longing. When my mind and reason are confused and troubled, refill them with your Word and its power to overcome all my doubts and fears. For without you and your saving Word, all of my life is but trouble and sorrow; with you and your holy gospel, even the shadow of death is made light at the end of day with your peace and the joy of forgiveness and the promise of eternity with you in heaven. Amen.

The Boy Jesus in the Temple

I.

Luke 2:43-46 – After the festival was over, while his parents were returning home, the boy Jesus stayed behind in Jerusalem, but they were unaware of it. Thinking he was in their company, they traveled on for a day. Then they began looking for him among their relatives and friends. When they did not find him, they went back to Jerusalem to look for him. After three days they found him in the temple courts.

What a fascinating account! It is the only one we have of Jesus from the time of the return from Egypt until some 30 years later when he began his earthly ministry. The family had gone to Jerusalem for the Passover; that was the great festival that celebrated Israel's rescue from death and from Egypt by the blood of a lamb (Exodus 12) and thus pictured the real rescue to come through the slaughter of the true Lamb of God, Jesus himself.

Jesus is 12 years old. That was the age for a boy to celebrate the Old Testament equivalent of confirmation. That rite made a boy responsible to the law, to both know it and keep it. And know it he would! The custom required a boy to memorize large portions of the Old Testament, some say as much as the entire first five books of the Bible at the least!

Just think of it! Jesus, in his human nature, memorized the books of which he was, in his divine nature, the author! Just think of it! He went to celebrate the Passover knowing full well that its purpose was to picture him and his work of redemption to come!

But now the great festival celebration is over and it is time to go home. He had come to Jerusalem with his parents in the company of countless other pilgrims from Nazareth and the rest of Galilee. How everyone had looked forward to it! Joseph could visit with carpenters from neighboring villages and no doubt with relatives from nearby. Mary could visit as well and perhaps go shopping for things that just were not available in little Nazareth. Who knows? Perhaps the parents of John, Zechariah and Elizabeth (her relative), were still alive; if so, they would certainly be there. What a treat it would be for them to share stories of their two growing boys! And then how this celebration of Passover must have overwhelmed the souls of Jesus' pious earthly parents; for on some level they must have had at least a glimmer of the ultimate reality that Passover was really all about their son.

But wait a minute. Mary and Joseph leave the hustle and bustle of crowded Jerusalem and head back home with the neighbors and the relatives—and leave Jesus behind! How is that even possible? Who does something like that? They thought he was somewhere in the crowd accompanying them back to Nazareth? They have been entrusted with the care of God's own Son and they just expect that he is around somewhere? To be sure, as God's own Son he could take care of himself, but he is in his state of lowly humiliation, a growing boy both physically and spiritually (Luke 2:52) and they knew that. No, there is just no excuse for it; even today such behavior would win the charge of child neglect or endangerment!

And so there we have it: Jesus' parents weren't perfect. They were—well, how can we say it?—so very like us. They had gotten so used to having Jesus with them that it was possible for them to forget that he was their responsibility and their priceless treasure—the focus, the center, the all in all of their lives. Yes, and even in the great celebrations of their religion, which were really all about Jesus, they had gotten so taken up with the fringe, albeit real, pleasures of friends and family that Jesus got sort of lost in the shuffle. And so, even when they realize what a horrible mistake they have made, they do not go to the most obvious place to find Jesus, to where his Word is; they run here and there, hither and yon, looking for him with growing anxiety that he was lost—and more important, that they were responsible for losing him! What fear, what guilt, what anguish must have torn at their hearts during those three long days of searching!

Is it too much to suggest that the behavior of Mary and Joseph on this occasion serves as a useful object lesson and reminder for us? We have celebrations too that are really all about Jesus. And those celebrations are often accompanied with the real joys of time spent with friends and family that he has given us, joys for which otherwise there is often too little time. It's Christmas. It's Easter. It's the baptism of a child or a confirmation. It's a wedding. Yes, it could even be a funeral. All of these times are occasions that God provides in the course of our pilgrimage on earth for celebration with his gifts of family and friends. But always, and most important, at their center is . . . Jesus! It is his birth at Christmas and his resurrection at Easter that are all-important. At a child's baptism or confirmation, it is Jesus who is the real sponsor and author of all the blessings that accompany the celebration. At a wedding it is Jesus who is the all-important third party to the new family. And at a funeral it is Jesus who is the Redeemer from death and the author of eternal life in heaven.

But it's easy to forget that. It's easy to make Jesus the secondary element of the occasion (or as Luther likes to put it: just the foam on the beer!) and then—then to leave without him! Then, perhaps exhausted from the hustle and bustle of the celebration, we go back to everyday life, wondering whether it was really worth all the bother. When that happens, it's time to go back to Jerusalem and to look for Jesus again. It's time to look for him, not in the tinsel and the outward finery of a festival but where he is always to be found. Look for him in the Word. Look for him in the sacraments. That's where he has promised always to be. That's where he has promised always to find you!

> Dearest Jesus, forgive the times when even in my religion, I have been so absorbed by the externals that I left you behind. You have entrusted yourself to me in your Word and sacraments so that there I should find and treasure you. Give me this grace and favor that I ever and again may return to find you there. Give me this grace and favor so that in finding you, I may take

you again back into my everyday life with family and friends, in work and in pleasure. Give me this grace and favor so that being found by you in your gospel, I may more and more come to see that you are indeed the all in all of my earthly pilgrimage; for you are the source and center of all that I treasure in life here and look forward to in heaven hereafter. Amen.

II.

Luke 2:46-50 – After three days they found him in the temple courts, sitting among the teachers, listening to them and asking them questions. Everyone who heard him was amazed at his understanding and his answers. When his parents saw him, they were astonished. His mother said to him, "Son, why have you treated us like this? Your father and I have been anxiously searching for you." "Why were you searching for me?" he asked. "Didn't you know I had to be in my Father's house?" But they did not understand what he was saying to them.

What a thrill it would have been for us to be there to see the 12-year-old Son of God and Mary's son with the great teachers of the law, listening to them and asking them questions. Luke tells us that far from dismissing this boy as unworthy of their attention, they listen to his questions and his answers and are amazed. Apparently, a crowd has gathered. All look on with wonder at this child. He had been there in the temple before, 8 days and then 40 days after his birth, and at those times amazing things had happened too, but few noticed. At least some of these teachers who now listened to him so attentively had been the same ones who heard of the star leading the wise men and who had, through Herod, instructed them to go to Bethlehem to find the child—but they themselves did not go. And now, without their connecting any of these dots, here is that selfsame child in their midst. At the age of 12 he listens, he speaks, and they listen! Would that their listening would last!

And now on to the scene come Mary and Joseph. How astonished they must have been by what they saw and heard. For three days they have been looking for him. And now they come to the temple. Do they come there in desperation, as it's the only place left that they hadn't looked? Do they come to pray for their rescue from their sin of neglect or for the rescue of their son, perhaps lost to them for good? By this time they must have been in a real panic. But there he is! And no one has asked him, "Where are your parents? What are you doing here all alone?" The only ones in a panic about those questions are Mary and Joseph. They are not interested at this point in the learned discussion Jesus is having with the great teachers in the temple. They are not interested in the amazement of all who saw and heard him there.

Instead, Mary blurts out what—to her mother's heart—was the only thing that mattered. In a mixture of deep relief and considerable annoyance, she forgets her responsibility and that of Joseph in this whole business and puts all the blame on Jesus! Jesus' words in answer to his mother put the responsibility back where it belongs. But look at how gently he does it. There is no preteen outburst. He knows who he is and they know too. And therefore, there really isn't any excuse for their annoyance. If anyone should be annoyed, he should be; after all, angels had told them quite plainly who he is, even before his birth. And they had seen the message confirmed in the worship of the shepherds, in the words of Simeon and Anna, and then in the worship of the wise men. They had been to Egypt and back again, and through it all, they had had the opportunity to live with this amazing child, the sinless Son of God. But Jesus doesn't beat them over the head with any of this. He just reminds them in the clearest and most gentle way possible of what they should have expected. But even then the heads and hearts of Mary and Joseph continue to spin; they have no answer for him.

We have been calling to mind our own religious celebrations. We have given thought to the possibility that as Jesus got lost in the shuffle of that great Passover celebration, perhaps he has been lost too by us at times, even as we celebrate great religious events during the year. Then when we go back to our everyday life from a hectic Christmas, a busy Easter, or even from a joyful Baptism or confirmation or wedding, we are worn out. We are left wondering if all the bother was worth it. And so our three days pass without a lingering afterglow. And why? Because Jesus was lost—or rather, he who always finds us in his Word and sacraments has somehow been left behind.

When that kind of weariness comes over us this year, perhaps we should remember the answer of the boy Jesus in the temple—the answer he gave to Mary and Joseph—slightly reworked to fit our own situation: "What are you so anxious about? Why are you so worn out and wondering if it was all worth the bother? Did you forget that I was God's gift to you in Christmas, God's life for you in Easter? Have you forgotten that Baptism is all about an eternal inheritance bestowed on you and the one baptized because I was there? Have you forgotten that it was the treasure of my grace and pardon that the one who is confirmed reaffirms? Have you left behind the Bridegroom of the church at the wedding celebration?"

When we look at it that way, we can feel a smile come over our souls. We can breathe again a sigh of relief. We can look at the boy Jesus in the temple and answer, "How kind of you and how gracious that you put up with all my nonsense. How kind and how gracious that when I make the secondary things most important, you let me experience weariness and frustration so that I will look again for you and be found again by you in your Word and sacraments. How kind and how gracious that you give me a lifetime to learn with Mary and Joseph these lessons over and over again. Thus over and over again, I come to you in repentance. And over and over again, you find me and fill me with joy in the promise of your presence with and for me in the gospel.

> Even so, Lord Jesus, be patient with me, be patient still. Only in heaven will I finally catch on to everything. And only there will I at last see how truly patient you always were with me. And for that grace so underserved, I worship you even now and give you all thanks and praise. Amen.

III.

Luke 2:51,52 – Then he went down to Nazareth with them and was obedient to them. But his mother treasured all these things in her heart. And Jesus grew in wisdom and stature, and in favor with God and man.

And so the Son of God demonstrates yet again his humility! We might have expected this first line to end differently; we might have had it go this way: Then he went down to Nazareth with them and *they* were obedient to *him*. Or maybe this way: Since they had shown themselves unworthy, Jesus stayed in Jerusalem and found a better set of parents to care for him. Or how about this: Once they got back to Nazareth, he never let them forget their mistake, but held it over their heads for the rest of their days.

But that's not the way Jesus is. It's not the way he was then with Mary and Joseph. It's not the way he is now with you and me. Jesus demonstrates both his humility and his holiness in his perfect obedience to the Fourth Commandment. And in the process, he prepares himself for the day when he will redeem us from our breaking of that commandment. He submits to his earthly parents, even though he was in a better position to tell them what to do than they could ever be to instruct him. He puts to shame the child who thinks he could run the household better than his parents and so treats them with contempt. The child sometimes is right—sometimes he could run the household better than his parents—but that's not the role God has given him. The church member who thinks he'd be a better preacher than his pastor and so speaks ill of him—even if he's right, that's not his role. His role is to help his pastor in any way that he can. The wife who is sure she should be the head of the family instead of her dim husband—again, she may be a better head than he, but that's not way God has arranged things. Her assignment is that of helping him be a better head of the family than he could be without her support. The husband who imagines that his wife is there to serve his every whim and fancy—that's not his assignment. His assignment is to treat her the way that Christ treats the church: with love and respect and all possible care.

We all have roles in which God has placed us: roles in the home, roles in employment, roles at church and in the state. Those change over time, to be sure. But as long as we occupy a role, even if we could do better the assignment of another in a different role, part of our life as a Christian is to imitate the humility of the child Jesus. He served. He helped. He didn't backbite or hold over their heads their obvious faults and failures. Isn't it amazing how often the life of Jesus puts such a different spin on our own lives? We would scarcely think of it that submission and respect is an important and noble work were it not for Jesus' obedience to his so flawed parents. We would hardly have it occur to us that arrogance towards those who exercise authority in the home, at work, in the church, and in the state is any kind of sin were it not for Jesus' quiet gentleness towards Mary and Joseph.

And how do we know that he showed such a quiet gentleness in his submission and obedience as he grew into an adult? "And Jesus grew in wisdom and stature, and in favor with God and man." In lowliness he veiled divine wisdom and became a student. In humility the God-man lived and walked among other children and young adults. And all of it he did in such a way that none could reproach him. He grew in favor with God; his obedience in his human nature was perfect. He grew in favor with people; those who saw him and lived with him had only good to say about him. They made no harsh reproach of, "He thinks he's better/smarter/holier than everyone else!"—even though that was all true and no doubt even obvious. In short, his love for his Father and for us was complete in every moment.

> Lord Jesus, I can only marvel at your example of humility. I can only be amazed at the humility you still show, even now in glory. For you do not despise me in my imperfection, my imagined wisdom and importance. You do not even hold all my foolishness and all my sins forever over my head. But in grace and mercy, you still stoop to dwell with me in kindness that forgives my faults, in mercy that shields me from the full consequences of my folly, and in love that never abandons me or lets me go. Oh, that I might grow in wisdom from you in your Word, in appreciation of your Father's favor given by your

forgiveness granted in the Word and sacraments, and in favor with those around me who may come to see you more and more in my humble service! Amen.

The Baptism of Jesus and His 40 Days in the Wilderness
I.

Matthew 3:16,17 – As soon as Jesus was baptized, he went up out of the water. At that moment heaven was opened, and he saw the Spirit of God descending like a dove and alighting on him. And a voice from heaven said, "This is my Son, whom I love; with him I am well pleased."

Here is a truly beautiful and amazing event in the life of Jesus and in our lives too. Jesus was conceived and born without sin. Jesus committed no sin—no not one in thought, none in word, not a single one in deed. Jesus' entire existence was one of loving obedience to the Father in accordance with the law of God and in service to all mankind. Nevertheless, he goes to be baptized by John the Baptist, who preached repentance and administered Baptism for the forgiveness of sins. Though needing no forgiveness for himself, Jesus insists that John baptize him. Jesus' baptism would be yet further evidence of his perfect submission to the will of his Father. Indeed, that baptism serves as a sort of inauguration into his public ministry, a ministry that will end in his death and resurrection for us and for our salvation.

But look at how it all takes place. A president is inaugurated or a king is crowned with great pageantry and powerful displays of military and political might. But Jesus? See how he enters into his most holy office of Redeemer. He goes to this man who is clothed with rough camel's hair, a man living on locusts and wild honey. There is no pomp. The angels do not form an honor guard or a choir. It may be that some of John's disciples or a few other people were there. But, if they were there, they merited no mention in the account of the simple ceremony performed by a simple man. John baptizes this Jesus, one who also appeared as nothing special even though he was the only really important person in the world.

And then it happens! God rips open the curtain that separates time from eternity, heaven from earth. And he speaks! Yes, and the Holy Spirit humbles himself as he takes the form of a lowly animal, a common dove. Nobody special was at the baptism—just the Holy Trinity! And listen to what God says: "This is my Son, whom I love; with him I am well pleased." So there we have it—a perfect testimony from God the Father that this is indeed his Son, not Joseph's. How proud this Father is of this unique Son! This his Son clothed in human flesh and blood, a true man born of the virgin, is spotless, sinless, and perfect in every way. For without perfection, God could not be pleased with him. Indeed, without his being God's eternal Son, he would never have been perfect in the first place.

But now, for all that we could yet say about this wondrous event, we want to cry out in ecstasy: *Lord Jesus, take me with you into your baptism so that the Father may say of me what he said of you; grant that the Holy Spirit may attend my baptism too!* And here is the amazing fact of the matter: Though at our baptism we never uttered such a prayer, that is nevertheless exactly what happened there! This is a fact that we call to mind when we remember Jesus' baptism; God was most surely present at our baptism too. There God said in effect: *Yes, most certainly! Yes, absolutely, in your baptism I was there. In your baptism, all unseen by human eyes, the veil between heaven and earth was ripped open, and the difference between time and eternity became insignificant. And yes, in your baptism too the Holy Spirit descended, and I spoke; Jesus is my only-begotten Son, and in your baptism you became my adopted child because of all that he did for your salvation.*

Is that not a wondrous thing indeed? It's exactly what St. Paul says in Roman 6, Galatians 3, and Titus 3. It is all so beautifully expressed by Paul when he sums up the life we received at Baptism. He says, "Your life is now hidden with Christ in God. When Christ, who is your life, appears, then you also will appear with him in glory" (Colossians 3:3,4)!

So there you have it. Your baptism too, so simple in its outward appearance, was and remains a most glorious event in your life. Nothing can compare with it in splendor or in effect. Jesus was there. The Father spoke. The Holy Spirit was active. And all of it was to bring you into a blessed fellowship with God through the washing away of your sins for time and for eternity. All of it was to confirm for your whole life long the love of God designed just for you. For your baptism was no accident of time and circumstance. God ruled over history to hide you in Christ, to cloth you with all of his righteousness and holiness, to dress you in royal robes as an heir with Christ of heaven. And one day you will actually see it! It is no less true just because you can't see it now; God has spoken and he does not lie. Ahead of you is that glorious day of Christ's appearing when the embrace of the Father and the Spirit's perpetual presence in Word and sacraments will be yours to enjoy perfectly and forever.

So then, what was your baptism like? Were there a lot of people present to celebrate your adoption by Jesus' Father? Was it perhaps just parents and the pastor? Whatever the case may be, even though you were probably too young to remember it, it was an amazing day in your life. Jesus was there. His baptism began his public ministry of winning your salvation. And at your baptism all the fruit of what he did was given to you. Jesus took you in his arms, as it were, and placed you in the lap of his Father. The Holy Spirit stirred within your soul to create—even before you could speak or think much about it—a trust in the merit of the Savior and a love for the Holy Trinity. There couldn't be a better day in your life than that.

> Dear Lord Jesus, as I call to mind your baptism and thus call to mind my own as well, may your Holy Spirit stir in me a deep gratitude for this sacred washing. Yes, whenever I wash my body outwardly, may I think on the sacred washing you gave me in my baptism. For there you took away the spiritual death and doom that was mine in the sinful nature inherited from Adam and Eve. There you even gave me the promise of forgiveness for my whole life long. There you washed my naked body and soul and dressed me in your own holiness and righteousness. There you made me a dear child of your Father by faith created in Baptism, faith that trusts you alone for my salvation. Oh, preserve to me ever these precious fruits of your work and your gift in Baptism. Grant that I may grow in thanksgiving to you for your saving work and the saving gospel in Word and Sacrament by which alone I am yours for time and for eternity. Amen.

II.

Matthew 4:1,2 – Then Jesus was led by the Spirit into the wilderness to be tempted by the devil. After fasting forty days and forty nights, he was hungry.

But wait! The story of Jesus' baptism is not over. It has another side to it that is also astonishing. As already noted in passing, his baptism is really his inauguration into his public ministry. But we might want to give God some more advice here: *Is this any way to inaugurate your Son into his public ministry?!* For what happens in our world when a high official is inaugurated? There's a parade. There's a party. There's a celebration for all and sundry to see how wonderful and how powerful the new president or governor is. Wouldn't this inauguration have been a wonderful time for some form of testimonial from people who would echo the Father's testimony at the baptism? Wouldn't this have been a fine time for Mary to step forward and rehearse for an attending crowd what she knew and had experienced? She could have brought all present to wonder and awe as she told of the angel's announcement of his coming. She could have spoken of the worship of the shepherds and then of wise men from the east. She could have told everyone about the testimony of Simeon in the temple, about the preservation of the family on the flight to Egypt and during their time there. What wonderful stories she might have told about Jesus' childhood. And others too could have come forward to tell what they knew and had experienced with Jesus during his first 30 years.

But that's not the way it was for Jesus. He had not come to be exalted in this life. No, exactly the opposite was his lot in life. His life was a march to the cross. The Holy Trinity had promised and prepared for this work since the fall of Adam and Eve in the Garden of Eden. And now the time had come. God is eager to get on with it, to get on with the work of our redemption! And so, immediately—without delay, minus any kind of outward celebration or glory—the Holy Spirit urges him on into the desert. In fact, St. Mark in his gospel uses a very strong verb; he tells us that the Holy Spirit sent him (literally, cast him out!) into the desert. And for what purpose? To be tempted by the devil!

What a beginning for his redeeming work! It begins as it will end—with struggle, with battle. Unseen by anyone else, Jesus goes into the desert. He will devote himself there completely to a loving obedience to his Father. And he will show it as none of us is asked to, as not one of us ever could: For 40 days and 40 nights he will eat nothing. In his human nature he will rely on his Father to sustain him.

At the end of the 40 days, he was hungry. This hunger shows us that he was not just some phantom with what appeared to be a body; no, he was a true human being. And even though miraculously sustained during that 40-day fast, he nevertheless was hungry at its close. We are not to think of his work for our redemption as some sort of easy shadow boxing. No, the entire work will require a struggle, a battle of heroic dimensions. And it is a battle that he must not lose, not even in its first skirmishes, because our salvation is at stake here!

And so Jesus goes from his baptism not to glory but to his first steps on the way to the cross!

To a certain extent that's the way it is for us too. We too do not go from our baptism to outward glory. To be sure, in our baptism we become God's own children by adoption. But we follow Jesus into the wilderness, as it were, to be tempted by the devil. We are not driven there to win a victory for our salvation; that was Jesus' work and his alone. But we do follow him into battle—into a lifelong struggle against the temptations of the devil. As Jesus' struggle was real, so too is ours; it too is no shadow boxing.

What then shall we say? Will we run away from the battle? We know only too well how unfit we are for it in our still-fallen nature. Will we try to pretend that there really is no battle, that we are already close enough to good enough as we are? After all, we have gotten used to whatever faults we may have—and God will just have to get used to them too.

Oh, may it never be! We do not need to run away, even if we could. For Jesus in the struggle has been victorious—victorious as our substitute. He won his victory so that he could give it to us by forgiving—as he already has in our baptism—all of our failures in the struggle. In his human nature he won where we have lost, and he won *for us*.

Nevertheless, there is still a battle for us. Pretending that, since Jesus won the victory for us, we are now free from the battle and can sin as much as we want is to throw away his so dearly won struggle on our behalf. That's one of the great paradoxes of our faith: Our victory is won entirely by Jesus, but to refuse to struggle in the wilderness and instead to embrace and wallow in our sins is to throw away that already-won victory.

So then, clothed in the victory garment of forgiveness and with the status of adopted children of God—of brothers and sisters of Jesus—we follow after him to the struggle that will only end with the crown of glory in heaven. Of course we are not alone in the battle. Jesus is there with us, he who has already won our victory. So we will not shun the fight. We count it as an honor—or at least the Christian part of our nature that was born and created in us in our baptism counts it as an honor—to show our love and gratitude for victory by striving after submission to the Word of God with heart and soul, with mind and strength.

Jesus, in his own struggle, will show us how.

> O great Victor, my champion in the battle, my Savior and my Lord, grant me grace so that I do not shun to follow you into the wilderness. By your victory for me, grant me ever greater zeal in following you. I know how weak I am and how ready my sinful flesh is to shun the battle and surrender to the devil; by your love for me in your battle, grant me renewed desire and strength for the struggle. Amen.

III.

Matthew 4:2-4 – After fasting forty days and forty nights, he was hungry. The tempter came to him and said, "If you are the Son of God, tell these stones to become bread." Jesus answered, "It is written: 'Man shall not live on bread alone, but on every word that comes from the mouth of God.' "

Just as Jesus has taken you along to his baptism and given you all that he has merited as God's beloved Son and your Savior in your baptism, what happens to him after his baptism happens to you too. As you have shared in the glory of his baptism, so he bids you share in the struggle—the battle—that follows it. And here is perhaps the most surprising thing of all—yes, a most comforting thing at that: What follows for Jesus and what follows for us is, in a way, a good thing!

And just what is it that follows? Satan comes with an intriguing series of temptations. While Jesus no doubt was tempted all through the 40 days and nights of his fast in the wilderness, we are told of only three temptations. And these temptations are recorded precisely because they are the ones that we must struggle against every day our whole life long. In fact, few temptations are there that get very far from these three. That's why the writer of Hebrews can say that Jesus was tempted in every way just as we are and that he fully understands us from his own experience (Hebrews 4:15).

The first temptation: Jesus, in his human nature, is understandably hungry after this long fast—no doubt very hungry. While his divine nature had preserved him from starving to death during those days, he was not spared the sensation of great hunger. Now, the devil suggests to Jesus, would be a good time to step out from behind the veil that hides all of the divine power and majesty that Jesus possesses as the second person of the Trinity. After all, *if* you really are the Son of God, then it should be no small thing for you to satisfy your hunger by turning these stones into bread. After all, why should you suffer? Who is going to see? Who is going to know? It will just be our little secret. Here, now, *if* you really are the Son of God, prove it!

Oh, how clever! First the tempter wants to introduce doubt about truth, about reality. That's a favorite tactic of his, one he used with success already in the Garden of Eden. Do you hear an echo as you follow Jesus into the wilderness? You are, by faith and by your baptism, a dear child of God. That's a fact. God promised it and said so. And he does not, cannot, will never lie or deceive us. Well, *if* that's really true, then why should you suffer when there seems no real point in it? Why should you have needs unmet and wants unsatisfied? Shouldn't God overturn all your financial reverses, all of your personal setbacks with family, friends, and coworkers? Shouldn't you have the success and the happiness you see others enjoy—others who deserve it less than you?

But wait! You don't have all those things you should deserve *if* you are such a dear object of God's love. Instead, you have trouble after trouble. You have problems that just don't go away or are only gone to be replaced with other problems. You have needs and wants ever unsatisfied, frustrations with this one and that, underserved opposition from here and there. And to top it off, you get nothing but ingratitude from those you try to help. Well then, only one conclusion is possible: God doesn't love you after all and you really aren't his dear child! When all is said and done, you are alone in the world, alone in the wilderness. You'd best grab what you can while you can. You can't trust God to provide for you! A child of God? Fantasy! Illusion! Pie in the sky!

How does Jesus deal with the bottom line temptation to doubt the truth, to doubt the reality of his relationship with God his Father? For starters, he doesn't do what we so often do and what becomes a critical ingredient in our frequent falls into sin. He doesn't toy with the temptation. He doesn't even consider it. His answer is swift and to the point: "It is written"! That's the beginning and the source of every victory! What God says in his Word is true, regardless of what seems to be true in a moment and on the outside. It's beyond all doubt true, fixed, and sure—the only real reality! And what is it that is written that has to do with this particular temptation? "Man shall not live on bread alone, but on every word that comes from the mouth of God"! It was his Father and the Holy Spirit who had sent him into the wilderness and to this particular time of fasting and struggle. And so his Father could not abandon him there. He had his Father's promise implied in the sending. And that's all he needed. At other times he would eat and drink as any human being does and needs to. And at those times his body would be sustained by such eating and drinking, just as God sustains us normally by our eating and drinking. But—and that's the point—the eating and drinking of itself sustains no one! It is the Word of God and his promise that gives the food the ability to do that. Apart from what comes from the mouth of God, nothing going into our mouths would do us any good at all. And so Jesus answers the devil and reminds us that the real source of earthly life and sustenance is not bread that perishes; it is what comes from the mouth of God, from his promises, from his Word.

Our champion has won! Our hero has the victory! Moreover, his answer was not just perfect for him; it is perfect for us too. We so easily imagine that our life consists of things fleeting and perishable. *If I have enough and more to eat, if I have this problem solved and these wants satisfied, then I will have life and be happy.* But it isn't so—unless God in his infinite love and compassion is pleased to grant it. And even then, it is God who has satisfied us with good things. And it is God who has taken some of them away at times, sometimes for a long time, so that we will come back again to what St. James said so well: "Every good and perfect gift [yes, including the times of need and temptation and loss!] is from above, coming down from the Father of the heavenly lights, who does not change like shifting shadows" (1:17).

In times of plenty and prosperity, there is no *if* about it: By faith you *are* a child of God. In times of want and need, of pain and loss, there is no doubt about it: By his promise in his Word and at your baptism, you *are* a child of God. So say grace at mealtime and open your mouth with thanksgiving that, not by bread alone but by God's Word and promise, the bread sustains. By his Word as well, all your other needs he satisfies; for it is, as it were, by the word of his mouth that he sent them. Friends and family satisfy. Days of good health by which we work and are able to enjoy leisure—they all come from him. In times of seeming lack and loss, we still give thanks that he abides true and will sustain us by his grace and promise, just as he has in the past, in good times and bad.

> Even so, Lord Jesus, my champion in the struggle against Satan and all his lies, I give you thanks and praise that you won this battle and won it for me. I confess with sorrow the times I have lost in the struggle to trust, in spite of all outward appearance, that God is really my dear Father because of you. Let me in this hour rejoice to reenter the battle against such doubts when they again assail me. Teach me yet again to trust that, having you and your Word, I have life—the only life that really matters. So grant me still victory over the silliness and the vice of imagining that life is found in anything or anyone else. For me that truth—that reality—will always be a struggle. Pardon and forgive me as I stumble, and ever raise me up to enter again the fray. Amen.

IV.

Matthew 4:5-7 – Then the devil took him to the holy city and had him stand on the highest point of the temple. "If you are the Son of God," he said, "throw yourself down. For it is written: 'He will command his angels concerning you, and they will lift you up in their hands, so that you will not strike your foot against a stone.' Jesus answered him, "It is also written: 'Do not put the Lord your God to the test.' "

Now here is an intriguing temptation indeed! It is, in fact, a temptation to fall into the sin opposite the sin suggested by the first temptation. The first temptation was a temptation to doubt the promises of God. This one is the temptation to misuse and pervert the promises of God. This time Satan is a theologian! He doesn't run away from church but to it. He doesn't flee from the Bible but takes it into his foul and filthy mouth with the intent of perverting it. He is the first heretic and the father of all heresy; for heresy takes part of the Bible out of its context and twists it to a meaning opposite of God's intent.

And so just what is the temptation here, and what is the perversion of God's Word? First notice that again the temptation begins with an attempt to cast doubt on the truth with that little word *if*. But this time, Satan wants Jesus to prove that truth by a false trust in God's promises. The temptation is this: *If* you really are the Son of God, then you should be able to do whatever you want; God will be obliged to come to your aid, even if what you do is contrary to his Word. For look here! He has promised always and everywhere to come to help and rescue you, even sending angels to get the job done for him! See, the Bible even says so!

Of course, as always when Satan uses the Bible, he leaves out what doesn't fit his purpose. And so he does here too; Satan is quoting from Psalm 91:11,12. Verse 11, however, reads, "He will command his angels concerning you to guard you *in all your ways."* The phrase "in all your ways" is critical to a correct understanding of God's beautiful promise in this psalm. What should "your ways" be? They should be ways that submit to the Word of God, ways that seek only to think and speak and do what worships him and serves our neighbor (Psalm 1). The opposite ways are those which cast aside the law and the gospel and then expect God to prosper us in our sins.

For us it works like this: Satan takes us too into the temple of God's Word and into the heart of Jesus where God lives and where his promises dwell. He reminds of the cardinal truth of God's Word and permits us to make the happy confession of faith: "Jesus loves me, this I know; for the Bible tells me so!" And then he adds his little twist that is so death-dealing and devastating: "Jesus loves me, this I know; *and this is all I want to know!"* Now I am free to do exactly as I please. I can sin boldly and with reckless abandon; for Jesus loves me, and he has promised to forgive me. So it doesn't matter what I do. I can cheat. I can lie. I can lust and follow my lust. I can throw all caution to the wind and chuck the law of God behind me. I don't really even need church anymore; for I know that Jesus loves me, whether I hear his Word or not. Yes, I can even pick and choose what parts of his Word I will follow and what parts I'll just forget since some just don't suit me. I can cast myself down from the peak of the temple—of the gospel. For God is obliged to save me *for* and *in* my sins. Oh, to be sure, I'll repent later on, and God will forgive me so that I can freely do it all again!

Who hasn't thought that to one degree or another? What temptation, be it great or small, doesn't have that whisper of the devil somehow at its heart? Using the most precious promise of forgiveness, the devil seeks to drive us away from the Word of God; he wants us to imagine that God is a fool who doesn't take his Word seriously and really doesn't expect us to take it seriously either. That way, all false doctrine and all godless living is made easy, in spite of God's serious warnings against such presumption (Galatians 5:19-21).

And what is Jesus' answer to this temptation? Again, he does not toy with it for an instant. Again, he who is the real author of God's Word takes it in hand and triumphs over the temptation. He quotes the bottom line, so to speak, of God's stern warning against the temptation to arrogant presumption, to imagining that God gives us his gifts and ultimately himself so that we can despise him and cast his Word aside with reckless abandon. "Do not put the LORD your God to the test" (Deuteronomy 6:16)! That says it all, doesn't it? Don't throw God's promises in his face and then "trust" that he will let you play him for a fool!

To be sure, "Jesus loves me this I know; for the Bible tells me so." And that is our great comfort in our struggle—not a license to sin. What a blessed relief it is that Jesus won the victory over the temptation and did it for us and in our place. But he didn't do it so that we would never have to struggle against the temptation. Quite the contrary, he did it both to save us and to show us how to endure and win in the struggle.

So then, go indeed to the peak of the temple; go to be with Jesus where he is to be found: in his Word and sacraments. Hold him in them close to your heart. And then with him do battle against the temptation to put God to the test; for he will indeed let you suffer the consequences of your sins if you cast his Word aside. Cling to every doctrine, lest you lose it all—for that's the tragic consequence of a smörgåsbord approach to his Word. Hold fast to all that he has said also in the law. And strive for a faithfulness to his Word that imitates his own faithfulness to it. That you will never do this perfectly goes without saying; that you would brag about failure, however, should not come into the mind of one who has known the blessed peace of forgiveness and the joy that comes from all of the blood-bought promises of the gospel.

> Lord Jesus, let me hold ever before my eyes your love and mercy; let the sight of your holy cross and passion, which proved your perfect faithfulness to all of God's promises for my salvation, move me to love all of his Word. Yes, and by that Word help me to strive after an ever more complete imitation of your victory in the wilderness until I at last come to enjoy your victory perfectly in heaven. Amen.

V.

Matthew 4:8-10 – Again, the devil took him to a very high mountain and showed him all the kingdoms of the world and their splendor. "All this I will give you," he said, "if you will bow down and worship

me." Jesus said to him, "Away from me, Satan! For it is written: 'Worship the Lord your God, and serve him only.'"

Another temptation, one with which we are all too familiar! In this temptation Satan shows his real colors: he is a liar! The world isn't his to give. He is a murderer of souls! For to worship him in a rejection of God's Word is to die and to follow him into the eternal death of suffering in hell. Could there be a victory more important than this one for Jesus to win? Our salvation depends on it!

But for all of the death and deceit in it, the temptation is a very clever one. Just think about it: Jesus had come into the world to win the world. Jesus deserved all of its glory and its splendor; after all, he created the world! Satan says in effect, "You can have it all even in your human nature; you can have it right now, and you can have it cheap! All you need to do is perform one act of worship, just bow down this once. Think of it: No further need for a wilderness of struggle; no further need for hunger or want; and most blessed of all, no need for the agony of the cross! I just want to help you! Here's a shortcut!"

Again, the whole business is a lie, albeit a very clever and seductive one. Were Jesus to listen for an instant, we would all be lost forever. But he wins the victory over the temptation again by answering it with the Word of God, here with the essence of the First Commandment. With his answer and in his victory for us, he gives, as it were, a swift kick to the devil and with the Word of God drives him away. Jesus will not toy with the idea of taking a shortcut. He came down from heaven willingly. He entered the wilderness willingly. In perfect love to his Father and for us, he wants to trudge every step of the way to the terror and horror of the cross; he will not shun a single bit of the pain our sin deserves in order to pay for our redemption.

Oh, that we would engrave it on our foreheads and inscribe it deep into our hearts, doing it out of love for this our Savior who won the victory for us: "Worship the Lord your God, and serve him only"! For the temptation of the liar and the murderer of souls to take a shortcut is ever present with us. In fact, no matter how often we fall for it and then see that Satan did not and could not deliver on his promise, we still have to do battle with the temptation again and again. We never fully succeed in giving Satan the swift kick with our clinging to God's Word. We always seem to leave him enough wiggle room in our souls to return yet again with the same lies and the same temptations.

Think about it: How often don't our sins follow on his suggestion, "Here, let me help you out a little; here's a shortcut to success, to happiness, to getting what you really deserve in life." The suggestions come early and last a lifetime: "Here, just cheat a little on the test and you'll save yourself the disgrace of failure and the consequence of having listened to me last night when I tempted you to be lazy in study." Then: "Here, just a little stolen passion and you won't feel so frustrated; you'll be happy and loved." Or: "Here, chisel a little at work and a little on your taxes; after all, everybody does it, and you deserve a break once in a while. And just think of how much happier you will be with a gain the boss or the government will never really miss." Or: "Here's a shortcut to popularity/importance/deserved revenge for that person's meanness to you: Just gossip and cut that one or those people down; they've got it coming and deserve it. And you'll feel so much better for letting them have it! Besides that, people will learn not to mess with you if they know what's good for them."

None of us would have difficulty adding to the list of lies that Satan suggests and recognizing that our sinful flesh is only too willing to listen when Satan offers us his shortcuts to success and happiness. But his promises are all lies. Satan only has the ability to hurt, to harm, to destroy. And we should have learned that long ago. For sooner or later all of his promises, when followed, end badly—and that is by God's own gracious design! God permits the temptation to give us the opportunity to prove our love and loyalty. And on those occasions when we fail and fall, he lets us suffer sooner or later the painful consequences of our folly. He does that both to bring us to repentance and to strengthen us for the next series of Satan's lies. The wonder is that the cycle has to be repeated in our lives our whole life long; we never fully learn the lesson. Is not the grace and mercy of God amazing?! Is it not sufficient reason to yell at the top of our souls, *"Away from me, Satan! For it is written: 'Worship the Lord your God, and serve him only.'"*

> Lord Jesus, what a fool I am, how slow to listen and to learn! What can I do but worship and adore you for your patience with me? What can I do but give you thanks and praise that you won the victory in the wilderness and then went to the cross to give me your victory. Forgive me, forgive me; be patient with me, be patient still and to my dying day! Strengthen me with your Word and sacraments that more and more I may learn to drive the devil away as I cling most gladly to your Word and the promises that never lie or deceive. Hear me still for the sake of your own grace and all the victories you won for my salvation! Amen.

VI.

Matthew 4:11 – Then the devil left him, and angels came and attended him.

What a perfect end to his struggle in the wilderness. The devil was defeated by the Savior's use of God's Word—defeated and sent away. To be sure he would be back again. But for a moment Jesus had peace in his victory.

And then look what happens: "The angels came and attended him." What a sign that is of how serious and intense Jesus' struggle had been. At its close and at the end of his 40 days in the wilderness, he is exhausted in his human nature. So great is his victory and so profound his exhaustion that the holy angels appear to serve him. What a sight that must have been. What an honor and what a joy for the holy angels that they should come down from heaven and serve their Creator and Lord! Did they bring him food and drink for his hungry body? Did they come with words of the Father's pleasure at his victory? Did they come to show him a picture of the cross and the empty tomb by which he would win the final victories for us and for our salvation?

We cannot now know the details of this wondrous service that the holy angels rendered to their Lord and our Savior. But this much we can know: Jesus entered willingly into a battle that would be exhausting and that would continue for the coming three years. His Father also willed it and so did the Holy Spirit. Jesus went straight to it from his baptism. All of his energy was devoted to it. Not for an instant did he flinch from the struggle or turn away from the pain yet to come. And even in the midst of it all, he knew the Father's comfort and the angels' presence.

Oh, that we could just get a little closer to an imitation of his zeal. Oh, that we could just love him a little more like he loved us. Oh, that we would be just a little quicker in our answers to the devil's temptation—answers rooted and grounded in loyalty to God's Word and love to our Savior. Just think of it: All that he did was done not for his own outward glory but for us and for our salvation. When we serve one another, our service is usually less than half as zealous as our service to ourselves. But not so with him. It is all for us. It is all done with 100 percent attention and devotion. The plain fact of the matter is—and it's a shock to realize it—that Jesus has always been more anxious for our salvation than we ever have been! And he has always loved us incomparably more than we have ever loved him! For we are never so quick to shun temptations that offend him and ultimately hurt us. Nor do we ever cling to his Word, the great weapon of defense against temptation, enough to overcome in every battle. Far from it! We can but marvel that when the angels came to serve Jesus after those 40 days, they didn't ask him this because of what the angels know about us: "Are you sure you really want to do this for the likes of those you have come to save and at so great a cost?"

Yes, marvel at the love of the Savior in his coming down from heaven for us! Marvel at his victory in the wilderness for us! Marvel at that love so much greater than ours that not for a moment was it ever less than perfect; it was perfect even to the cross, perfect even now! And then as we marvel, let us follow after him—even though we stumble all the way—in growing love and loyalty to him and to his Word. For have you not noticed it? When we struggle against our temptations, when we cling to his Word faithfully, he keeps the promise he made to Nathanael: he lets us see the Son of God with the eyes of faith and lets us experience the help and protection even of the holy angels who come to our aid (John 1:51). And always shining over it all is the sign of his cross by which our stumbling and falling is forgiven, by which we are assured of the ultimate victory that he has won for us in his death and resurrection.

We cannot serve the lowly Jesus as did the holy angels at the end of his struggle in the wilderness. Nevertheless, we can and do bring him joy—most importantly—when we receive him in his Word and sacraments. And then secondarily, we bring him joy as well when we serve those around us as we might wish we could have served him in the wilderness. For where is he hungry and needy now but in the hunger and need of people around us? Where is he weak and exhausted now but in the weakness and exhaustion of those around us? Where does he need a kindly word now, except in the ears of those who have not heard the gospel or who need to hear it still?

> Lord Jesus, much as I wish it were otherwise, I can never love you here on earth as much as you loved me before the world began and then in all that you have done for me and my salvation. But this I ask of you: Grant me your Holy Spirit in the Word and sacraments that my use of them and my love for you may grow and increase until I finally reach the goal your love has always had for me—the joy of seeing and worshiping you face-to-face in heaven. Then while I am here, give me still the honor of doing battle in the wilderness, giving thanks for your presence and the protection of the holy angels and serving you through service to all around me. Hear me, I pray, for the sake of your own perfect love and grace and mercy. Amen.

He Manifested His Glory in the Calling of the Apostles

After his baptism and his time of testing in the wilderness, Jesus began the earthly ministry that would end with his suffering, death, and resurrection for us and for our salvation. In the approximately three years that led up to his Lenten passion, Jesus *manifested his glory*. He did that by what he did and what he taught; through both his teaching and his deeds, he demonstrated that he was indeed the Son of God sent to be our Savior. Let us then consider what he said and what he did to *manifest his glory*. In the process we will have ample opportunity to give him advice on what we think he should have said and done—and surprise, surprise!—he will show us his divine wisdom and our fallen foolishness. In so doing he will do for us what he always does in his Word: he will lead us to abandon our own imagined wisdom and to learn a little better to trust him and the Word by which he offers himself to us and for us as Savior and Lord.

I.

Luke 6:12-16 – One of those days Jesus went out to a mountainside to pray, and spent the night praying to God. When morning came, he called his disciples to him and chose twelve of them, whom he also designated apostles: Simon (whom he named Peter), his brother Andrew, James, John, Philip, Bartholomew, Matthew, Thomas, James son of Alphaeus, Simon who was called the Zealot, Judas son of James, and Judas Iscariot, who became a traitor.

During the first months after his baptism and the temptations in the wilderness, Jesus went about teaching and even performing some miracles. As a result of what he said and did, many began to follow him. Some thought that he was a great teacher or prophet. Some early on recognized that he was much more than that. Some, or perhaps all in this second group, had been disciples of John the Baptist. They had heard John's preaching of the coming Messiah. They had even been there when John pointed to Jesus and identified him as the true Lamb of God who had come to take away the sins of the world (John 1:29-36).

Now after some time has passed, Jesus is ready to begin his seminary. In it there will be 12 men chosen especially by him. They will spend most of the three years before the first Lent with Jesus. He will teach them and they will be witnesses of his mighty deeds, through which he would show himself to be the Son of God and the Lamb of God.

Notice how solemn the event is at which he appoints his apostles. It begins with the holy Son of God separating himself from all earthly interests and concerns. He goes to be alone with his Father—to be alone with him in prayer. What a night of prayer that must have been! Jesus is about to appoint his apostles; the very word *apostle* means "one who is sent." These are the preeminent ones that he will later send out into all the world with the message of salvation. He speaks with his Father about it. The choices will not be haphazard. The creation of the church, his bride, will take place through their work. Some of them will even end up writing books of the New Testament. God has prepared all of human history for this momentous time of Jesus' coming and work (Galatians 4:4), so the ground must

Epiphany

be well and properly laid for these 12 very special men to learn from Jesus and to be filled with wisdom and zeal for the proclamation of the gospel message throughout the world. There is little wonder that he would spend the night in prayer, discussing the whole matter with his Father. For his Father is just as eager as he is for the success of their mission.

What, then, should we expect the outcome of their discussion to be? Should we not expect that he will pick the finest men of the land for his apostles? Wouldn't we think that they would be the most holy of men, the smartest in the country, the strongest and most courageous in character, the most charming in personality? Surely they must be the best that he could find, the best of the best.

But look! That's not who he picks at all! We might even think that if he asks for volunteers from among those he has as disciples, he could have a more fitting company of apostles. But the choice is not to be left with men; it is his choice alone. He would even emphasize that point later on when he reminded them, "You did not choose me, but I chose you" (John 15:16).

And so what kind of men does he pick? It's such a nondescript, unimposing, frail, and fault-ridden lot that when all is said and done, we know almost nothing about them! Few of them left any footprints in the world's muddy history. After Jesus' death and resurrection, we know a little about Peter and a bit about John. But for the rest of them, we know only that they took the gospel into the world, preached and taught, suffered, and died. But where? How? We have some traditions about a few of them, but nothing solid. In fact, on their memorial days the church gives thanks that they did whatever they did, even if we don't know what that was (e.g. the prayer for August 24th, St. Bartholomew's day is typical: "Almighty God, your Son, Jesus, chose Bartholomew to preach the blessed gospel of salvation. Grant to your Church also in our time faithful pastors and teachers to proclaim the glory of your name. . . .")

Then there is this: One of them will be betray him! And Jesus knew that from the beginning! Surely this is no way to start, no way to begin showing forth the glory of the Son of God. And Judas, the betrayer, is only the worst of the lot; the rest of them don't exactly shine even after their training is almost finished. Peter denies him; all the rest forsake him and flee in his hour of trial; Thomas doubts his resurrection, and for at least a time, the rest were not all that comforted by it. Read the gospels and you will see—time after time—occasions when we might suggest to Jesus, *Why in all the world did you pick such a flawed bunch to begin with? And now that their character is apparently incapable of major improvement, why don't you cut your losses and replace them?*

Thanks be to God that we were not there to advise him! Thanks be to God that Jesus, neither then nor now, shares our quick reproach of his choices! St. Paul explains it all so well: "But we have this treasure [i.e. the gospel] in jars of clay to show that this all-surpassing power is from God and not from us" (2 Corinthians 4:7). The clay jar in which valuables were hidden was supposed to protect the treasure, but it's just the opposite with the treasure of the gospel: it protects those so fragile jars. Then when it comes out of the jar, it is the treasure of the gospel that works the miracle of faith—not the jar!

So we don't know much about the apostles. They don't shine except with the martyr's crown. Not their brilliance but Jesus' radiance shines in their work. Not their power but his is manifest in the creation of the church. Not even their memory but his alone is what grounded the church and grounds it still.

Thank God for that indeed! For if faith and the survival of the church depended on the apostles' brilliance, their virtue, and their power, then the church would have perished long ago. But no; Jesus takes frail and fallen mortals, the likes of you and me, and by his Word and sacraments, creates and preserves the church. He does it through the apostles' teaching and through our faithfulness to it. And so the jars of clay then and the jars of clay now and the jars of clay through all eternity sing praise to Jesus: the ultimate, real, and only treasure. They magnify and extol the mercy and grace of the lowly and all-glorious Son of God, our Savior. For it has pleased him to use them and to use us also for a work that angels might well have wished for themselves.

> Lord Jesus, it pleased you to make the apostles holy by your blood and to send them out to bring us that same holiness through the proclamation of the gospel. I am no less frail and flawed than they were. Be still gracious to me that I too may have the honor of sharing the treasure of your saving gospel with those around me. Then, in union with the church, let me share it with countless throngs throughout the world who are in need of it as much as I am. Amen.

II.

Matthew 4:18-20 (ESV) – While walking by the Sea of Galilee, he saw two brothers, Simon (who is called Peter) and Andrew his brother, casting a net into the sea, for they were fishermen. And he said to them, "Follow me, and I will make you fishers of men." Immediately they left their nets and followed him.

Jesus called his apostles on more than one occasion. In the last reading we saw their solemn installation, as it were, into the apostolic band. Here

Epiphany

we see him calling Peter and Andrew on an earlier occasion. He calls them to follow him and, at the same time, indicates what he is calling them for. They will not just learn; in due time they will teach. They will not follow for their own benefit but ultimately for the benefit of countless others in a mission now theirs only by promise.

But there are interesting hints about the character of the ones called and of the work they will one day do. First of all, these two and a number of the others are fishermen—how inappropriate! They are untrained middle-class businessmen. Wouldn't it be better if he would call the learned from Jerusalem, perhaps even a mix of Pharisees and Sadducees to show how broad-minded and ecumenical he can be? At least they would be better educated, have a better class of relatives, and some of them at least would be recognized by all as holy men. For everyone knew that the Sadducees were scholars not only of the Bible but of Greek learning and culture as well. Besides that, many or most of them were related to one another and connected to the chief priests and even to high government officials. And the piety of the Pharisees was famous worldwide; no one could match them in obvious virtue and external holiness. But fishermen? Hard workers, yes. But famous for learning, for connections, for virtue—no, not so much.

And then there is the promise: "I will make you fishers of men." Who would want that? After all, fish are unmanageable and messy; you pull into the net good and bad alike, and it's often hard to tell the difference. Some of the fish even damage the nets. Moreover, the work is very hard and there is no guarantee that anything at all will be caught. Indeed, to call those they catch "fish" is no great compliment either—fish are good for nothing until they are dead! They are a lot of work. They are messy and smell. Rarely do they provide, at least on an individual basis, much benefit. Indeed, often the ones caught are no good at all—even dead—and have to be thrown back into the water. The apostles themselves were often proof of this point. How often dealing with them was messy and seemed barely worth the bother!

Oh, the amazing grace and mercy of our Savior! He calls into his service and entrusts his precious and saving gospel not to the angels nor to the smartest, the most clever, the strongest, and the most obviously holy. No, he calls apostles and then those who publicly carry out their work after them from among those who recognize more and more—the longer they live and serve—that all they have is a gift of grace. If they should be so foolish as to imagine that they deserved their high office as pastors and teachers of the church, well, that would be their greatest sin and disgrace; they would have learned nothing from Jesus' Word and less still from their own experience with it. So the greatest honor is to be called an apostle or one sent by Jesus with his life-giving gospel. And that greatest honor is best received when those who have it recognize that their assignment is all about Jesus! Yes, and whatever success the message has in those who hear it, that too is all the work of Jesus—given the lowliness of his messengers, it would have to be!

Look how eager Peter and Andrew were to heed Jesus' call. That too is evidence of the power of the gospel. They are willing to give up what was a difficult but nevertheless middle-class occupation and life. And for what? To follow after this lowly looking Jesus who promises them nothing but a more complicated and difficult version of the life they already had. For what could that mean to be a fisher of men other than a lot of trouble and frustration and little reward? Certainly there is not much in the way of outward glory. But there is the mysterious lure and power of the gospel: it always gives what it commands! Jesus called and commanded and by his gospel of grace, moved them to accept that call and command. The apostles still had a lot to learn about him and about their assignment and about the cost both to Jesus and later to themselves. But still, John the Baptist had pointed to Jesus and declared that he was the Lamb of God who takes away the sin of the world. By Jesus' own words and deeds, they saw that he was indeed the promised Messiah, their Savior. And so, burdened with the baggage of their own obvious limitations, they nevertheless heard his call and by the power contained in it, they followed him. That's the way it still is with those who hear his call and become with them fishers of men.

Let the rest of us give thanks that Jesus did not entrust the preaching and teaching of the gospel to the smartest, the most clever, those outwardly the most and only holy people. If he had, we fish would fear even more than our conscience sometimes makes us fear; we would fear that Jesus would surely not want us or love us or call us to receive the fruits of his own suffering and death and resurrection. We would fear as well that we should never share the gospel message. For who would want to hear it from the likes of us? It would feel as though the power of the gospel to create and sustain faith and its rich capacity to comfort and console in all times of life and in death itself depended on us. In the abundance of his grace and mercy, Jesus came to save us all. In the abundance of his kindness and understanding, he showed through his choices of fishermen and fish that his call includes us too.

How good of him, then, that he would not take our advice about the types that he should call either as fishermen or fish!

> Yes, Lord Jesus, in all that you say and do, you show your glory not by choosing the best but by choosing fishermen who long

only for your grace and mercy. And then you crown their work with such success that I too am among those lured, captured, caught, and kept by the Word that kills with the law and then makes me so joyfully and fully alive by the message of your forgiveness. Oh, help me to remember with gratitude the work of the fishermen you send, that I do not add to their troubles by my own foolish pride. To that end, do not let me forget that I am just a fish, always needing to be killed with the law and made alive again and joyful only through that saving message of your gospel. Hear me for the sake of your own infinite compassion. Amen.

He Manifested His Glory by Deeds That Taught
Turning Water Into Wine at Cana

I.

John 2:1-5 – On the third day a wedding took place at Cana in Galilee. Jesus' mother was there, and Jesus and his disciples had also been invited to the wedding. When the wine was gone, Jesus' mother said to him, "They have no more wine." "Woman, why do you involve me?" Jesus replied. "My hour has not yet come." His mother said to the servants, "Do whatever he tells you."

Now this is indeed a strange and beautiful way for Jesus to begin his public ministry, to begin manifesting forth his glory! He is about to perform the first of his many miracles. All of them will have this in common: They prove that he is indeed the almighty Son of God, and they all demonstrate that his is a mission of love and compassion for the fallen children of Adam and Eve. And the people helped by his miracles will all have this in common: Their condition is desperate, and they have no hope of human help.

But wait a minute. This situation doesn't seem to really fit any of those criteria. It's just a wedding. The circumstance is just an occasion of embarrassment for the hosts of the wedding feast and the newly married couple. The banquet will end and so will the embarrassment. It really doesn't seem to be an event of sufficient importance for Jesus to bother himself with it. Not long before this he had spent 40 days of fasting and temptation in the wilderness, and now he should care whether there is enough wine for a wedding banquet? People there had not gone hungry or thirsty. And there may indeed have been some who ate and drank more than they should have. Maybe that was one of the reasons the wine supply ran short.

Then there is the matter of Jesus' mother. She, in spite of the weakness we noted in her on that visit to the temple when Jesus was 12 years old, understands who he is and what he can do. But this request seems so out of place. Jesus himself says so: "Why do you involve me?" A literal translation of the Greek text is a bit sharper: "What is there between you and me" that you think you have the right to expect that I should do something about this situation? His relationship with his mother is no longer limited by the Fourth Commandment; their relationship has changed now that he has begun his saving mission. Though still obliged by the law to respect and honor his mother, he is no longer subject to her the way he was when the family returned to Nazareth from Jerusalem that time so long before.

Still there is so much that is surprising and fascinating about this incident. As is typical of everything that Jesus did and said, there is no end of things to ponder, no end of things to learn. Even the words of Mary on this occasion are a wonder to us. Jesus had not yet publicly performed any miracles. Why, then, did Mary make this subtle request that Jesus do something about this situation? What did she expect?

Perhaps that's a good place to begin thinking about Jesus here. Mary knows that he is the Son of God. Mary knows that he therefore will always do what is right. She knows that on the basis of all that she has experienced, from the moment the angel promised that she would be his mother to this moment. She knows that in him is the perfect match of love to his Father and love for people. On that basis she speaks to him. She doesn't directly tell him what she wants him to do. She places the problem before him and trusts that he will know what to do and will do what is right.

Is that not a good place for us to begin when we speak to Jesus? We too know who he is. On the basis of all he did and said—especially on the cross—we know even better than Mary did at that moment how powerful and full of compassion he is for us. Nevertheless, the day comes when there is a problem. It may be big or small. It may be a problem in a moment or one that has lasted a long time. If we think of Jesus in the moment, this thought might come: *This really isn't something he would care about; I'll muddle through as best I can and take what comes.*

But again, we know Jesus. We know his might and his mercy. We can call to mind what Peter said: "Cast *all* your anxiety on him because he cares for you" (1 Peter 5:7). That's how a life of faith and prayer really begins. We invite Jesus to stay, he who has already come to live with and in us with his Word and sacraments. We invite him to be present in every moment of our lives. As at the wedding of Cana, most people did not see who he really was, so most people today do not really see him as present, as the center of and the reason for our lives. In fact, we often don't see it either! But then in his might and mercy, he permits or sends needs into our lives that we cannot satisfy by ourselves. And with those he taps us on the shoulder to remind us that, in fact, we cannot satisfy any longing, whether for the body or the soul, without him.

And so we give thanks that by needs small and some not so small, he reminds us that he is there; he gets our always-so-distracted attention. What, then, shall we do, we who know him to be our Savior in all things great and small? What else but bring the need to him, a need of which he is already fully aware? What else but speak to him as Mary did? She didn't spell out what she wanted or expected him to do; she knew that he could figure that all out by himself. She simply stated the problem. So do we. A long-drawn-out explanation isn't necessary. Even less necessary is a prescription, giving him instructions on exactly what he should do and when he should do it.

Jesus, of course, could and did read his mother's mind. He knew that her remark had in it an implied instruction. But see how gently and yet firmly he set her straight. He didn't address her as mother but called her with a general term, "Woman." His role was set. He was not subject to her, but she to him. And so we too come to him in this hour and say,

> Lord Jesus, let me feel your tap on my shoulder in problems big and small. Let me thank you for each of them when they remind me that you are not far away or indifferent. Give me this wisdom so that in every time of need—in every situation in life—I look to you for help. Give me also this grace so that in every time when I am aware of no need at all, I remember that this too is all your doing. Even so, now I come to you; this is the need of the moment. Do what you will. Do what you want. For that will always be proof of your love and mercy. That will always end up giving me further reason to thank and praise you for the greatest gift of yourself for my salvation and then for this gift of your abiding presence in grace during every moment of my life. Amen.

II.

John 2:5-10 – His mother said to the servants, "Do whatever he tells you." Nearby stood six stone water jars, the kind used by the Jews for ceremonial washing, each holding from twenty to thirty gallons. Jesus said to the servants, "Fill the jars with water"; so they filled them to the brim. Then he told them, "Now draw some out and take it to the master of the banquet." They did so, and the master of the

banquet tasted the water that had turned into wine. He did not realize where it had come from, though the servants who had drawn the water knew. Then he called the bridegroom aside and said, "Everyone brings out the choice wine first and then the cheaper wine after the guests have had too much to drink; but you have saved the best till now."

Among the many lessons this account teaches us, this one is especially comforting and, in a way, unique among the miracles of Jesus: Jesus is most generous! Consider all the ways in which he shows his generosity in this miracle, and note the perhaps similar ways in which he has shown his generosity in your own life.

For starters, he is generous to his mother. She had presumed on a relationship that was changing as Jesus left home and began the active work of the world's salvation—and hers too. He tells her: "My time has not yet come." Time for what? Time for fully revealing himself as God's Son and our Savior. He had teaching to do, proof to present of his special grace and power, and suffering and death to endure. Nevertheless, he grants her implied request. And she, on her part, in spite of his gentle rebuke, trusts that he will. How kind of him. How generous. "Lord Jesus, I know I have no right to ask this of you, but . . ." And he listens. And he acts.

Then there is the manner of performing this miracle. Gallons of wine! Not the cheap stuff either! Of course it is not Jesus' intent that the guests should guzzle themselves senseless. He could have made sure that such was impossible by providing just a little wine or wine that was passable but not really all that enjoyable. But he doesn't do that. The responsibility for moderation is left to the guests. For his part he will give what he alone always does—yes, what he gave already in the creation of the world: the best!

And so he rescues the bridegroom and his family from any possibility of embarrassment. There is no reproach: "Well, the bridegroom should have known better how much was needed; at the very least he should have made sure that no one drank so much that they would run out." No, there is none of that. Instead, Jesus provides in full measure and provides the best there was to be had. How relieved that bridegroom must have been. Yes, and how surprised at this turn of events. He himself does not know how it came about. He can only thank God that it did. How generous of the Lord!

Have you known that kindness and that generosity from him too? "Lord Jesus, this time and that I have been a fool. How often, even without a prayer from me, you have saved me from myself; just so, without any prayer or thought from the bridegroom, you so generously rescued him from embarrassment at his wedding banquet. How kind of you and beyond any merit in me! How beyond generous you are." And so it is—in needs both great and small. Jesus is there.

There are, to be sure, so many times when we need to learn and do learn of his mercy in days of suffering and loss. But not all of our days are days of pain and misery. Jesus was there at a wedding. There are days of joy and gladness for us too. And Jesus is there. The pity is that we too often fail to recognize his presence, to recognize that he has given us that day and all the joy that comes with it. Was he stingy at your baptism, your confirmation, your graduation, your wedding, your birthday, your anniversary, this happy occasion and that happy occasion? Doubtless he was not. He did not make you skimp at every turn and feel guilty over the least pleasure. No, he was generous, whether we recognized him there or not! Is that not a generosity that is unique? Who but Jesus would insist on providing us with such joy and gladness as we have had in our lifetime when he knew that we so often would miss the fact that he was its source, just like the bridegroom? Yes, *generous:* A word too small for the reality, but it's the best we can do.

> O most gracious, most generous Redeemer, would that I could remember all of your acts of generosity and loving kindness in my life. If I could, my days would pass in unending thanks and adoration for all that you have done for me: things great and small, things most often unrecognized by me at the time and forgotten by the end of the day. Nevertheless, you have never failed me or forgotten me. You have not grown weary of demonstrating your generosity to me in every breath I take, in every pleasure I enjoy, in every moment of gladness, in the beauty of creation, in the kindness of friends, and in the company of loving family members. On and on it goes, all this proof of your kindness and your generosity. And why should such generosity on your part even surprise me? After all, you spared nothing to satisfy my greatest and eternal need, the need for forgiveness and for the saving Word and sacraments that bring you and forgiveness to me. It is good for us that heaven lasts for an eternity; that's how long it will take for me to know all you have done and then to give you thanks for it. Forgiveness and eternal life are the beginning, middle, and end of your generosity. But it never stopped there. Lord Jesus, all I can say is this: Thank you! Amen.

III.

John 2:7-11 (ESV) – Jesus said to the servants, "Fill the jars with water." . . . The master of the feast tasted the water now become wine, and did not know where it came from (though the servants who had drawn the water knew). . . . This, the first of his signs, Jesus did at Cana in Galilee, and manifested his glory. And his disciples believed in him.

Of the many lessons to be learned about Jesus at the wedding in Cana, let's consider just one more. Jesus manifests his glory by hiding it! Did you notice how he performed the miracle? There is no great show, no puffed-up performance, no, "Look here all of you at what I am about to do!" None of that. There is the simple command to the servants to fill these 20-gallon-plus water jugs.

Then once the miracle has been performed, everyone, Jesus included, keeps quiet about the source of this amazing deed. Somehow even Mary manages to suppress what must have been the very natural urge to proclaim to one and all, "See what my son has done!" The servants say nothing either; perhaps they expect that no one would believe them anyway. And Jesus' disciples are quiet too. Who has ever heard of such a thing? Don't we expect great benefactors to have their names on the buildings they built? Isn't it just a matter of course that large donations have their source trumpeted so that all will know the glory of the giver? Yes, and for the rest of us too, isn't it altogether normal and natural that we would like some credit, some praise, some appreciation for even little things that we do for others? Indeed, how many with the passing of time become bitter and resentful when they think that their merits and benefactions have been forgotten or not sufficiently appreciated? And how many fail to be generous or as generous as they easily could be because they expect that they will not be adequately thanked or praised? Even in our churches many years ago there was the annual publication of what some called "the scandal sheet;" it was a listing of what each member had contributed that year, so that the generous would be praised and the stingy shamed.

But there is none of that here. As so often before his suffering and death, Jesus wants not awe in the face of wonder-works but faith in his person as the Son of God and the Savior—faith that comes not from miracles but from his Word. And so "he manifested his glory, and his disciples believed in him." The miracle was not an end in itself; it was but a means to this end: that his disciples would see proof in the miracle of what they knew from his Word, that he was the Son of God and the Messiah.

We can learn a lot from Jesus' example here. Oh, to be sure, there's not necessarily anything wrong with it when someone expresses their appreciation for what we have done. It can rightly warm our hearts if we don't covet it and didn't do the good thing just so that we could be praised for it. In fact, we often do all too little of thanking and expressing our own appreciation for those who have been kind to us or helped us in ways great or small. But still, we can learn to put into practice what Jesus did and what he told us to do in Matthew 6, namely, to avoid seeking glory from men for what we do for him.

But even more important than that, at least in this text, we can learn to look at all that he does in our life that is hidden from the view of others. Think of all the times when your blessings of good days and rescue in what seemed to be bad days could come only from his generous hands. No one saw that it was Jesus alone and Jesus all along. No one but you was aware of how great your need and how abundant his blessing. No one but you could look into the face of Jesus and say to him, "You did this just for me, didn't you?!" And so, though it should never come as a surprise, it often does. The disciples knew who Jesus was from his Word; they learned from what he did that he never disappoints and is always present with his mercy, his generosity. It's like that for us too. We learn and believe that he is our God and Savior from his Word. And then we learn it again from his every act of rescue and his every deed of kindness throughout our lives, in things great and small. It may be a crust of bread or a piece of cake. It may be a breath of fresh air, especially after an illness when we could scarcely catch a breath. It may be a quiet evening with loved ones. It may be rest after hard work or the satisfaction of a job well done. It may be the pleasure of watching little children laugh and play without a care in the world. The list could go on all day. In it all Jesus is there, revealing and hiding his glory at the same time. In it all he is giving us reason every hour of the day to pray:

> Lord Jesus, no one else may see your grace and mercy and perhaps few will understand it when I speak of it. But I know it and see it every day: You are my Redeemer from sin, death, and hell. You are the one who has rescued me times uncounted from disaster and taught me in times of trouble to trust in you alone. You are the giver of every good and perfect gift, from the best banquet of my life to the cup of water when I was thirsty and the slice of bread when I was hungry. You are the companion when I am lonely, the protector when I am afraid, the deliverer when I am in danger, the comfort when I need to suffer pain, the consolation in the hour of death, the life from the grave when I must pass through that dark valley. O grant me yet this kindness that I learn to shun vain glory from others when I have done what pleases you and to praise

you alone with word and deed for all that I am, all that I have, and all that I have the honor to do in service to those you have placed around me. For the sake of your own generosity, be pleased to hear and grant my petition. Amen.

(For further reflection and prayer on the themes considered here, the reader will find Psalm 145 very timely.)

Healing a Leper

I.

Mark 1:40 – A man with leprosy came to [Jesus] and begged him on his knees, "If you are willing, you can make me clean."

What an amazing way for Jesus to show his glory and to teach us! At the wedding of Cana, he showed it with incomparable generosity. Here he will show it with incomparable compassion. For here is a man who is disgusting to look at. Leprosy entailed the outward rotting of the flesh, beginning with the hands and feet and then extending over more and more of what was left of the body, until all was lost and the leper was released from his misery by death. Moreover, since leprosy was highly contagious, its victims were outcasts from society—even from family. The lepers had only the company of other lepers, if that. They stayed at a distance from other people and were obliged to cry out if others came near, "Unclean! Unclean!" If they failed to do that, they could expect to be stoned to death.

They were indeed unclean, but not just physically. Leprosy was considered a visible picture of the invisible ruin of mankind by sin; just as leprosy made the body loathsome, so living in sin made the soul and ultimately the body utterly repulsive, especially to God. Both the leper and those living in sin were the walking dead.

But now consider this leper and consider Jesus' interaction with him. Look at that leper! What boldness, what daring! He approaches Jesus and his disciples. He risks being stoned to death for approaching without the warning cry of "Unclean!" Nevertheless, he comes near. But what does he really have to lose? He is doomed either way, whether by being stoned to death or by dying from his dread disease. Only consideration for those who might be infected by his presence could keep him away from people. But here is Jesus. Perhaps his relatives or friends had called to him from a distance and told him about Jesus. Jesus is, at any rate, one about whom he has heard; he has heard that Jesus can perform miracles, heard that he is kind and doesn't turn away the poor and needy. However the leper knew about him, prompted by what little he knew, he boldly steps forward.

And listen to his prayer. It is one of the most perfect prayers recorded for us in the Bible.

Falling on his knees he cries out, "If you are willing, you can make me clean." On his knees with face to the ground, he is a picture so perfect of our proper approach to Jesus. It is a picture that reflects total, absolute unworthiness on the one hand and desperate need on the other. How else should we come into the presence of God, we who deserve nothing but wrath and punishment because of our spiritual leprosy? But that's only half of it. His prayer is beautiful because it expresses a total reliance on Jesus' mercy. By implication it trusts in that mercy—else why would he have risked coming in the first place? "If you are willing—and that is my desperate hope. But if you are not willing, what then? Then I must bear my sorrow and my suffering, even accept it still with the trust that you are merciful, in spite of my continuing misery!"

Again, what an amazing prayer—one well worth remembering and repeating often! When we come into the presence of Jesus while looking at ourselves, we see only needs: spiritual needs and temporal needs as well. We cannot do a thing to rid ourselves of the leprosy of sin that corrupts body and soul. We are helpless even as we pray, "Give us this day our daily bread." It all lies in Jesus' hands to give or to withhold. But, and that's the more important point, we do not come expecting him to withhold. Indeed, we've gotten so used to his granting that we fall into the bad habit of taking his pardon, compassion, and generosity for granted. For we too have heard and heard often of Jesus' grace and of his mercy. Hundreds of times we have come seeking help for our leprosy, and never has he cast us aside or turned his back on us. No, with each confession of our sin and shame, he has held before us his own suffering for our cure. And with a thousand repetitions of "Give us this day our daily bread," he has bountifully provided all that we need and more. For our troubles in life, he has been our strength and stay. For our struggles he has been our help and support. For problems that seemed impossible to solve, he has been there with deliverance, often different from what we asked, but always what was best for us. During our tears in loss, he has been there with the assurance that he remains our great treasure who one day will more than—and eternally—replace anything and everything that we have lost.

This leper reminds us to come as he did. So we come, we come still, we come again and again. Looking at ourselves as we ought, we see only need, only despair. But we have heard of him. We have seen him in Word and sacraments. We have experienced his faithfulness to who he is: our God, our Savior, our all in all. And so we do not just look at ourselves. Even more we look at him. And in looking at him we pray with full confidence, "If you are willing, you can make me clean!"

O dearest Jesus, give my soul eyes that see myself as I really am. Let me come ever with the leper, recognizing that my needs in body and soul, for time and for eternity, are absolute. And then give my soul eyes as well to look to you alone with trust and confidence in your Word that you remain my ever faithful God and Savior. With despair in myself and, at the same time, joyful confidence in you, let me ever pray for pardon and for grace, for rescue and for strength to stand up again so I am ready to live trusting in you and then in joyful and thankful submission to your Word and will. Amen.

II.

Mark 1:41,42 (NIV 1984) – Filled with compassion, Jesus reached out his hand and touched the man. "I am willing," he said. "Be clean!" Immediately the leprosy left him and he was cured.

Hang on to each word of this remarkable account. "Filled with compassion!" The Greek verb used here has the meaning, "his insides were churned, turned over." See how fully Jesus enters into our humanity! Who hasn't had that churning of the stomach when confronted with some tragedy or disaster? But in Jesus the sensation is as the English translation relates it: He is *filled* with compassion. Not just, "Jesus felt a little sorry for the fellow." Not, "Jesus was so disgusted that he felt obliged to help the wretch." But he was "filled with compassion." Not a particle of the body and soul of the God-man was left unmoved by what he saw and then what he heard from the lips of this poor man.

Yes, and then he gives evidence most striking of that compassion that filled his body and soul: "Jesus reached out his hand and touched the man." What shock waves must have spread through whoever else was there to witness this amazing deed. Touch a leper? Who would do such a thing? They were loathsome to see and disgusting to smell. But Jesus touched him—not after he healed him but before! We are told that the human need for touch is one of the most important needs that people have. Without human touch people shrivel up and die inside. In the "olden days" caregivers in orphanages were told to pick up the babies and hold them; for if they just fed and changed them and never held them, the babies would die. This leper had not been touched since he had come down with this dread disease. But now, Jesus touched him! How that simple act must have sent a shiver through what was left of his diseased and half-dead body. Surely if we had been there, we would have pulled Jesus' hand back in shock at the act. But how beautifully that simple act teaches us of his compassion—a compassion that filled him, a compassion that is as total and absolute as is the man's desperate need and wretched condition. And then Jesus heals him—heals him perfectly, fully, completely.

Oh, what a beautiful lesson, what a consoling way for Jesus to manifest his glory (John 2:11). He is "filled with compassion." That's what brought him down from heaven in the first place. And we are the objects of that compassion no less than was the leper. Who wouldn't wish, when weighted down with guilt and burdened with one problem after another, to experience the touch of Jesus, to feel his hand on head and shoulder or perhaps even his warm embrace? When in our weakness we might fear that he would turn away from us in disgust—as indeed we deserve—who would not feel the soul leap for joy at the sensation of Jesus' touch?

But wait: We have felt his touch, felt it often. For he was there, picking us up in his arms at our baptism. And he has been there really and truly with his body and blood, not just to touch us but to feed us with himself in the Sacrament of the Altar. Yes, closer to us is his touch than that of any other. "For in him we live and move and have our being" (Acts 17:28), and "your life is now hidden with Christ in God" (Colossians 3:3). How could he prove and express any better this truth that also toward us he is "filled with compassion"? It is all the more amazing, given the sad fact that we are never thus "filled with compassion" toward the repulsive and undeserving or even toward those not repulsive and underserving! For it's all too true that for ourselves, given our fallen nature, we will always have more pity than for anyone else. Nevertheless, this always describes Jesus' attitude towards us: He is filled with compassion; he longs to bend down and touch us, and he does so repeatedly in Word and sacraments. That we do not think of it or remember it, that we are so often unaware of it altogether, has more to do with our own faults and failing than any unwillingness in Jesus.

But for today let us put aside our own coldness and instead delight in his compassion. For today let us find ourselves falling at Jesus' feet and remembering with delight that he is not far away and indifferent. Let us cherish in our hearts and minds the blessed reality that he is always mindful of each of us. Still, even in his glory at the right hand of the Father, he is filled with compassion at the thought and the sight of us. For today let us keep it in mind that he touches us, takes us by the hand, and raises us up.

Then for today let us rise up with him, resolving to get closer still to an imitation of that love and compassion towards each and every one around us, whether or not we think them deserving and especially if we think them altogether undeserving. That's how we mirror for others the way he is with us. That's the way he wants to be with them too. And it is by our compassion with word and deed that he wants to touch those around us. Far be it from us to shun those for whom he is filled with compassion. For hidden in compassion is the glory of the Savior to us and then through us.

> O most compassionate Savior, I can never fully realize, much less appreciate, the totality of your compassion for me. And too often I am forgetful of your always gracious touch in your Word and sacraments. Nevertheless, at this hour I know it from your Word and I give you heartfelt thanks and praise for all of your compassion and tender mercy. So strengthen me by this your grace so that with you I may rise up to a closer imitation of that compassion in my life with all those around me. Yes, let me be to them, however dim, a reflection of what you always are with me. Hear me for the sake of your perfect compassion. Amen.

III.

Mark 1:43,44 – Jesus sent him away at once with a strong warning: "See that you don't tell this to anyone. But go, show yourself to the priest and offer the sacrifices that Moses commanded for your cleansing, as a testimony to them."

What an astonishing turn of events! See how Jesus manifests his glory! He wants it kept a secret, just like at the wedding in Cana. Who does that? If we get a trophy, it goes up on the mantelpiece right away so that all may marvel, not at it but at us. If we do something really special, at least in our own eyes, we expect a little glory at least—a little acknowledgment of how wonderful we are. Oh, to be sure, we know enough to pretend it doesn't matter, but deep down inside it really does matter, doesn't it?

But Jesus? Here again as in the last verses, the verbs are very strong. He strictly, even sternly tells the man to say nothing about what had happened. What should the leper so miraculously and fully cured do instead? He should obey the law of the Lord (Leviticus 13, 14). He should go at once, not home, not to family and friends to share the good news but to the priest as the law required. There he would be restored legally by their declaration to civil society, to his family and friends, to the happy fellowship of worship in the temple and the synagogue. After that there would be plenty of time to rejoice in this gracious gift of the Savior and to share the message of who had given it with one and all. But that time was not yet.

And why not yet? Jesus gives the reason: The man is to go and keep the law "as a testimony to them" (i.e. the priests). The temple priests had early on expressed hostility toward Jesus and his message. But Jesus, for his part, as long as possible is "filled with compassion" even for these men who opposed him and who—and Jesus knew this too—would one day conspire to have him put to death. But their wickedness could never be charged to Jesus' will. No, quite the contrary, he wanted to do everything to bring them to repentance. What a powerful testimony both to the fact that Jesus was God's Son and to his compassion for all, even his enemies, this would be: The leper would present himself to the priest; they had never seen the likes of it before, that a leper was made clean. That just didn't happen. Lepers died. But now if this once-in-their-whole-experience thing happened, they would certainly have to ask the leper, "But how did this happen? How did you become clean? We only know of the miraculous cleansing of Naaman in the Old Testament" (2 Kings 5). Then the leper could point to Jesus as the one who had done this otherwise impossible and unheard of act of both might and compassion.

That would indeed be a powerful testimony to the priests of who Jesus really was: not just the almighty Son of God but the Son of God filled with compassion for all—for lepers and for enemies no less! His compassion would even consist in this: If Jesus had such power, power even to cleanse a leper, let those who would oppose him hear a warning. If they were not moved by the compassion of Jesus, at least this would be a start—that they would fear his wrath against those who would reject this mighty one. That would be a powerful preaching that calls to repentance. Then, having recognized their folly—indeed their wickedness in ridiculing and opposing him—Jesus could then show the extent of his compassion still further: He would forgive them!

That's the way it is with his compassion. Again, he is filled with it; it extends to the one who comes in recognition of the absolute condition of helplessness and need. It extends no less to the one who needs still to be crushed by the law so that, seeing his need, he finally bends his stubborn neck before the Savior, who is so anxious to raise him up again.

What, then, shall we say of ourselves as we encounter Jesus—or better, as he encounters us—in his Word? If our sin and guilt says, "No, he would never want one so foul and corrupt as I am," then we understand ourselves well and his law has killed us with despair just as it is designed to do. Then we will look at the leper so dead; and we will look too at the priests so equally miserable and undeserving, even though they did not recognize it. And in seeing Jesus' compassion toward them, we will take heart. We will cry out, "Lord Jesus, I know you are willing; make me clean; wash away all my sin with your compassionate forgiveness; satisfy my need so great, my longing so desperate, and raise me up with your touch in the gospel in Word and sacrament." He will not turn us aside. He will be compassionate still. For that is the promise of his Word, of the one who will never lie to us or deceive us.

Then we will understand still better and anew why we never say, "No point in sharing the gospel with that fellow; he is too far gone and won't listen anyway—he will probably just laugh at us and continue to mock the Savior who died even for him." No, such a thing we will never want to say. We want only to show the Savior's grace. We cannot know who will someday receive it by the power of that message or who will spurn it through their own fault and their own stubborn will. That we have been raised up by Jesus' compassion is always a miracle of grace. On his promise to us we rely. On that same promise and in union with the church, we continue to show the compassionate touch of the Savior to all in the message of repentance and forgiveness.

> Lord Jesus, keep me from ever taking your compassion for granted. Bring me, by the recognition of my need, to repentant longing for your pardon. And then with joy at your faithfulness, move me both to a more faithful clinging to your Word and to the happy task of sharing it with those who know it and those who know it not. I ask it of you that, in me and through me, your glory in the gospel may be made manifest. Amen.

IV.

Mark 1:45 – Instead [the leper] went out and began to talk freely, spreading the news. As a result, Jesus could no longer enter a town openly but stayed outside in lonely places. Yet the people still came to him from everywhere.

We might well think that there could be no further evidence of Jesus' compassion than what we have already seen in his touching the leper, in his healing him, and then even in his desire to give testimony to his enemies. But there is still more!

First of all, consider the depths of human perversity. As soon as the leper, whose prayer had been so perfect, has received the Savior's touch and his healing compassion, all of a sudden he thinks he knows everything better than Jesus! He joins the ranks of those who want to give advice to God. Jesus did not want the report of the miracle spread far and wide for a second reason. The first reason was so that once the priests had certified the man as clean from his leprosy, the priests would have a powerful testimony of Jesus' might and compassion. The second reason was so that people would not flock to Jesus as they would crowd around a curiosity or a wonder-worker. He wanted to win them primarily with his Word; the miracles should have the purpose of demonstrating that he was indeed the promised Messiah. The Word was the most important thing.

But the leper thinks he knows everything better than Jesus, and Jesus' stern warning he simply casts aside. We can understand his joy and his desire to proclaim the wonders that Jesus had done for him. But it is always and alone Jesus' words that should direct our feelings, our reason, our consequent words and actions. By ignoring what Jesus told him—yes, told him strictly and sternly—the cleansed leper got in the way of Jesus' all-important mission of preaching and teaching the message of repentance and forgiveness.

But wait a minute. Didn't Jesus know that exactly this would happen? Of course he did—and accordingly with his stern words, did all that he could to prevent it, short of using his almighty power. He gave the man a unique opportunity to show his gratitude by a difficult but by no means impossible obedience. But, if Jesus knew what was going to happen, if he knew that the man was ultimately going to get in the way of Jesus' mission, why did Jesus cleanse him in the first place? After all, even the man's prayer ("If you are willing") gave Jesus a way out. Jesus could even have explained it to the man: "I am not willing because I know that you will misuse my gift; better you stay a humble leper than that my gift would give you the occasion of becoming one who thinks he is smarter than his God and, worse still, one who would get in the way of my preaching and teaching!"

Oh, do you see it yet again, what it means that Jesus was "filled with compassion"? Yes, and have you not experienced it yourself a thousand times? Have you not noticed that with every gift that Jesus gives us, he runs a risk—a risk of which he is well aware, even at the time of his giving it? He runs the risk that we will forget the primary purpose of his gifts: that we be joyful in thanksgiving and then use his gifts not just for our enjoyment but in the service of others. He thus runs the risk that we will love the gift more than we love him; he takes the risk that the gift will get in the way of devoted obedience to him and his Word.

Think about it: We pray for friends, family, health, a measure of this world's wealth, this rescue, and that pleasure. And then what happens when he grants our prayer? The gifts so longed for are cherished more than their giver. Now we have more time for friends and family and less time for devotion to his Word and prayer. Now we have more time and resources for entertainment than for church and for service to those in need around us. Now we clutch to our hearts the treasures gained and granted, as though they were the reasons for all our happiness and to lose them would be a total disaster. All of a sudden, like the cleansed leper, we know better than Jesus what will make us really happy and life worthwhile. The hymn verse "Jesus, Jesus, only Jesus can my heartfelt longing still" (*Christian Worship* [CW], 348) gets pushed to the back of our mind.

And what of the work that Jesus wants to do in those around us from our example? He encouraged us to use life and all his gifts to us in such a way that people "may see [our] good deeds and glorify [our] Father in heaven" (Matthew 5:16). But that doesn't get done. And why not? Because those around us do not at all realize that we give Jesus all the credit for those things in our life that have made it what it is; they do not understand from the way we live with them that it is Jesus himself who is the chief and only lasting gift, and his Word and sacraments the most important things to us in our life.

But nevertheless, mark well Jesus' compassion! He knows that so often we will cherish his gifts more than we cherish him and, in effect, think that we know better than he does how his gifts to us should be used. And still he does not deny our prayers. Still he grants us daily bread and so much, so much more! Will we ever get to the point on this side of heaven when we make the best possible use of all his gifts? No, doubtless we will not, given our fallen nature. But perhaps we can get a little closer to a grateful heart that marvels more and more at his compassion in granting us so many blessings, even when we have forgotten that they are his gifts. Perhaps we can get a little closer to the point of enjoying his gifts with him, in connection with him; he certainly wants that too! And then maybe, bit by bit, we may grow in the thoughtful and grateful use of his gifts to his glory. That happens when those around us come to recognize that we see all we are and have as gifts from Jesus. That happens when those around us come to benefit from the ways that we use his gifts—our abilities, talents, and treasure—in service.

> Dearest Lord Jesus, would that I see in each moment the truth that it is to your compassion that I owe all that I am and have. Would that I spend more of the time and energy you give me in both thanksgiving to you and in loving service to all around me. In this hour at least, let me look at your holy cross and recognize that on it, you have shown a compassion for me and for my salvation that endures for all time and for eternity. And then help me grow in gratitude for that gift of salvation and for all that you have given me my whole life long as a manifestation of your glory in compassion. Amen.

Driving Out Demons

I.

Mark 5:9-13 – Then Jesus asked him, "What is your name?" "My name is Legion," he replied, "for we are many." And he begged Jesus again and again not to send them out of the area. A large herd of pigs was

feeding on the nearby hillside. The demons begged Jesus, "Send us among the pigs; allow us to go into them." He gave them permission, and the impure spirits came out and went into the pigs. The herd, about two thousand in number, rushed down the steep bank into the lake and were drowned.

We want now to begin a series of devotions on one of the most interesting, beautiful, and comforting chapters in the gospels. Mark 5 from beginning to end shows us Jesus manifesting his glory in what he did. Both what he did and how that reflected his glory are astonishing.

For starters, we have here the account of Jesus casting out demons from a man possessed completely—body and soul—by Satan's minions from hell. In the way that they possessed the man we get to see the true nature of the devil and of his intentions as he moves and works among us and, tragically, also in us. One of his tricks is to get people either to deny that he and his minions exist at all or to portray himself and them as cute little fellows with horns and pitchforks and who nevertheless have a sense of humor. Even worse, the devil is presented as man's ultimate friend (e.g. in the philosophy of Nietzsche and others)! Indeed, that's how he presented himself already in the Garden of Eden and then even to Jesus in the wilderness.

That picture has no relation, however, to reality. We get the true picture of Satan and his coworkers in this account of the demon-possessed man. The man is in every way a wreck. His whole life is one of unending pain and torture. He resides (to say "he lives" would be an exaggeration!) among the graves of the dead. He howls, he rants and raves mindlessly. He is, to be sure, strong; he cannot be captured and tied down with ropes and chains. But all of his strength is devoted to pointless violence from which he derives neither pleasure nor benefit. His every thought and word and act bespeaks torment for himself and for any who knew him or would come into contact with him. His whole existence is counter to all reason, to all that is good, to all true pleasure or happiness.

And there we have an accurate picture of the devil and his work. The devil is incapable of any good thing. He is devoted entirely to causing misery and destruction. To play with him and to toy with his temptations is to invite ruin in this life and even more in the next. There is no denying his cunning and his power. Each of us, if we thought about it, could write a book on the subject of the ruin he brings when either we have foolishly and wickedly followed him or when we have seen the wreckage he has brought to the lives of some we know who did so.

The folly and the wickedness of following him is highlighted in this section of the account when the demons, recognizing the incomparably superior power of Jesus, ask him to do them a favor: Don't send us away from here; for if you do, we will suffer even more misery than we do already and have suffered since you cast us out of heaven (Luke 10:18; Revelation 12:7-9). Their request is altogether irrational. Their whole existence is one of unalterable misery. For they have been forever separated from the grace and love of God because of their rebellion shortly after their creation at the beginning of time.

Given, then, their perpetual and unalterable misery—and that's all they have to share—what folly and how wicked that we should follow them! Deceit and destruction, misery and torment away from the grace and love of God is all that they can deliver, in spite of their promises of happiness, if we just pay heed to their temptations. St. Peter teaches us well when he reminds us that the devil is like a roaring lion seeking only our destruction (1 Peter 5:8).

Why, then, would Jesus not only listen to but even grant the request of the demons in this account? Yes, and why would he permit their continued existence and, worse yet, their hellish activity among us even to this day?

Consider well the glory of our Savior by what he does here! By granting their request he lets us see the destructive folly—the utter lack of reason and sense in the devil—even when it comes to his own supposed well-being. For what happens when Jesus grants their request? They enter swine and plunge to the ruin of the swine. For their part the demons continue in the hell that is their proper reward for their evil. At the same time, Jesus shows his own power as incomparably greater and, yes, different than the power of the devil. Satan and his hosts are capable only of destruction; but Jesus uses his power to save, to help, to bless, to bring a happiness that lasts in time and continues for all eternity in those on whom his blessing rests.

Who, then, should we follow? Will it be the devil, who intends only our ruin and whose temptations are designed to give the opposite of what he promises? Will we never learn that he is as Jesus said, a liar from the beginning and the "father of lies" (John 8:44)?

Behold the glory of Jesus: of ourselves we will (and how many times have we proven it?!) follow the irrational and destructive voice of the devil. But Jesus has a voice too! And his is the voice that speaks truth, and that truth rescues and saves us from the consequences of our own folly and wickedness.

Jesus calls us to himself. He comes to us—yes, comes as he did to the demon-possessed man. Did you notice it? All the attempts of people to tame and save the poor man were pointless; the demons were too powerful for human efforts to expel or control them. Pass all the laws you want.

Threaten people if you must. No mere human effort can control or tame or expel or overcome the devil. But Jesus comes with miraculous power in his words. His words drove out the legions of demons that so thoroughly possessed that poor man. His words already in our baptism performed the same miracle. He drives out the devil to make room for himself to dwell with us and in us. His words repeated to us again and again call us back to his love and his forgiveness; he calls thus in spite of our ongoing folly, when we have listened to the lies of the devil in cahoots with the world and our own fallen sinful nature. What grace! What glory!

But why does Jesus permit the devil to keep coming back to us to continue his irrational but so powerful and destructive work among us, even in us? May we see it here: He permits it so that we may come to know more and more how total, how absolute, how desperate is our need for him. He permits it so that we may come to know more and more how great his love for us is that he came to redeem us. He permits it so that we may come more and more to recognize our total dependence on his Word and sacraments for strength to resist not only the devil but our own still sinful nature as well. He permits it so that our thanksgiving for his rescue and our love for him may increase from day to day. He permits it so that we may learn to look forward to our final and permanent rescue from the devil—and all the damage he does—in the heaven from which the devil has been forever expelled.

> Lord Jesus, let me this day see your glory in your promise of forgiveness for me when I have been foolish and wicked enough to listen to the destructive voice of the devil instead of to your saving and healing voice. Let me see your glory even in this so that, by the power of your presence in Word and sacraments, I do resist the devil and his temptations, even though imperfectly. Let me see your glory in this so that your powerful forgiveness makes perfect my so imperfect obedience. Hear my prayer that your glory may be made the more manifest in your continuing grace and mercy. Amen.

II.

Mark 5:14-17 – Those tending the pigs ran off and reported this in the town and countryside, and the people went out to see what had happened. When they came to Jesus, they saw the man who had been possessed by the legion of demons, sitting there, dressed and in his right mind; and they were afraid. Those who had seen it told the people what had happened to the demon-possessed man—and told

about the pigs as well. Then the people began to plead with Jesus to leave their region.

Consider here the only two possible responses to the glory that Jesus shows when he comes to us with his powerful and saving Word:

On the one hand, we have the man who was demon-possessed. Could there be a sharper contrast than between the way he had been and the way he is now? No more mindless raving all night long. No more naked thrashing about in his home among the dead. No more violent tearing of cords and chains from any who attempted to control him. Now he is at peace. Now he is clothed and sensible. Now he is where all of us long to be: at Jesus' feet! The contrast between his two states is a good one for us to think about. Many of us have been with Jesus ever since our baptism a few days or weeks after we were born. We are so used to his kindness, his generosity, his patience with us. We know even before we make confession of our sins that he is going to be gracious, that he will point us again to his holy cross and passion as the payment in full for all of our sin and guilt. We are so used to his providing for us even before we ask him for anything, even when we don't ask him for anything. And so it becomes easy for us to take it all for granted.

But look at the demon-possessed man before Jesus came to him, before Jesus set him free from the devil's hateful and torment-filled clutches. We need to call to mind that that would be our condition if Jesus had not so graciously and richly blessed us with his Word and sacraments. It is a rich blessing indeed if you have never been so completely in the devil's clutches as this man was with all the attending torment. It is only the grace and love of Jesus that keeps that from happening. That is a blessing we ought not forget or take for granted, given what we have deserved for the times we have toyed with the devil's temptations and so lightly given in to them. It is Jesus in his Word—and yes, even in his rule over history—that stays the hand of the devil and keeps him from making us miserable in this life and then dragging us by the throat into the torment of hell.

So instead of what we deserve by nature and what we fully merit by our own choices to sin, what do we have? We have Jesus. We go to bed at night at peace. The devil cannot claim us, for Jesus is there. We sleep securely. For whether we wake or sleep, Jesus has clothed us in his righteousness, the perfect righteousness of forgiveness. When we wake, it is not torture and torment that greets us in the new day. No, it is another day to walk with Jesus, yes, to follow him in the battle against the devil's seductive lies. It is another day to cling to Jesus' saving Word and to serve in the confidence that he blesses all that is done in his name and to his glory. That's one response to his Word. It is a miraculous response worked by Jesus himself and his Spirit through his Word.

But there is an alternative response. Look at these people in our reading. The demons' request of Jesus had been utterly irrational and Jesus granted it to demonstrate their folly. But now what of these people? They are still listening to the voice of the demons that Jesus has just vanquished! Is that not an amazing thing? They are as irrational as were the demons! Those who were responsible for the swine run to tell their employers and any who will listen what had happened. They do not want to be blamed for the loss of the swine. The loss, to be sure, was an altogether legal loss from the standpoint of the Law of Moses (assuming that the owners of the pigs were Jews). For Jews were forbidden to eat or touch pigs. When Jesus brought about destruction of the pigs, the loss was altogether deserved. And now what should be the reasonable reaction from both the keepers and the owners of the swine and then from all who saw or heard of this miracle? The owners should have recognized their sin and seen in the destruction of their illegal property the consequences that should befall them eventually if they continued in their sin.

But that's not what happens. Instead, they are afraid. Their fear in the presence of one so mighty that just with a word he could put a legion of demons to flight should have brought them trembling with a cry for mercy and forgiveness. And the sight of the demon-possessed man now clothed and at peace at Jesus' feet should have encouraged them and given them hope of pardon in answer to their plea for mercy. But that's not what happens.

What about the rest of the people, those who saw and heard the tortured cry of the demons and saw the destruction of the swine—what about them? They saw the blessed, most happy result of Jesus' words and deeds on the poor wretch who before had been the scourge of the neighborhood. Should they not also have sat down at Jesus' feet, eager to learn still more, anxious that he should bless their souls as he had blessed that man's body and soul? How utterly rational, and how beautiful it would have been had they offered the prayer later prayed by the Emmaus disciples: "Stay with us, for it is nearly evening" (Luke 24:29). But that's not what happens.

Instead—who can bear to hear it?—they plead with him to leave! What an amazing thing that is. And yet, how altogether common and familiar to us. We see it all the time: People who have made a mess of their lives by listening only to the destructive voice of the devil. They hear the gospel message of pardon and peace in Christ—and they want none of it. It's not that the Word of Jesus in his gospel was weak or ineffective. It's not that Jesus was not earnest and sincere in his call to the banquet of forgiveness and eternal life. No, not that. It is, rather, that even though his Word has the miraculous power to convert and to change, it is not irresistible. Those who receive it have only Jesus' love and grace and the power of his Word to thank for it. Those who refuse it have only themselves to blame for the ruin they bring to themselves for time and for eternity.

Tragic as it is, most are like that majority who witnessed the blessing of Jesus and his Word. Most prefer the destructive lies of the devil to the saving peace of the gospel. We see it all around us. We see it in our whole culture and society that is determined to share in the doom and the destruction that Satan brings: ridicule aplenty for the Word of God, praise and toleration for all that contradicts it. Then there is a refusal to see that the downfall and ruin of individuals and whole nations is the fruit of that wicked choice.

What shall we say to these things?

> Lord Jesus, help! Lord Jesus, save us! Save us from our own folly by which we so easily fall prey to the destroyer's voice. Save us from our own wickedness by which we toy with his temptations and then justify our sins with the excuse that we couldn't help it and that others are a lot worse than we are. Save us from all that contradicts your life-giving and saving Word. Bring us to rejoice before all things when we get to sit at your feet and hear your voice in the gospel. To you may our hearts and voices rise in thanksgiving now and forever. Amen.

III.

Mark 5:18-20 – As Jesus was getting into the boat, the man who had been demon-possessed begged to go with him. Jesus did not let him, but said, "Go home to your own people and tell them how much the Lord has done for you, and how he has had mercy on you." So the man went away and began to tell in the Decapolis how much Jesus had done for him. And all the people were amazed.

A truly amazing end to an amazing story! But before it ends, we want to take Jesus aside and give him some advice: "Now would really be a good time for you, Lord Jesus, to show your glory by another miracle—one of power, one of judgment. Rain down on these wretches your divine wrath; let them feel thunder and lightning! Let the earth open up and hell swallow them alive for their wicked rejection of your grace and goodness! It would serve them right and serve as a good object lesson and a warning to any and all who would be tempted to follow their example!" Haven't we wanted to give him that advice at times during our day in the face of such utter wickedness, in the face of so much ridicule of his Word and the few believers left who still want to follow him?

Yes, that's the advice we might want to give to Jesus. But, as he does so often, he does the opposite. And thank God for it! Otherwise, in our times of wickedness and folly, we too would have been destroyed long ago. For we too have had our days when the irrational allure of temptation proved too much for us. At such times we set aside the Word of the Lord for the sake of pleasure or to avoid being ridiculed or to save ourselves from the pain of some struggle against our own sinful flesh.

But look here! See how Jesus deals with their petition that he leave. He did indeed leave in answer to their request. He did not rain down his wrath on them. That day might come eventually, but not just yet. And look how he worked to prevent the ultimate doom of these people who preferred their pursuit of the devil in unbelief to the blessings of peace and pardon in Jesus. Jesus shows his glory in grace as he answers another prayer; it is the prayer of the only reasonable man in the story—the formerly demon-possessed man. Quite understandably, he wants to stay with Jesus, to go with him and be his student. His is an altogether rational request. And what is Jesus' answer? He denies the man's prayer! But why? Because he still loves these miserable people whose only prayer was that he should leave! Yes, and he loves this man who wanted to go with him too. In such love both for this man and for these wicked people, he gives the man a holy assignment that in the end can only fill that man's heart with joy. He tells the man to be his apostle to the man's family and then to his friends and then to all those around him. "Tell them how much the Lord has done for you," Jesus commands. Yes, let them know of Jesus' love and compassion; tell them of his power exercised in saving, as opposed to the devil's power, which is only exercised in destroying and bringing misery to people in this world and in the next.

We are told that the man happily did what Jesus told him to do. And did you catch the little addition? Jesus said, "Tell them how much the Lord has done for you!" But the man told them all that *Jesus* had done for him. He got the point: Jesus was the Lord, his God and his Savior. Mark tells us that in response, the people were amazed. Were they amazed so much that when they later heard the whole story of Jesus' saving work they came to believe it? Wherever Jesus' Word is preached, it always will bear fruit for eternal life in at least some.

How can we help but marvel at this whole account? In it we have unreason highlighted. There is the unreason of the demons that brings misery to themselves. There is the unreason of the people who listened to the devil instead of to Jesus and thus deprived themselves of the peace that Jesus came to give them. And then there is the unreason of Jesus himself! He refuses our reasonable advice to destroy and in his unreason, wants only to give the opposite of what people deserve: he wants to help and heal, wants to pardon and redeem! Oh, most blessed unreason! Then there is the demon-possessed man himself. He is the only "reasonable" one in the whole account. And Jesus gives him to be his ambassador with the message of Jesus' beautiful, saving, unreasonable gospel!

How kind, how generous, how gracious of him. He still does that. Though he has removed his visible presence, he has not left us orphaned. He still sends those he has rescued from the devil and from unbelief to tell us what wondrous things Jesus has done for our peace and our eternal rescue. Oh, that our reason might be bent—as was that formerly demon-possessed man's reason—to the service of declaring and living the saving gospel in an irrational, perishing, unbelieving world! For Jesus has not yet granted a prayer that we too might sometimes offer up, the prayer that we would be taken home to see him face-to-face in heaven. Not yet. Someday, but not yet. Go and tell your children and your grandchildren and as you have the opportunity, tell other relatives, friends, and coworkers what amazing things the Lord—Jesus—has done for you. And if you can't spell it out for them, at least when you can, say what Andrew said to his brother: Come and see (John 1:39).

We can't close our consideration of this miracle without noting at least briefly yet another way in which Jesus manifested forth his glory by what he did here. Obviously he showed forth his glory by his use of his healing power and by all that he told and showed these people of God's love and grace for them. But just beneath the surface is this other manifestation of his glory when we think about this whole story: Jesus manifested forth his glory by his deep humility.

Just think of it. Anyone else would have been instantly angry at these people. Anyone else would have listened to our advice that they should be destroyed at once and on the spot. Anyone else would have accepted the healed man's request to leave that wretched place and those wretched people so that he could continue to praise Jesus and learn from him. But that's not the way that Jesus deals with our fallen condition. For now in his humility he lets himself be rejected so that he can come yet again to us with his message of peace and pardon. For now he lets us suffer at times the consequences of our own sin and folly so that we may long for his return with the message of grace and salvation. For now when we are crushed by the law and by our accusing conscience, he returns quickly with the assurance that his whole and earnest desire is that we enjoy his forgiveness and come at length to be with him forever in heaven. What humility can compare with that of the Son of God who needs nothing and no one but who nevertheless gives himself freely for us and for all!

> O dearest Jesus, you are almighty and need nothing; yet you stoop to me, to one who is poor and lowly, one who deserves

nothing and needs everything. In your Word and Sacrament you give me yourself and all that you have stored up for me of peace and joy in this life and then the perfect enjoyment of peace and joy with you forever in heaven. By that same Word and Sacrament, grant also this prayer that I remember with joy and thanksgiving all you are for me and to me, and that in remembering I grow in the earnest desire to share your wondrous love and grace wherever and whenever I can. Amen.

Healing a Sick Woman

I.

Mark 5:32-34 – Jesus kept looking around to see who had done it [who had touched him]. Then the woman, knowing what had happened to her, came and fell at his feet and, trembling with fear, told him the whole truth. He said to her, "Daughter, your faith has healed you. Go in peace and be freed from your suffering."

Again, what an amazing story and how rich in comfort for us! Read the entire account in Mark 5:24-34. The case of this woman is sad indeed. She had some sort of bleeding disease, had it for 12 years. Imagine the toll that it had taken on her body, how it had sapped all her energy and made it difficult to carry out the most common of tasks. Worse still, this sort of bleeding disease made her ceremonially unclean; like the leper, that meant that she was a virtual outcast from society. A healthy marriage and family life were impossible. Attendance at the temple and probably at the synagogue too was likewise out of the question. Her condition was not one that she would want to talk about. There was no help for her. Oh, it wasn't that she hadn't tried to get help. She had gone to doctors, one after the other, for 12 years. She had exhausted whatever savings she had. And for all of that, she was no better, only worse off than she had been before.

And now Jesus appears on the scene. She has heard of him. She knows that he can help her. Perhaps she had even come close before. But to actually approach the great man and tell him her problem and then ask for his help? No, that was out of the question. But here, today, there is a crowd pressing all around him. A high-ranking official of the synagogue has come to Jesus, pleading for his help; his daughter is at the point of death. He pleads with Jesus that he would just come and lay his hand on the little girl so that she would be healed. So the crowd pushes and shoves as Jesus begins to follow Jairus to his home. Everybody wants to see what Jesus will do.

Now here is this poor woman's chance! With the crowd pushing and shoving, she can inch her way through it. Maybe, just maybe if she can just touch him—no, just touch his robe—maybe that will be enough. After all, what does she have to lose? No one will see or notice her. She won't have to expose herself to the embarrassment of saying what was really wrong with her and then to the upturned noses of those who would hear her.

And it worked! She touched his robe. Instantly she could tell that her bleeding, for the first time in 12 years, had stopped! She didn't just feel a little better. She felt well, fully cured. Oh, how she must want to sing, to jump for joy. But that would never do. She will just slink away as unnoticed after this amazing miracle as she had been before.

But Jesus will have none of that. No, he has much greater things in mind for her than she had imagined or wanted or hoped for. And so he stops. He looks around him for the one who had touched his robe. It is not as though he doesn't know who did it. It's not as though the miracle had happened sort of magically, without his consent. He knew what had happened and he willed it to happen. But he wants to give this woman so much more than she came for. And he can only do that if she will come forward. And so he calls her out, no doubt looking right at her. She knows that she cannot escape this encounter with Jesus.

But wait just a minute! This won't do! Jairus is an important man with a desperate need of help for his daughter. This isn't the time to stop along the way. Everyone is pushing and shoving and in a hurry. There is that pained look on the face of Jairus, who fears that Jesus may get to his home too late to help. Wouldn't this be a good time for Jesus to just let things go, to let the poor woman go on her way? She certainly wouldn't mind. Why not just let the miracle of her healing be between God and her? She would be healed and grateful. Even Jesus would benefit. After all, Jairus was important. And to help him with the crowd witnessing his power, well, that would certainly increase Jesus' own popularity and the willingness of people to listen to him. But what is gained by taking time for this poor woman?

But that's not how Jesus sees things—thank God! He doesn't listen to the prayer of important Jairus just because he's important. And he doesn't treat this poor woman with any less concern or respect just because she is poor and lowly, too humble and fearful to approach Jesus as directly as Jairus had. As Jairus' prayer had Jesus' undivided attention, so too does the need of this unhappy woman. Think about that when next you teach a little child to pray. Jesus gives that child—so unimportant in the world—his undivided attention. Think about it when next you pray. Come into Jesus' presence if you want, sneaking up behind him, almost unsure if he would want to be bothered with you. And then, thinking of Jesus and this woman, know with certainty that in Jesus' way of thinking, he has nothing that he would rather do than hear you pray. That's how he manifests his glory: He deals with us, with each one of us, one at a time, and he does that according to our need: both the need we bring to him and the need of which we may not even be aware.

> Lord Jesus, how kind you are, how filled with grace and mercy! Forgive me all those times when I didn't pray because I thought myself too unimportant for you to bother with. Forgive me all those times when my prayers were merely mechanical because I didn't really think about your love for me or because I didn't recognize my own need. Instead, by this picture of you with this woman, bring me to rejoice and give thanks that you always know me and my needs far better than I do. Trusting in that love proven so completely on the cross, I come now for pardon and lay before you all my cares, my fears, my doubts. For the sake of your own perfect merit, I know that you will hear me and give me both forgiveness and everything else that I need for this life and the next. Amen.

II.

Mark 5:33,34 – [She] fell at his feet and, trembling with fear, told him the whole truth. He said to her, "Daughter, your faith has healed you. Go in peace and be freed from your suffering."

Our amazement at this incident is not yet finished. Picture it again in your mind: The woman has been found out—the last thing she would have wanted. But there is no escape from the look of Jesus. Trembling, she falls at his feet, and she "[tells] him the whole truth."

Just imagine that! The crowd is still all around. Jairus is in a hurry. And here is this poor woman at his feet, scared half to death. Inside of her is this strange mix of exultation that she is cured and dread that perhaps she had done something wrong; in any event, she would have to give an account of what she was and what she had done and do that in front of Jesus and this crowd. And so she blubbers forth "the whole truth." Do you wonder how long that must have taken? She has had 12 years of pain, of weakness, of frustration with doctors, of hiding from people, of a sense of not only helplessness but of worthlessness. And now it all comes out! Why had God dealt with her thus? There was this doctor and then that one and then another and another. There was the exhaustion of her body and of her money. There was the fear of what would become of her in the end, now that all her money had been lost. And now this! In an instant she is well. But would she be punished for what she had done so carefully? Was Jesus angry that she had touched him, touched his robe?

Listen to Jesus! See how he manifests forth his glory in a unique way in his encounter with this woman. His words to her show that he understands us, really understands us. He knows us inside and out. He knows that this woman had a need even greater than her need for physical healing. She needed to know that he understood her. She needed to know that, in understanding her, he had nothing but love for her. Who do you know like that? Who do you know who understands you 100 percent and has nothing better to do in the world than to stop everything else and tend to your needs even without your asking? Indeed, few are there; perhaps there is no one who understands us that way. Truth be told, we probably don't even want someone to know us that well. For we fear that if they did, they would go away annoyed, perhaps even disgusted.

But look here. How well he understands this woman's fears and doubts, her self-loathing, and perhaps her despair of ever being wanted by anyone, even by God. Jesus, with just one little word, cures all her fears and gives her so much more than she had sought. That one word? *Daughter!* It is a word of such tenderness. It is a word so full of understanding for her particular, unique situation. She was probably at least as old as Jesus was. But he, this great rabbi—yes, God clothed in our flesh and blood—calls her "Daughter"! She is God's daughter. She may have felt abandoned by God in her distress. But God had never forgotten about her. Her need was to him as the need of a dear daughter to a father. And he knew just the perfect time for meeting that need. He would meet it in such a way that for the rest of her life she could be thankful even for those 12 years of misery! For how else would she have come to know the love of God in the person of her "brother," God's only begotten Son—a love of God that was intended just for her?

And then these added words so rich in comfort, so filled with joy for her and for the rest of us too: "Your faith has healed you. Go in peace and be freed from your suffering." Wow! All that he had done for her, he attributes to her faith. And where did that come from? Was it from her merit, the result of anything that she had done for Jesus? Clearly it was not. Her faith so highly praised was his gift to her. It was a gift that, unknown to her at the time, he had created by the words she had heard earlier from or about him. On the basis of what she heard and saw in him, he had created such a trust in her heart that she dared to approach in the first place, even though it was in such a weak and fear-filled way. And now this gift of his he praises in her as something of the greatest importance to him.

Then he reassures that faith still further and blesses it and her still more: "Go in peace and be freed from your suffering." Peace was something she had not had for a long time. No peace in her body. Perhaps less still in her soul: she may have thought her long-suffering was the result of her sin, that God was somehow punishing her. But now Jesus has called her "Daughter"! What a way of declaring that her sins are forgiven, that her status with God is that of a dear and beloved child! She never could have had that peace were it not for the suffering that drove her to seek Jesus and then to hear from him these sweetest, these most powerful words. So in peace she can leave. In peace her suffering of both body and soul have been relieved and removed.

Is there no one who understands you perfectly? Is that, in fact, the way you want it, lest if someone knew your inmost being they would turn away, annoyed or disgusted? In truth if there was someone who knew and understood you perfectly, what use would it be to you? They either would be unable or unwilling to satisfy your inmost needs.

But here is Jesus. He calls you Son! He calls you Daughter! And he does that while understanding you perfectly! He does not turn aside or go on his way to people you might think deserve his understanding, his attention, his mercy, and his love more than you ever could. No, he has it all for you no less than for another. In his Word and sacraments he gives you this faith, which trusts that he is telling you the truth: "For you I came! For you I suffered the torments of the damned! For you I died and rose again! For you I have ruled over history so that you have needs no one else knows about or understands. And I let you have those needs so that despairing of yourself you would turn to me and trust me to meet them." Couldn't you write a book about the times in life when you looked into the sky and wondered why God let this or that happen to you that brought you down so low? Couldn't you write a book about the times when, in such need, you cast yourself at his feet and pleaded for his mercy—and he showed it. He rescued and relieved you and gave you peace again; he gave you strength sufficient for the day until such time as the suffering would be relieved, even if the relief was the promise of heaven at the end. Listen to him here: He praises the faith that he has created and sustained all this time. He bids you go in peace in the assurance that he understands, that he answers your prayers, and that he gives you peace in his pardon, peace in the assurance of his constant presence in grace, peace in the promise of perfect rescue and relief in heaven.

> Even so, Lord Jesus, grant me still that peace, which is found by faith and found in your wounds and Word alone. I dare to ask it not on the basis of my merit, but on the basis of your merit and your promise. Amen.

Raising Jairus' Daughter

I.

Mark 5:35,36 – While Jesus was still speaking, some people came from the house of Jairus, the synagogue leader. "Your daughter is dead,"

they said. "Why bother the teacher anymore?" Overhearing what they said, Jesus told him, "Don't be afraid; just believe."

We have not finished yet with this beautiful manifestation of Jesus' glory, this so consoling a truth that he understands us. And in understanding us, he does not turn away but with his words draws us ever closer to himself.

Jairus had begged Jesus to come and lay a hand on his daughter so that she would be healed. But Jesus didn't need any instructions from Jairus, well-intended though they were, on what he should do. It would have been quite enough if Jairus would simply have told Jesus of his need and then said, "Amen," rather than instructing Jesus on what he should do. Jairus doesn't understand that yet. And so Jesus causes the events to play out just as they did.

Jairus is anxious. He wants and has, in effect, told Jesus to hurry up, lest the time when he could help runs out. Then this woman shows up. The hurried procession stops while Jesus gives her his undivided attention, as though he had nothing better to do and no one more important to deal with. We can't help but wonder what anxious, what fearful, perhaps even annoyed looks crossed Jairus' face and thoughts crossed his mind as this woman went on and on about her troubles. But Jesus pays him no mind. The right time has not yet come. Jairus still has something to learn about himself and, just as important, about Jesus. He has to learn patience. He has to learn that God's time for rescue is always the best time. He has to learn that time itself and what unfolds in time is ever in God's keeping. He has to learn that it is even in love that Jesus delays his help, so that Jairus would learn exactly these lessons. They were no doubt hard lessons for Jairus, but necessary. They are hard lessons for us too and no less necessary.

But then Jairus' friends come and inform the anxious father that time has run out. The child has died. No point in bothering Jesus any further. Think of those friends just for a moment. Their advice to Jairus on the matter tells us a lot about them. They had no trust in Jesus as the Son of God and the Lord of life and death. It may be that they had thought it a waste of time to come seeking Jesus' help in the first place. And now they bring this tragic news and their heartless advice. To be sure, all of the outward evidence is in their favor. The reality of who Jesus really is and of the way that God deals with us in our weakness—that remains hidden.

We may have experienced it or at least are aware of those who have. The situation is hopeless; the condition beyond all help. There comes the response, "All that is left for me is to go to church; all that remains for me is to pray and to tell God what he should do—and quickly." Someone will always be on hand, whether people we know or the devil's voice inside of

Epiphany

us, to answer: "What's the use of that? You've got to make do as best you can in this life. If there is a God, he wouldn't have let this mess go as far as it has in the first place. To expect—if there is a God—that he is going to care about you now, well that's just a waste of time."

What is Jesus' answer to Jairus' anxious fears and ours? What is Jesus' answer to the advice of Jairus' friends and of the devil himself? It's all so simple. It's all so seemingly impossible. "Don't be afraid. Just believe." Again, the outward evidence gives every reason for fear. The child had been critically ill, and there was no help for her. And now the child has died. Fear, we should expect, will soon be replaced with despair. But Jesus says, "Just believe!" Believe what? Believe that you have not called on Jesus in vain. Believe that Jesus knows exactly what he is doing. Believe on the basis of all that you have seen and especially all that you have heard from him that what he does is always best. Believe that what he does is always done in love. Believe that that love of Jesus is not just a warm and fuzzy feeling but that it is directed at each individual who is drawn to him by his Word. And then believe that his love is ever active in planning and providing just exactly what that individual needs.

Yes, Jairus, yes Tom, yes Susan, just believe! Just trust Jesus, casting all your fears at the foot of his cross, even with this prayer: "I have no clue how all this will work out to my good; I have no instructions that I might give you, Lord. I just lay it all at your feet. I trust you. Do what you will. That can only be for my good here in time and forevermore."

That believing, that faith, clearly could not come from Jairus. It had to be implanted, created, and sustained by Jesus' powerful Word itself. And so it was. Jairus cast aside the cynical, unbelieving counsel of his friends. He continued his journey home with Jesus, even though his mind and heart are filled with questions yet unanswered. He trusts, he believes, and he does that in the face of all the evidence that counsels only fear, only despair.

That, exactly that, is the nature of faith: it trusts Jesus' Word, in spite of all the contrary evidence. I see in myself sin and guilt. But Jesus in his Word brings forgiveness. I see in myself the seeds of death. But Jesus promises eternal life. I see in my everyday existence all kinds of reasons for fear, for doubt, for anxiety, for despair. But Jesus promises his abiding presence with me in Word and sacraments, a presence in love and grace; that all remains true whether I see that in a moment or it remains shrouded behind a cloud or in a veil of tears. Yes, exactly that is always the nature of faith: "Don't be afraid. Just believe."

> O almighty and ever-gracious Jesus, turn my eyes from what I see in myself and all around me. Turn them to focus on you and on your Word, by which alone I come to the joyous

confidence that in spite of any and all evidence to the contrary, you remain my Jesus; you remain still my God and only Savior; you abide in life and death my reason for rising above fear. Your Word continues as the source of all my confidence in life. To you be praise and glory forever so that I trust you and your Word above all that I may think or feel outside of or contrary to your so powerful and gracious gospel. Amen.

II.

Mark 5:40-43 – After he put them all out, he took the child's father and mother and the disciples who were with him, and went in where the child was. He took her by the hand and said to her, *"Talitha koum!"* (which means "Little girl, I say to you, get up!"). Immediately the girl stood up and walked around (she was twelve years old). At this they were completely astonished. He gave strict orders not to let anyone know about this, and told them to give her something to eat.

And so the scene unfolds. Jesus arrives at Jairus' home. But things now are so different from what they had been such a short time earlier. For one thing, Jesus has somehow gotten rid of the crowd that had pressed around him and been so eager to see what would happen at the home of Jairus. Did the crowd go away in silent sympathy for Jairus when his friends came and told him that his daughter had died? Or did Jesus himself somehow manage to send them away? Either way, Jesus arrives at Jairus' home only in the company of Jairus and three of his disciples.

And what does he find when he gets there? Another crowd. This time it is a crowd of professional mourners, weeping and wailing at the death of the little girl. For that was the custom in those days: funerals were conducted the same day as the death. A prominent or wealthy family would hire professional mourners as stand-ins for the relatives and friends who could not attend the funeral at such short notice. When Jesus arrives, he informs the professional weepers in anticipation of what he is about to do that the child is not dead but sleeping; immediately their tears turn to riotous laughter and ridicule. Here is another time when we might be inclined to take Jesus aside and suggest to him, "Let them have it! No one should just get away with such bold ridiculing of the Son of God!" After all, who hasn't been tempted to suggest that to Jesus more than once these days when he and his Word are so ridiculed and mocked at every turn? But that is not his way. The day will come, but not yet. In his humility he veils his power and might that he could have so easily, even justly, used for death and destruction. He simply dismisses the mockers.

Then without any pomp, without the least show, he goes quietly with the parents and three disciples to the room of the little girl. And there—see how gently it all takes place—he just takes her by the hand and calmly tells her that it is time to get up. Jairus had been eager to give instructions. Jairus was in a hurry. The crowd earlier was curious, and the crowd at Jairus' house loud and laughing. But here is Jesus. He understands it all. He teaches Jairus faith and patience. He does what he wants to. And what he wants to do is help and heal. He wants to bring life where there was only death, only fear, only despair.

The miracle is perfect in every way. The little girl gets up and starts to walk around. There is no period of recovery, no days of recuperating and regaining strength. No, she is completely well. Her parents are amazed. Perhaps they shouldn't have been so surprised. After all, what did they expect would happen? Jesus is there. He is the Lord of life and death. Nevertheless, we can certainly understand their amazement. After all, we too cry day in and day out for pardon. We too have been in situations where our other prayers were offered in fear that perhaps the prayers would not be heard or do any good. And then, lo and behold, contrary to all our merit, Jesus forgives us in his Word and in the sacraments. Then, lo and behold, our other fears and doubts are allayed when Jesus brings, in his own good time, the rescue we needed; as he does here, he so often does it in ways far different from those we might have asked for.

But our amazement isn't finished yet. Jesus tells them the opposite of what he told the demon-possessed man earlier in the chapter. He told that man to go and proclaim the mercy of God, which Jesus had shown to him—to tell everyone about it. But here he sharply commands that the parents tell no one what had happened. But why the difference? The demon-possessed man lived in a predominantly gentile region; Jesus rarely went there. Moreover, there were no widely held dreams there of some great Jewish messianic kingdom that would be ushered in when the Messiah came. But here in the Jewish homeland, such dreams were common. Jesus does not want to foster any notions that the fulfillment of those dreams was his reason for coming. And so he charges the parents of the little girl to keep silent. No doubt when friends and neighbors saw the little girl well and running and playing in the neighborhood, they—and the laughing professional mourners—would conclude that, after all, she had not died but had just been sick and now had recovered. Jesus' miracles were intended to confirm that he is indeed the Son of God and the Savior, but he did not want his miracles to get in the way of his reason for coming. For he came not to win popularity or worldly power but to be rejected. He came not to have a good life but to suffer. He came not to embrace life but to give it by dying. And so, quietly, almost in private, he raises up the little girl as he raises us up: simply by speaking, simply by his Word.

And then note this final, beautiful touch: He told her parents to give her something to eat! Now is that not an odd thing? Couldn't they have figured that out by themselves? Of course they could and would have. But so complete, so thorough is Jesus' understanding of her condition and ours that not the slightest, seemingly most insignificant detail escapes his notice and his tender care. Oh, that I would remember this in every hour of my life. He who inhabits the praises of saints and angels in heaven is not too busy to be bothered with me; he knows and understands me down to the least bite of bread that I last ate. And he in his grace and perfect love provides it all: the life-giving bread of the gospel for my forgiveness and eternal life, and the bread on the plate that sustains me for the next five minutes!

> "What a friend we have in Jesus" (CW 411)! O precious Savior, how lightly those words fall from my lips. How unaware I am so often of the depth of your love for me and care for my body and soul. Even in this hour you attend to my next breath. And you do it all so quietly, so without fanfare, that I am unmindful of your goodness and generosity. O Jesus, dearest Jesus, at least in this hour let me bow low in adoration and thanksgiving for all your blessings, the many known to me and the even more unknown. This much I do know: They all come to me because of your merit, not mine, and because of your generosity and goodness and grace. Amen.

Mark Chapter 5 Summary

It is just not possible to exhaust the beauty and the richness of this chapter as in it, Jesus manifests his glory by teaching us through what he does. We see in all three miracles so much about ourselves and so much about him. In all three miracles we see a need most desperate. We see the need for rescue from the chains of the devil and the shackles of our sins. We see the need for help in bodily sickness and affliction. We see the need for rescue from death. We see the need for someone who really understands and knows us—and loves us in spite of how well he understands and knows us! For none of these needs can we find help in ourselves. For none of them is there any merit or worthiness in us that deserves help from God. But for all of them there is rescue—rescue and redemption in Jesus. And see how he does it all. He accomplishes everything with his Word. By his Word he puts the devil to flight, that devil who seduces us so often and even with our willing consent. With his Word he raises up the woman, who knows only of her weakness and unworthiness, when he calls her "Daughter." With his Word he vanquishes the death of the little girl and the doubt of her father.

We notice too in each one of these miracles the detailed care and understanding of Jesus for the individual. Each individual in these three miraculous events has different needs. There is the obvious need of the demon-possessed man for rescue, which he certainly cannot accomplish for himself. There is the need for the spiritually demon-possessed people who begged Jesus to leave—their need to hear of Jesus' love and grace in spite of themselves. Yes, and there is the need of that healed demon-possessed man to give thanks and to share the blessings he had received from Jesus and his Word. There is the need of the woman with the blood sickness to receive so much more than the cure for her disease of the body: her need of healing for her soul and downcast spirit. There is the need of Jairus to discover that Jesus is more than just a healer whose hand and presence is needed to accomplish anything at all.

We cannot help but notice in each of these cases that the desperate need proved to be a great blessing. For without their need they would have learned nothing of Jesus' person as the Son of God. Without their need they would not have experienced the power of his Word to help and heal. Without their need they would not have seen his grace and mercy, his yearning to rescue. And we note in wonder that in each case, the blessing that Jesus brought was far greater than what could be expected or even what was sought.

All of that should give us pause. We don't know why that man was demon-possessed. We don't know why that woman had to suffer so long. We don't know why Jairus and his wife needed to go through the anguish of their little girl's fatal illness. But Jesus knew all of that. And Jesus permitted or sent all of that for the ultimate blessing of each of those individuals.

Yes, that should give us pause when we want to give advice to God or to complain to him about our lot in life or about someone else's lot in life. Our pause is not one of mindless resignation, such as that expressed in the adage, "Whatever will be, will be." Rather, it is the pause of faith formed by the Word of God and by Jesus' work through it in our lives. We would so like our lives to be smooth and untroubled in this world so that heaven itself would be mere repetition. But if it were, we would never make it to heaven. For the simple fact is that it is need that drives us to the foot of his cross with the cry for grace, for mercy, for rescue.

And so while we give thanks to God for all of his many obvious gifts and blessings, may we not forget to give thanks as well for those times when the gifts and blessings seemed far away or gone altogether. Those times can be the most blessed of all if they bring us to an often absent awareness of our need so constant and so absolute (Romans 5:1-5; Hebrews 12:1-11). Pain of any kind points us to the pain that Jesus willingly endured for us. The guilt of sin remembered drives us to the remembrance of his pain in paying for our sins. Loss of worldly comfort and security reminds us that here we are but pilgrims—always a bit uncomfortable, always insecure apart from his gifts and his protection; ultimately our comfort and security is only perfect and eternal in the heaven he won for us by his death and resurrection. Pain, sickness, or loss of any kind can be a healthy antidote to the worship of this world and the things, even the people, in it.

So we look to Jesus both for our redemption and for our example. All that we tend to hold so dear, he shunned for our sake. All that we want to shun and avoid, he embraced for our sake. We want health and life—and that isn't necessarily bad—but he embraced death. We want comfort and ease; when we have and see them as his gifts of grace, that isn't necessarily bad either, but he most often had no roof over his head and depended on the generosity of others for his daily bread. We want a life with faithful friends and family always at our side and ready to defend and help us; when we have them, they are indeed beautiful blessings of God. But he, without complaint and for our sake, was abandoned by all, betrayed by some, denied by others, forsaken ultimately even by his Father.

And now in our time of pilgrimage, he so watches over us—over each of us as individuals—that he knows in detail that never escapes his mind and heart what we need of good things and ill. In grace and mercy and love, he sends need so that we will finally see that in him, we have everything we need and more. It is a blessing indeed when we have passed some years mixed with the sweet and the bitter and then can look back on them and say, "So much turned out so differently than I had expected or even wanted; Jesus has done all things well!"

> Lord Jesus, you have made my pilgrimage here an adventure indeed. For all the crosses you have sent and for all the pillows on which I have rested my weary head, I give you thanks and praise. For the comfort of the gospel in my guilt, for daily bread to quiet my hunger, for people who have helped me and who I now may serve, I give you thanks and praise. For all of it is by grace. All of it you purchased for me on the cross. Blessed are you my God and Savior forever and ever! Amen.

Rejected in Nazareth

Luke 4:24-30 – "Truly I tell you," he continued, "no prophet is accepted in his hometown. I assure you that there were many widows in Israel in Elijah's time, when the sky was shut for three and a half years

and there was a severe famine throughout the land. Yet Elijah was not sent to any of them, but to a widow in Zarephath in the region of Sidon. And there were many in Israel with leprosy in the time of Elisha the prophet, yet not one of them was cleansed – only Naaman the Syrian. All the people in the synagogue were furious when they heard this. They got up, drove him out of the town, and took him to the brow of the hill on which the town was built, in order to throw him off the cliff. But he walked right through the crowd and went on his way.

It is early in Jesus' three-year ministry. Already he has become famous. And now, in this text, he returns to Nazareth, where he had been raised and where a number of his relatives still lived. On the Sabbath the famous hometown rabbi enters his home synagogue. In accordance with the custom of the day, he, as a visiting rabbi, would be invited to speak on the lesson for the day. After reading the text from Isaiah and pointing to himself as the fulfillment of the promises of God made there concerning the coming Messiah, everyone is impressed. They are, however, impressed only outwardly: "My, how well he speaks! And just think how surprising that is, given that he came from here and that we know his relatives!" Then, proving that they understand nothing of what he said, they ask him to perform in Nazareth the miracles that they had heard he performed elsewhere.

Now here we should not have to give Jesus any advice. Clearly it would be wise and prudent of him to do exactly that. If they would see the miracles with their own eyes, then they would draw the right conclusion from his sermon, the conclusion that they missed on first hearing, the conclusion that Jesus is indeed the promised Messiah of whom Isaiah wrote.

But look what happens! Jesus does the exact opposite. Instead of acceding to their request and winning them over with a powerful display, he antagonizes them! He knew full well how it would gall them to be reminded that in Old Testament times, God showed mercy to heathen outsiders by miracles not granted in Israel. For the Jews considered themselves in every way superior to all such. Certainly as fellow citizens of Jesus, they should be worthy of his miraculous displays before anyone else. But now to have it pointed out that they compare poorly with the heathens of Sidon and Damascus, well, that's just too much!

Lord Jesus, had you just asked us! We could have saved you from this disgrace, this embarrassment, this almost untimely death! Why didn't you win them over with a miracle or two? Or if you didn't want to do that, at least don't insult these people who think they know you so well and deserve so much better from you. After all, they did like your sermon, even if they didn't get its main point. Besides that, people who have become famous and even popular should be careful not to jeopardize their popularity by saying things that they should realize will only antagonize their listeners.

But Jesus will have none of it! To be sure he does perform one miracle that day: He escapes! The almighty Son of God will die, but it will be at the time and in the manner of his choosing. Jesus disappointed the people who thought they knew him so well. They wanted a Jesus who would tell them how nice and special they were. That he showed them their sins and called them to trust in the only one who could save them—that angered them enough to want to kill him.

There are still many, like the people of Nazareth, who think they know him so well but find themselves at times disappointed or even angry with him. Are any of us in their number? "Why does he always have to remind me of my sins and call me to repentance? I think I'm good enough—or close to it—the way I am! It's so irritating in the liturgy to have to confess week in and week out that 'I am by nature sinful and unclean!'" Or: "Why doesn't he do for me what I have noted that he has done for others? Why doesn't he grant my will and my wish and my prayer the way that I think he should?"

But that's not the way it is with him. With him and for us, it is always this: the Word, the Word, the Word! Listening to him, that is our task. For faith is kindled by listening. It is a faith that has as its heart and core repentance and the longing for the forgiveness so freely offered in the Word and sacraments. And it is a faith preserved in the storm and stress of life by listening. Such a faith survives even death itself by listening ever and again to his gracious voice: *In me are all the promises of God fulfilled; in me is forgiveness. In me is peace. In me is life and salvation. Once you have me, you have the fulfillment of all the good that God has promised; all the rest you will see me sort out for your benefit in good time—the time of my choosing, not yours.*

So then, don't be disappointed or angry with him. Listen to him. Abandon your own feelings and opinions—whatever is contrary to his Word—in favor of the Word of God Incarnate. He truly will never disappoint those who trust him. When giving Jesus advice takes the place of listening, then so much, sometimes all, of the blessing and benefit he intends to give with his Word is lost. Jesus' experience in Nazareth certainly demonstrates that point.

> Therefore Lord Jesus, most gladly I confess it: I am indeed by nature sinful and unclean. But you are perfect and holy. Forgive not just what I have done. Forgive first and foremost and each day what I am—a sinner. Then I will be perfect and holy too; for when you have forgiven me, it is your own holiness

and perfection that the Father sees when he looks at me. Then grant me this grace that I set aside all the silly notions I have about what I think you could have done better in my life; grant instead this favor that I cling to your Word, and trusting in your grace, gladly bend my will to yours. Hear me for the sake of your grace and mercy. Amen.

Cleansing the Temple

I.

John 2:13-19 – When it was almost time for the Jewish Passover, Jesus went up to Jerusalem. In the temple courts he found people selling cattle, sheep and doves, and others sitting at tables exchanging money. So he made a whip out of cords, and drove all from the temple courts, both sheep and cattle; he scattered the coins of the money changers and overturned their tables. To those who sold doves he said, "Get these out of here! Stop turning my Father's house into a market." His disciples remembered that it is written: "Zeal for your house will consume me." . . . "Destroy this temple, and I will raise it again in three days."

Here Jesus does what he didn't do in Nazareth. There he didn't show the wrath that ultimately comes to those who use their outward connection to God as an excuse for continuing to live for their sins. But here Jesus does show that godly and righteous anger and by doing so, he calls us to long for forgiveness. At the same time he demonstrates that he wants from us a life that reflects our joy and gratitude for the forgiveness he so dearly won for us and that he has freely given in his Word and sacraments. Consider how all that comes together.

When Jesus acts as he does here, we want to exclaim, "Good! You showed them who was boss and let them have it as they deserved! To your temple, God's dwelling place on earth, you came. Filled with zeal for your own house, you cleansed it of what was so obviously unholy in it. You did it not gently but with a whip! Grubby and greedy moneymakers all were those you drove out of your temple in your holy zeal; the fact that they sold animals to be used in sacrifice and exchanged filthy Roman coins for coins that would be more fitting for use in your house did not hide from you the greed that was behind all that they did."

But upon reflection we might still have a complaint to make. After all is said and done, what good did it do? Jesus left his temple, and as soon as he was gone, the grubby and the greedy returned to take up their places at the sheep stalls and money-changing tables. Oh, to be sure, he came again to his house during Holy Week and again drove out the buyers and the sellers (Luke 19:45). But that really didn't do any good either. In short order they got their revenge, crying out with their masters, the chief priests, and others, "Crucify him, crucify him!"—after which they again picked up their business where they had left off.

What point then was there in this cleansing of the temple and in the cleansing of it again during Holy Week? There are a number of lessons to be learned here. For starters, Jesus is so often pictured as "gentle Jesus, meek and mild." And to be sure he is that; he is that to the sinner who falls at his feet in confession and who longs for pardon. He is that to the tortured soul driven by temptations and passions he or she seems almost powerless to control, who pleads day and night for mercy and for strength. He is that to the one whose problems and pains in life know no solution but that of finding the courage to endure. Such come to him and plead with him for grace and mercy.

To all such he is indeed "gentle Jesus, meek and mild." He turns none away. He pours forth forgiveness and peace of conscience on those thus afflicted, like gentle rain falling from heaven on a dry and thirsty land. He gives strength sufficient for the day to the one exhausted by life's problems, cares, and sorrows. For his assurance stands stronger than the mountains: he casts out none who come to him. He remains forever as Savior, the helper of those who put their trust in him.

But "gentle Jesus, meek and mild" is not the picture we should have of him in the face of a mere outward connection to his Word while still clinging to or defending or making excuses for our sin. For those who do this, there is the whip of judgment. For them there is the anger of the holy and righteous Son of God who will not be mocked and will not suffer his Word to be scorned or treated with contempt. The cleansing of the temple with a whip puts to silence the devil's lie that what we do doesn't matter to God; it refutes the deadly deceit that somehow Jesus could never be angry with anyone and that ultimately everybody ends up in heaven, no matter what they did with Jesus and his Word.

Yet still there is this question: What good did it do for Jesus to cleanse the temple with such vigor, when the wicked just returned to their evil as soon as his back was turned? The answer is perhaps not at once obvious to us. But just think about it: Jesus' cleansing of the temple certainly shows us that he will not forever put up with abuse of his Word and with those who make their sins the goal of life. At the same time, however, Jesus' cleansing of the temple shows us that in this life, punishment and the reassertion of the law converts no one.

What a lesson! In the history of the church there have always been people who wanted to use force and law to cleanse not just the church but also the world outside of the church. Let's just pass some laws. Let's burn the heretics at the stake. Let's force people to lead a godly life with the church as the lobby group in the government that will turn the country into a "Christian" country. It never works. Forced outward submission there may be for a time, but the heart remains the same, and soon the behavior will resume its wicked course.

So Jesus cleanses the temple to show the need for a change of heart, a change that can come only when the whip brings the cry for forgiveness. That such a cry was not heard after this first cleansing of the temple points to his patience. He does not destroy these wicked people completely. He gives them time to come to see their need of inward cleansing that can come only with the gospel. When that doesn't happen, he cleanses the temple yet again, yet again showing patience. A cleansing of destruction, however, one day would come if his patience and his grace continued to be spurned.

Jesus' cleansing of the temple should indeed remind us that God, in due course, judges. He sends in his own time and in his own way the whip of purging against those who use his Word as a cover for their own greed and vice. That should serve as a warning to all of us to put away hypocrisy that has the name "Christian" while the heart still belongs to that same greed and vice. The cleansing of the temple is a call to take all of God's Word seriously. It is reminder that sometimes our losses and sorrows in this life are calls to turn away from the greed that betrays an idolatry of the world and the things in the world. And such sorrows point us and drive us to the cross of our dear Savior for forgiveness, which alone can make us clean again.

Finally, Jesus' cleansing of the temple reminds us that our task is that of preaching and teaching his Word in all of its truth and purity from hearts devoted to the message of his grace and goodness. For that is what brings us and others to a repentance that clings in faith and joy to his salvation. That's why it is so important to keep preaching and teaching pure Scripture, drawn from the Word of God alone and not from human opinion or preference. To be sure, we don't hurt or want to kill those who pervert his Word, but we don't let them into our pulpits or schools or fellowship either. Physical and spiritual punishment for the perversion of his Word is in God's hands, not ours. When the time for such preaching and teaching has come to an end, God himself will intervene without any interference or help from us. That's what he did in the destruction of the first temple (2 Chronicles 36:11-20). And that's what he did in the year A.D. 70 in the destruction of the temple that Jesus here cleansed as a warning of what was to come.

> Lord Jesus, have mercy on us! Do not cast us off because of the times that we have failed to cherish your Word taught in

its truth and purity. Forgive us, forgive us still for the times our Christianity has been merely an outward show while inside the heart was still ruled by greed and vice. Be patient, merciful Savior! Let your cleansing of the temple warn us against the faith-destroying wickedness of thinking that we have been saved so that we could sin all the more boldly. By the greatness of your love on the cross and in all that you have done for us in our daily lives, move us instead to love and trust in you alone as both Savior and guide. Hear us, we pray, because of your great love and grace. Amen

II.

John 2:17,19 – His disciples remembered that it is written: "Zeal for your house will consume me." . . . "Destroy this temple, and I will raise it again in three days."

The zeal of his house consumed Jesus that day in Jerusalem. It consumed him so much because the temple had been God's visible dwelling place on earth in the many years before Jesus came down from heaven to be born the Son of God and Mary's son. God has always wanted a visible sign of his presence among men. He showed this when he commanded the people of Israel at the time of the exodus from Egypt to erect the tabernacle. That would be the place where God would meet his people. The temple built later by King Solomon and then rebuilt after the Jews returned from the Babylonian Captivity continued that visible sign of the presence of God among his people. There in the temple they would observe the sacrifices that pictured and promised the ultimate temple, Jesus himself. In him, as in no one else and nothing other, all the fullness of God lived (Colossians 2:9).

But that real and ultimate temple of Jesus' own body also had to be destroyed. And destroyed it was, just as Jesus had so often foretold and foretold in this reading as well. However unlike the destruction of the temple in Jerusalem in A.D. 70, God's real and ultimate dwelling place in Jesus' body would rise victorious from the grave and abide forever.

But now we have this problem: Jesus' body, that living and most holy temple, has disappeared from human view. Where, then, is God's visible presence among men now? Where is Jesus' own dwelling place on earth now that men can no longer see him?

Wonder of all wonders! You have become his temple, his dwelling place on earth (Ephesians 2:20-22, 1 Corinthians 3:16). What an honor! Could there be any honor or glory on earth that could even come close for comparison? Were you the richest person on earth, you would still be a destitute beggar apart from this honor. Were you the strongest and most beautiful among the children of men, you would remain dust and ashes—just an heir of death—apart from this honor. Oh, that we always could remember that and act accordingly! For just think of it: We buy the best house we can to live in, with as many comforts and conveniences as possible for us to enjoy. But God? He chooses to make us, mere mortals and sinners from conception and birth, his visible home on earth. Visible and yet hidden within us, he chooses to make himself known to us and comes to dwell *in* (not just *with*) us by means of his Word and sacraments. Hidden there he nevertheless makes himself known to those around us as we strive to live by his Word of forgiveness and then in loving obedience. We choose the best we can for a dwelling place. But he chooses those who know themselves to be utterly unworthy. And then by forgiving them and washing them in the blood of his Son, he makes them his fit dwelling place.

    And so you are beautiful in his eyes. You have been dressed in the perfect righteousness of Christ because your sins have all been washed away. Deep inside, as in the Holy of Holies at Jerusalem, you have the hidden and golden treasure chest of his Word. So powerful is that Word that day after day, year in and year out, it continues to cleanse you from all sin and stain by virtue of Jesus' sacrifice. So powerful is that Word that day after day, year in and year out, it preserves your trust in Jesus' merit in spite of the shrill cry of conscience and the accusing shrieks of the devil that because of your weakness and your guilt, you should belong to him. So powerful is that Word that day after day, year in and year out, it continues to inspire you to love him and to serve your neighbor. Trusting that his forgiveness covers all that is lacking in your love and your service and your worship, you move the tent of your body from place to place on this your earthly pilgrimage on the way to the heavenly Jerusalem.

    So consider it well: God dwelt in a tent in the wilderness and in Israel. The tent was moved from place to place and, in time, disappeared. God dwelt in the temple in Jerusalem. It was in so many ways splendid and yet so corrupt in the use people put to it that twice it was destroyed and leveled to the ground. For God was zealous for his house! Jesus still has a zeal for his temple, his visible dwelling place on earth. He does not want and will not stand for his temple becoming the dwelling place of the devil. He will not have it that his Word, the "holy of holies" within us, be covered over with greed and vice, envy and self-serving strife. When these threaten to take over, he sends a scourge to purify and cleanse his house so that his Word again may have the preeminence. He lets pain and loss bring his temples of flesh and blood to cry out once more for the life his flesh brings and the cleansing only his blood can provide.

So then, let no one think that this highest possible honor of being God's temple gives a license to wallow willfully again in the muck and mire from which Christ has cleansed us. Such a one shares in the delusion of the Jews in the temple at Jerusalem; the Jews imagined that just because they had that temple and with it a formal, outward connection to God, they could do anything they wanted with it. May we not join in their delusion, a delusion that ended in the final destruction of that temple and even the outward connection with God! Just such a destruction is the lot of those who imagine that they have been saved to sin, washed so that they could stay filthy.

Rather, may this ever be our goal: that Jesus cleanses us day by day from all that offends him in us, his temples on earth. And then may we, thus cleansed, still struggle against all in our minds and hearts, our mouths and actions that offends him and that is contrary to his Word. That's a lifelong assignment, one that will be perfectly carried out only when we have come to his temple in heaven. But it remains a basic truth for his temples on earth, those in whom he lives and rules by faith in his forgiving cleansing: we trust that cleansing alone for our salvation, and we strive to live as those in whom his zeal for trusting obedience remains the goal of our lives of worship. As you go through this day may you think back on it often: "I am God's temple on earth; he lives in me with his Word of grace and forgiveness. May those around me see in me one in whom Christ lives and reigns!"

> Lord Jesus, I beg of you, do not come at me with the whip and the scourge to drive out the greed and the noise from me, your living temple and dwelling place. Lord Jesus, be patient with me and do not destroy me because of my daily need for cleansing. Cleanse me, O Savior, cleanse me with your blood and passion. Have still according to your Word a zeal for your house that purifies it with pardon and not with the destruction it deserves. By that same zeal, that same grace and goodness, kindle in me also a godly zeal to live as your temple. May your zeal for my salvation find a response of zeal to do your will in love for you and for those around me. And finally, O zealous Jesus, seize me and swoop me up in the hour of death to your temple and everlasting dwelling place in heaven. There finally let me rejoice fully and perfectly thank and praise you for your saving grace! Amen.

He Manifested His Glory by Teaching
I.

Mark 12:28-31 – One of the teachers of the law came and heard them debating. Noticing that Jesus had given them a good answer, he asked him, "Of all the commandments, which is the most important?" "The most important one," answered Jesus, "is this: *'Hear, O Israel:* The Lord our God, the Lord is one. Love the Lord your God with all your heart and with all your soul and with all your mind and with all your strength.' The second is this: 'Love your neighbor as yourself.' There is no commandment greater than these" [emphasis added].

Jesus showed forth his glory by what he did. Who could possibly, or at least reasonably, argue with that. There is perfection in everything that he did. In it all there is nothing but perfect love for his Father, for his Father's Word, and yes, for all those with whom he came in contact. Even when he rebuked—rebuked with a whip as in the cleansing of the temple—his motive was always perfect love to his Father and to all of those around him. That all should come to repentance and receive his pardon and the Father's grace—that was his all-consuming passion.

Just as he showed forth his glory by what he did, so also his glory shines through with the brightness of the noonday sun in what he taught. That is so evident in every word he spoke. And it is most splendidly summarized for us in the discourses in the temple on Tuesday of Holy Week. We want to look at just a portion of that masterful summary recorded in Mark 12:28-37.

In the first part of that summary, Jesus is quizzed by an expert in the law. Jesus had just put to silence an assortment of religious authorities who had come to him with questions designed to trip him up. The authorities hoped that they could trap him into saying something that would either make the crowd surrounding him angry or give them an excuse to turn him over to the government as a rabble-rouser and a rebel. They failed at every turn. They failed as Jesus perfectly answered them on the basis of God's unerring Word.

But now a man comes to him from among them who is a bit different from the rest. He was impressed with Jesus' answers. He wanted more. He wanted instruction on the most important matter possible. His question really boils down to this: What does God really want from me? The Jewish legal system was a labyrinth of rules and regulations so complicated that it was impossible either to fulfill all the rules or to know which were the most important.

So this man asks Jesus: Out of all the rules and laws, what's the bottom line? What, when all is said and done, does God really want?

We want to know that too, don't we? We don't have a complicated legal system like that of the Jews in Jesus' day. But even with the Ten Commandments that so well express the mind of God and his will for us in our daily lives, we have our difficulties. What's the sum of it all? What covers all of the difficult situations and problems we have just with the Ten Commandments?

Listen to Jesus' answer! It's beautiful. It's brilliant. Jesus begins with the simplest and most important matter of all. Each word merits separate attention like a beautiful diamond in a setting of beautiful diamonds. So then, what's the bottom line of what God wants from me?

His first word is *hear!* That's what comes before everything else. Hear, listen! How often Jesus began his teaching with that word *listen!* God wants that before anything else. Who would have thought it? Certainly no one in the man-made religions of the world. All of them have as their first word, *do!* Do this: Wash with the Hindus in the Ganges. Do this: Make a pilgrimage with the Muslims to Mecca. Do this: Burn incense with so many in Asia to your ancestors. Do this, then do that. That's the beginning, middle, and end of all man-made religion to this day.

But Jesus says that this above all else God wants from you: Hear! Listen to what God has to say. At once he has cut off any argument or advice from us; he's not interested in that. This one thing he wants—that we should listen to him and hear his Word. And yes, it is the Word of God made flesh who is telling us that. Let all the earth keep silent to hear what he has to say.

And just what is it that he has to say that is so important? Jesus quotes from the national anthem of the Old Testament, from Deuteronomy 6:4. "Hear, O Israel: The Lord our God, the Lord is one." God calls his people by name. He addresses Israel, the people descended from Jacob. God had given Jacob the name *Israel* on that unique occasion when Jacob wrestled with God—with Jesus himself—so many years before Jesus' birth (Genesis 32:22-30). The name means "one who prevails/has power with God"! That's who should listen—those whom God has called by name, those he has chosen to have power with himself, those he lets overcome him because of his love for them! What an astonishing thought! God, the Almighty, who needs nothing and no one to complete himself, chooses to let himself be overcome!

And who is that now whom he calls to listen to him and to whom he gives such a blessing? St. Paul tells us that it's all those who share the faith of Abraham, Isaac, and Jacob: the faith in God as the only God and our Savior (Romans 11). What a joy! What a thrill! God calls us by name! God chooses us for himself and deigns to talk to us in his Word. And so rich is his love and grace that he lets us overcome him as we listen, as we hear his Word. For his Word is a promise of forgiveness, of life, of salvation, of triumph over sins we didn't know about and over sins we chose, over death we deserve, over the hell that we fully merit. We listen to his promises and overcome him as we cry out for mercy and for pardon. He will not say no. He cannot say, "No!" For here is the only begotten Son of God who has paid for our victory in those prayers. We have a long way to go—and a delightful road it is—before we will be finished with our all too brief consideration of Jesus' summary of his teaching. But for the moment, let this be enough: What does God want from you before everything or anything else? What's the greatest "work" that he desires? It is this: that you listen to him so that he can give you all that he promises when he calls you by name and claims you for his own.

> Lord Jesus, I am almost reluctant to speak to you. For what can I say? You overwhelm me with what you say. What you desire most is that I should listen to you. And in listening, this is what I hear: You call me by name; you love me so much that, just as Jacob of old overcame you, so too do I. For in accord with your promises and what you have earned for me, I lay claim to every grace and blessing in the heart of your Father. And you yield. And he will not deny me. So grant me this also: that as I hear you in your Word, I may listen with joy-filled attention and cling with heart and soul to all that you have to say. Amen.

II.

Mark 12:29 – "Hear, O Israel: The Lord our God . . ."

Listen, listen to this! The Lord is *our* God! What a perfect summary of the gospel! He calls us by name, the name Israel. He tells us as we listen that he has chosen us to be his own. He gives us a name which promises that we will have power with him and prevail in our prayers for grace undeserved, for mercy that knows no end.

And then he puts such a beautiful exclamation point on it as he explains how that all works: He tells us that he is *our* God! He belongs to us! He gives himself to us totally! That was the dominant theme of the Old Testament relationship that God kept on striving to have with his people. He described his gift of himself to them in so many different ways. He called himself the Shepherd of Israel, just as Jesus calls himself our Good Shepherd. He called himself the Bridegroom, always ardently seeking his bride, always giving everything that he is and has to her; that's the picture of Jesus that we have in the New Testament too (e.g. Ephesians 5:27; Revelation 21). He showed himself in Old Testament words and Old Testament history that he was the mighty victor and Savior of the people to whom he had given himself. That's certainly what Jesus is to us. All of those pictures and so many more apply to us—to the New Testament Israel of believers who trust his Word and embrace Jesus, the Son of God our Savior. He is the Bread from heaven who feeds us with himself (John 6). He is the one who goes beyond the picture in the Sacrament of the Altar and gives himself to us truly to abide with us and in us. He makes us—as we heard earlier—to be his living temples, his home on earth as he dwells in us by faith in his saving work and his life-giving Word. Already in our baptism he gave himself to us as he gave us a bath that washed us from every sin and stain and continues to cleanse from all unrighteousness (Titus 3:4-7).

Yes, we could go on and on with the glory that Jesus manifests in these words. All of the great rulers and important people in the world win glory for themselves. But Jesus wins glory for us just so that he can give himself and all that he has and is to us. He unites himself with us as the God who is *our* God by Word and sacraments. What an amazing thing! How altogether grand and glorious, how altogether different from any religion that people have dreamt up in their own vain imaginations. How vastly superior to anything we could ever imagine, much less earn or in the smallest part deserve.

But nevertheless, there it is: "Hear, O Israel: The Lord *our* God"! Do you ever wonder if your life has been worth half the bother of it? Does it really matter? Do you really matter? Nothing that you've done has changed the world. But still, here it is. You do really matter. For Jesus says here words that come from the mind and heart of God: He has called you by name. He has chosen you for his own. He has given himself to you so completely that you have won him over when trusting in the merit of his Son. Trusting in Jesus' merit, you called to him for grace, for pardon, for protection, for peace, for life, for heaven itself—and see here—you have won him over because he wants to be won over! And see, here in the person of this same Jesus is the ultimate and perfect proof of it all: He loved you so much that even his only begotten Son he has given not just to you but on the cross for you! Would you, could you, still imagine that your life has no meaning and is worthless? It has infinite worth because of God's gift of himself and all that he is and has to you, for you.

As to your life and accomplishments that may in your own eyes seem so puny and worthless, well, that's not how God looks at them. That point we will pursue somewhat more a bit later. But for now may it be enough to remember that we tend to judge everything only by outward appearance. But God looks at the heart, at the heart that listens to him. To that heart he gives himself. Such a heart can boast not in foolish pride but in grateful joy: God is *our* God! As you go through the day in whatever place God has placed you, call that basic truth to mind: I am his and he is mine! My work and my rest all have him in it and it is therefore worthwhile. He treasures it the way a father looks with pride on the little boy at his side who wants nothing more than to imitate him. He cherishes it as the mother cherishes her daughter's eagerness to help set the table. To the world such works are nothing. To the doting parent they warm the heart and bring a smile to the face. So is he to us. So is he for us, his own dear children who dare and delight to pray, "Our Father, who art in heaven!" Listen, then O Israel, O chosen of God in the gospel: The Lord is *our* God. And that makes all the difference.

> "How precious to me are your thoughts, God! How vast is the sum of them! Were I to count them, they would outnumber the grains of sand—when I awake, I am still with you. Search me, God, and know my heart; test me and know my anxious thoughts. See if there is any offensive way in me, and lead me in the way everlasting" (Psalm 139:17,18,23,24). Even so, Lord Jesus, let me hear in your Word and sacraments your thoughts towards me; then let me delight to surrender my sins to your forgiving grace, my worries and cares to your protection, my life to your resurrection and its promise of my own. Hear me as I rejoice to hear you and receive you in the hearing, which trusts all that you have said to me and done for me in your life and death and resurrection for my salvation. Amen.

III.

Mark 12:29 – "The Lord our God, the Lord is one."

Now here is another simple and beautiful exclamation point on this magnificent summary of the gospel message by which Jesus shows forth his glory. "The Lord our God, *the Lord is one*"! The point may seem obvious, and yet it is, at the same time, mind-boggling in its implications. God is one. There is no other. God is one. He cannot be divided up into fragments or particles of himself. God is one, the God who reveals himself in his Word as Father, Son, and Holy Spirit—three distinct persons in one undivided essence. We know that so well. We confess it all the time in the Apostles' Creed and in the Nicene Creed.

Now put that together with the other elemental truth: He is *our* God, this God who is one undivided and indivisible God. That means that when he gives himself to us—to you, to me—he gives himself completely. When you listen to him in his Word and when you respond in prayer, you have his undivided, total, complete attention! For he cannot be divided from himself. You don't just have a one ten-billionth of a fraction of him. You have the Lord, *our* God, the Lord who is one. Haven't you wondered from time to time if God is so far away and so busy with saints and angels that he probably has little time left for you? Haven't you wondered, especially in dark and troubled days, if perhaps you may have escaped his notice or attention? Well, here is your answer! No, it's not possible that he is too busy for you or that you have escaped his notice while he was busy with others that you think are more important and more worthy of his attention. For "the Lord our God, the Lord is one!" How God can give himself to you completely at the same time that I have his undivided attention, we leave to him! After all, he is God and he does and acts as it pleases him. He does and he acts as he has promised. For he cannot lie and he will never deceive us.

But how can it be, our sinful flesh answers back, how can it be? I am so weak. Sometimes my body is wracked with sickness. Other times my soul is tossed to and fro with one overwhelming temptation after another. And all of the time I am still on my best day a sinner. Under such circumstances, how can it be that, in my life, it is just as if God and I were the only ones and alone together? Look at the life of Jesus; look at the life of the church. What do you see there so consistently? It is this: God delights to hide himself in weakness and lowliness. He does this in the birth and life and death of Jesus. He does this in the simple words of the Bible. He does this in the common elements of the sacraments. He does this in the church that always seem so weak as to be on the brink of perishing altogether. To us it seems like a contradiction that God who is all powerful should prove it by dwelling in the midst of our sin, our weakness, our utter frailty.

Paul explained that seeming contradiction so well; when looking at his own life so full of weakness both on the outside and on the inside, God explained it all to him (2 Corinthians 12:9). It is by weakness that God shows his glory and his strength. The "weak" Word and sacraments last when all things in the world perish. The church that always looks like it is about to perish endures, while all who sought its ruin fall and die. And yes, you survive the flu and arthritis and cancer and one plague after another and the cemetery itself because he lives and gives himself to you for an eternal life and triumph. You survive one stumble and fall after another as he comes and reclaims you for himself day after day. You survive and triumph over death and hell itself because Jesus did, and he did it just for you! He gives himself to you not in fractions, not in a moment or two just now and then, but completely. For, *"The Lord our God, the Lord is one."*

What an amazing God this is who is ours by faith in Jesus' gift of himself to us! Who could think their life pointless or worth nothing with such a God as this? With what dignity the parent changes the child's diaper and teaches the child how to pray even before he or she has learned to speak.

What nobility in a man or woman who goes off to a job that seems to afford little satisfaction and less than an easy lifestyle. What an honor that boy and girl have in school who know that Jesus belongs to them and that both in study and on the playground, there is one who cares constantly and never gives up caring. For the Lord is *our* God, the Lord who is one in his essence is one in his will and desire to give himself to me completely. So let the world mock and bully the confessing Christian adult. Let the world dismiss as of no account the child defending someone picked on. Let those laugh who will at the persistent struggle of a teenager or aged saint to reflect the love and patience of Christ in life. We know the facts and the ultimate reality: "The Lord our God, the Lord is one;" he is ours, ours every day and hour, ours in our weakness, ours as the source of all our strength, even when we seem so weak.

> Yes, Lord Jesus, beyond all measure and all beauty are your thoughts towards me. When I am not thinking of you, you are still thinking of me. When I am foolish enough to imagine myself as so powerful and so wonderful apart from you, you do not abandon me because of my folly. Rather, you rule over all things to bring me low so that you can raise me again to that weakness which joyfully confesses that you are my God who gives me all that I am and have. You bring me again by the lowliness of your cross to a life that finds in you and from you its great value and worth. Lord Jesus, let me ever bow low, in wonder and thankful adoration, for this your astonishing grace and perfect love. Let me hear it in heart and mind and soul: You are my Lord, my Savior, my one true and only God. Amen.

IV.

Mark 12:30,31 – "'Love the Lord your God with all your heart and with all your soul and with all your mind and with all your strength.' The second is this: 'Love your neighbor as yourself.' There is no commandment greater than these."

Jesus always gives more and better than is asked of him. So here too: The scribe just wanted to know which is the greatest commandment of all. But Jesus gave him so much more. He told him first and foremost why what God commands should matter and why we should want—really want and desire above all things—to do what he commands. Why should it matter and why should we care? As we have seen, it should matter and we should care because of the gospel; it should matter and we should care because

God has given himself and all that he is and all that he has to us, to be our loving Father in this life and our blessed Savior for all eternity. His heart ever longs for our fellowship and so ardent is his love that he did not spare even his only begotten Son to win our salvation.

Therefore, it should be with a corresponding burning love that we wait with excited anticipation for Jesus' answer to the question asked: What is the greatest commandment? I can hardly wait to hear it and to follow it! *Listening* to his Word is what Jesus pointed to at the start. But then what? And here it is! It is a commandment altogether reasonable, given the already announced blessings of the gospel. It is this: *Love God as much as he has loved you!* That's all. That's it. And indeed, what could be more reasonable? Why should I love anyone or anything more than I love him or even love anyone or anything with a devotion that would subtract from the totality of the love he wants from me, a love like his for me? For wealth and health, friends and family, strength of mind and body—to the extent that I have them—are always and alone his gifts. They cannot save me in time, far less in eternity. They can only be enjoyed and that just for a season. Delightful as they are, they have this as their greatest benefit: They point me to the One who gives them. As sweet as they may make parts of my life, they serve best when they remind me of the beloved who grants them so freely, so generously, so altogether apart from my merit and worthiness.

But there is still more to this first and greatest commandment. And there has to be. For the very word *love* that is used here means "to seek the ultimate good and benefit of the one loved." But how can I love God in such a way that I accomplish something for his good and benefit? After all, he is all in all; no one can add to him or subtract from him. How, then, can I love him with my all in a way that benefits him and serves his ultimate good? Jesus' answer is full and plain and clear: "Love your neighbor as yourself"!

Could he have been more profound in his answer? His answer presupposes that I love myself. And who can deny it? By nature I love myself. By nature I seek my own ultimate good and benefit. That's why I breathe. That's why I get up in the morning. That's why I go to work and why I look for leisure, and why I strive to stay reasonably healthy, and save and spend time and treasure, and why I find and keep friends and family. Jesus accepts that reality: This is the way we are. God takes it as a given in the commandment to love him that we understand love best when we are thinking of ourselves—not of him! Is that not an astonishing thing?

But as always, Jesus never leaves us where we are by nature. By his Word he always aims at bringing us closer to where we ought to be. Are we already saints to whom God has given himself in the person and work of his Son? Are we already washed by him and cleansed of all our sin and guilt? Has even the sin of not loving him perfectly been not only understood but forgiven? Yes, to all of that. What, then, is left? If we have not loved God perfectly because our love for self always ends up subtracting from our love for him, what then is there that he still wants from us? If our whole understanding of what love is has been overwhelmed by his love for us and by the recognition that even if we could love him perfectly we would add nothing to him, what, then, does he still want from us?

He wants this: that we bend that rod of iron which is our love for self and aim it at our neighbor. So great is his desire for us to do this that he will count it as acting in love to him. For since we can do nothing to benefit God directly, he bids us benefit those he loves as much as he loves us. That's not hard to understand. "Do my loved ones a favor and I will readily count it as a favor you have done for me."

And why should I want to do that? We should want it because he is the Lord our God, the Lord who is one. That is, we want it because God has given himself wholly and totally to us and for us in Christ—in his life for us, his sacrifice on the cross for us, his promise of our resurrection, his assurance of heaven itself because he has gone there to prepare a place for us. It would take a heart colder than stone not to be moved, not to yearn and long to please such a God, such a Savior!

So we learn and come to understand what love is first and foremost by the way that God has loved us. How love is shown by devotion and tender care in human terms we learn just from the way we treat ourselves—always looking out for our own best interest and benefit. What, then, is it to love God? It is to surrender to him and to his Word completely. And how do we show it? By lavishing the same concern and care we have for ourselves on our neighbor.

Oh, how great is our constant need for his service to us in forgiving, and how great is the goal he sets before us in living! But for today, let us think on this and strive to make it our whole lives and desires: with the right hand may we take from him his gift of himself, of life and salvation granted in Christ and bestowed in the Word and sacraments; with the left hand may we strive to bend the iron rod of self-love to loving service given more freely, more willingly, more eagerly to those he has placed around us.

> Lord Jesus, how sweeter than honey and the honeycomb is your gift of yourself in Word and sacraments. How stark the contrast between your love so perfect and mine so prone to self-service, only self-love. Open my eyes and mind and heart to listen to your Word and so to bask in the sunshine of your grace that more and more I may desire and long for a heart and mind and strength that seeks, above all else, the honor of loving service to my neighbor. I ask it clinging to your promise

of your abiding love for me and the forgiveness you have in that love won for me. Amen.

V.

Mark 12:32-34 – "Well said, teacher," the man replied. "You are right in saying that God is one and there is no other but him. To love him with all your heart, with all your understanding and with all your strength, and to love your neighbor as yourself is more important than all burnt offerings and sacrifices." When Jesus saw that he had answered wisely, he said to him, "You are not far from the kingdom of God." And from then on no one dared ask him any more questions.

How very different this scribe is from the others that had asked Jesus questions in Mark 12! He asked, really wanting to know the answer instead of seeking by his question only to trap Jesus into saying something that could be used against him, either before the people or the state. So too his reaction to Jesus' words is so different from that of the other questioners. He is duly impressed. With some excitement even, he answers Jesus' answer by essentially repeating what Jesus had said; his words are a sort of "Amen" to what Jesus has said.

But what is even more interesting is Jesus' response to the scribe: "You are not far from the kingdom of God." Not far? Close, but not in it! The scribe is close because he now grasps what had been only confusing to him before. He wanted to know the bottom line of what God wants from us. And Jesus had told him. It is not merely outward observance of ritual. It is not even just an external decency in our lives with one another. No, what God wants is the heart. What God wants is the will. What God wants is our emotions. What God wants is that these—not the mere external observance of the law—be animated by a love to him that is translated into loving service to our neighbor. What God wants is that we measure our love for our neighbor first by his love for us and then by our own so attentive, so loving service to ourselves. Give to your neighbor a love like God's totally unselfish, self-giving love for you; give to your neighbor that attentive and careful service that you so readily and even without thinking lavish on yourself.

The scribe grasps that Jesus has answered his question with wisdom and insight. And so, certainly compared to the others who asked Jesus questions, he was "not far" from the kingdom of God—again, remembering that by definition, the kingdom of God is God's ruling activity by his Word in our hearts. But the scribe who is not far from that kingdom is not yet in it either.

And why not? As excited and happy as he was with Jesus' answer, he did not have the only really proper response to Jesus' words. And what response is that? It is the response of the disciples on another occasion when Jesus had so clearly shown them the law. It is the response of, "Who then can be saved?" (Mark 10:26). For the better I see the love of God for me in giving himself to me so completely, the greater is my recognition of how shabby my love is in comparison; I do not love him anywhere nearly as much as he loves me, nor do I ever come close to loving my neighbor as much as I love myself; guilt clings to me when I recognize that there is nothing—no work, no sacrifice, no ritual, no outward decency (no matter how close it comes to love)—that can make up for my failure to love God the way he wants to be loved.

Jesus' words to the scribe should have provoked him to ask Jesus what he meant by "not far." Instead we have one of the saddest passages in the Bible: "From then on no one dared ask him any more questions." Has your heart and mind ever been in that condition? You know what God wants from you. But you would rather not know it too well. The devil whispers in the ear, "You know enough already! Better that you not know much more. It would only depress you. It would only annoy you, these calls of Jesus for a commitment to him that is so total, so complete—so like his devotion to you! After all, you're a member of a nice parish. You give. You make a general confession. You go to Communion. You don't kick the dog or beat your spouse. That's close enough. The notion of the kingdom of God, of God really ruling in heart and mind and life, well, that's a little too deep for you."

And so grows the unspoken wish: May the pastor's sermons stay shallow and general. I don't want them to provoke too many questions about my own cherished beliefs apart from his Word or my habits that may be displeasing to God or my life with friends and family that reflect mostly my love for myself; I would rather not dilute the love I have for me by sacrifices of more than absolutely necessary for my neighbor. "No one dared ask him any more questions" can serve well as the superscription over much of our society and culture. Leave Jesus alone. He's a great teacher (but I'd rather not get to know his teaching) and a martyr to a noble cause. Let it go at that. Basically, I think he just wanted us to be good and nice to one another, just like every other great religious teacher in history.

That such is the attitude of those outside of the church—yes, and of all too many who think themselves inside of it—comes as no surprise to us. But may the world outside of the church and the worldlings inside of it not have as their excuse that they never met anyone who took Jesus all that seriously. May it not be that, in knowing me, they still have seen no one who lives to receive grace heaped upon grace and who has as their goal loving service that imitates the service of Jesus to us. For then the invisible inscription of our tombstone too will be: "Not far from the kingdom of God"!

Is it not abundantly clear in Jesus' teaching that he manifests forth his glory—not our own? Is it not abundantly clear in Jesus' teaching that I shouldn't want my own glory manifested? It's just too shabby, too stained, too far short of his glory in the love for me that he gives in the gospel. So then, I have all the more reason to delight in his work and in his Word and sacraments. For by them, again, he still gives himself to me and for me. By them he still takes away the despair that is mine when I look only at myself and replaces it with peace and joy in listening to and receiving him. By the motivation he gives in his love for me, I even want evermore to imitate his love in loving service to my neighbor, the neighbor that he loves just as much as he loves me.

> Lord Jesus, how painfully, and yet so beautifully, you make it clear: You love me so incomparably more than I love you, and still you do not cast me off! You are so much more concerned about my salvation than I have ever been, and you proved it by all that you did in your life and death for me; and still you guard and keep your Word and sacraments so that I receive what you died to win for me. Oh, grant it, please grant it, that by your love for me I may grow in a love for you that wants only to listen to you, receive grace heaped upon grace from you, and then serve those you love as much as you love me. To that end keep me listening to your Word, looking to your cross, and rising ever anew to life in you, with you, for you. Amen.

VI.

Mark 12:35-37 – While Jesus was teaching in the temple courts, he asked, "Why do the teachers of the law say that the Messiah is the son of David? David himself, speaking by the Holy Spirit, declared: 'The Lord said to my Lord: "Sit at my right hand until I put your enemies under your feet."' David himself calls him 'Lord.' How then can he be his son?"

Now this might be a good time for us to give Jesus some advice: Leave! Leave these wretches to their well-deserved fate! For you have given them a perfect and profound summary of God's love for them and of what God desires from them. And what's their response? Silence. There is no song of joy and thanksgiving for the gospel. There is no cry for mercy and forgiveness so desperately needed because of their failure to perfectly love God in response, much less love the neighbor as oneself. There is only stony silence that dares ask no more questions for fear that they will not like the answers. It's time to leave!

But that's not what Jesus does. Instead, he tries to provoke them to ask questions for which he not only has the answer but *is* the answer. He is not talking to "babes in the woods" when it comes to knowledge of the Bible. He is talking to people who know it well, who had memorized whole books of the Old Testament. And so he begins with what they know well and takes them to what they should have known from their Bible. He is talking to people who know the Bible so well and yet nevertheless had missed its central point.

In order to get them to see that central point, Jesus takes them to Psalm 110, one they knew by heart. They had thought about that psalm in a very superficial way. They recognized that it promised the Messiah, the Christ. But the Christ they thought it pointed to was the son of David and nothing more. They wanted such a son of David to fulfill their heart's desire of a restoration of David's kingdom with themselves, of course, running it and enjoying all of its wealth and power.

But Jesus takes them into the heart of the psalm and into the depths of God's promise to send the Christ. Indeed, who better to do that than Jesus, since he was exactly that promised Messiah? Listen to how beautifully he teaches by his questions the essence of God's promise concerning the Messiah.

To start with, he holds before them the whole of the Trinity in his discourse on the psalm. For the whole of the Trinity is devoted to our salvation. Jesus says that the Holy Spirit breathed these words of the psalm to David, words in which Father shows forth his glory by his gift to his Son. "The Lord said to my Lord"! The Father is speaking to the already existing Son of David, a Son who will not be born as a man until hundreds of years after David's death. Nevertheless, David speaks of that Son as already existing and calls that Son his Lord. How can David's son be also David's Lord? Only if that Son is himself God! Only if that Son has already existed as God from eternity to eternity! That's the conclusion that Jesus wants them to grasp, for starters. The Christ, the Messiah, will not just be a man who comes to create an earthly kingdom. He will be so much more! He will be God himself and yet the descendant of David—God incarnate, God in the flesh! That's what the Holy Spirit told David to write.

Just how much more the Messiah will be is indicated in what the Father says to his eternal Son: "Sit at my right hand until I put your enemies under your feet." So then, the promised Son, the Messiah, the Lord, will have enemies to battle when he comes. He will have enemies against whom he will fight—and lose! But after the battle is over and Christ has lost it in death, then his Father will raise him up to his right hand. That's not where losers are supposed to go, to the position at the right hand of the King! Losers go to the bottom of the heap, not to the top. But not so this Lord—Son of David and Son of God! He goes to the right hand, the position of victory and power, to enjoy forever the triumph that he won in his defeat!

And what of those who defeated him—what becomes of them? They are crushed. They are put forever under his feet. They will not pass into nonexistence; they will be for all eternity under his feet in misery. That's the opposite of what these Jewish leaders expected from their Messiah. They expected him to lead them in an earthly kingdom of triumph, of splendor, of worldly wealth and power. Instead, as Jesus explains the psalm, the Messiah will suffer defeat here and glory hereafter. But those who opposed him, who seemed so victorious over him in time, will endure unending humiliation in the hereafter.

Again, it needs to be kept in mind that Jesus is not speaking to people who were infants in their knowledge of the Bible and of this psalm verse. He is speaking to experts who should have been able to grasp what Jesus was saying and where he was trying to lead them with his question about the psalm. His question should have left them breathless and then eager with an insistent demand: "Tell us more! Answer for us the question that you have posed, a question we never thought about before."

But that is not at all what happens. They knew that Jesus was claiming to be that very Christ, the promised Messiah, spoken of and spoken to in the psalm. But they want nothing of him or of his attempt to teach them. Want it or not, within less than a week's time, Jesus will dramatically and most powerfully push this psalm and its real depth and meaning before them. At his trial he will declare it openly and boldly when they ask him if he is indeed that Christ here promised. He will answer, "I am. . . . And you will see the Son of Man sitting at the right hand of the Mighty One and coming on the clouds of heaven" (Mark 14:62). And then he will prove it by his resurrection from the dead.

Jesus manifests his glory by his teaching. To those who know little or nothing of his Word he comes in the humility of the manger. He comes in the lowliness of a kind and gentle and still so powerful invitation: "Come to me, all you who are weary and burdened, and I will give you rest" (Matthew 11:28). He comes with the "rest" of pardon and life eternal in the simple words and with plain water in Baptism. He comes with the gift of himself in common bread and wine in the Sacrament of his body and blood. He comes again and again so patiently, so filled with compassion and grace beyond measure.

Then, in coming thus he draws us closer and closer to his Word, which is a bottomless well of heavenly wisdom and power. He takes us ever deeper there into the heart and the mind of God in the way he tried to with the rulers of the Jews in this reading. He wants to bring us to see the more clearly his love for us and then to respond with growing love for him.

Oh, may we never tire of being thus drawn to learn of him more and more! May we never be among those who do not want to hear it anymore or who think they already know it well enough. Yes, may this alone be our horror and dread that we at length grow weary of him and resent his call to us. Then to our shame, having received so much of him and from him, we will end up like these leaders of the Jews; we will end up the enemies of the gospel, who defeat him by rejecting him in his Word. Then in eternity we too will languish among the enemies placed in shame and misery forever as footstools under his feet.

> O Son of the Father and David's Son, still draw me to yourself by your Word and sacraments. By these saving and so priceless means, give yourself to me and for me. By them increase always my longing to listen to your Word and to receive you in it. Deepen ever more my understanding that my love for you may be enriched by a growing knowledge of your love for me. Save me from myself and that perverse will from the devil, which would shove you aside and then make of me your enemy. Yes, O most holy Savior, do not let your love and your blood shed for me be in vain! Instead, make steadfast the resolve your Holy Spirit has worked in me never to depart from you but to remain faithful until that day when faith is replaced by the sight of you in heaven at your Father's right hand in glory. Amen.

The Transfiguration of Our Lord

I.

Luke 9:28-31 – About eight days after Jesus said this, he took Peter, John and James with him and went up onto a mountain to pray. As he was praying, the appearance of his face changed, and his clothes became as bright as a flash of lightning. Two men, Moses and Elijah, appeared in glorious splendor, talking with Jesus. They spoke about his departure, which he was about to bring to fulfillment at Jerusalem.

This is what we have been waiting for! Now at last Jesus really does show forth his glory, a glory that only God could have. What a sight that must have been. Never before in history had heaven and earth come so close together. And how fitting: Christ is the cause and Christ is the center of it all!

It is the middle of the night. Still ringing in the ears of the disciples are Jesus' very difficult words from eight days before. So weighty and important had those words been that nothing is recorded of what happened the following eight days. He had spoken of his own impending suffering, and death. And then he promised his disciples—what? glory? No, for them too there would be the cross. Those words stand out: **"If anyone would come after me, let him deny himself and take up his cross daily and follow me. . . . Whoever is ashamed of me and of my words, of him will the Son of Man be ashamed when he comes in his glory and the glory of the Father and of the holy angels"** (Luke 9:23,26 ESV). How hard it was for them to hear both the words about his cross and then words promising them a cross too. How hard for us to hear it too! Take up a cross? Who wants to do that? A cross crushes. A cross bloodies its bearer. A cross is the reward of the wicked and the despised, of those considered by the world unfit to live in peace or die with dignity. But there it is: Jesus' insistence—not a suggestion or a preference but an insistence on it. In fact, so insistent is he that he declares that a refusal to bear the cross will have this most dread result: Jesus will be ashamed of that person when he returns in his final triumph on judgment day. Two horrible-to-contemplate events are placed before Jesus' disciples that day and this: a cross now for a lifetime or shame for an eternity apart from the cross. Who can bear to hear it?

But now after eight days of letting these horrible alternatives sink in, Jesus takes three disciples with him up to the mountaintop to let them experience the ultimate and final end of it all. It will all be so worthwhile, this bearing of the cross in life. For look at the end of it all. There is Jesus in real glory. He has come to win that for himself and then to share it with all who carry their cross in that triumphal procession of death and resurrection after him. What a glorious sight! He shines like the sun with clothes blazing like lightning.

And look! There are the great prophets, Moses and Elijah! They have come from heaven to speak with their God and Savior on this mountaintop as he prays. Moses was the great giver of the Law; he now holds blessed concourse with the one who redeems from the curse of the law. Elijah was that so persecuted and hated prophet who almost gave up in despair; so futile had all his cross-bearing seemed. But now here he is in glory with the author of his glory, the Savior from the law and the deliverer from all of this world's pain and seeming frustration under the cross! Yes, what a sight! There he is at last, Jesus the Lord of glory, the center and whole point of the Bible with one of its human authors and one of its most faithful preachers.

What could they have to talk about, these three? Luke tells us: **"They spoke about his departure, which he was about to bring to fulfillment at Jerusalem."** In a way that's shocking. Jesus is clothed with glory.

And what do they talk about? The cross that Jesus soon and alone will bear! All that Moses wrote pointed to the need so desperate for the Lamb who would be slaughtered to take away the sins against the law. All that Elijah preached about repentance and all that he suffered for his faithfulness to the Word of God also pointed ahead; it pointed to a forgiveness that could only come through the far greater suffering of the far greater preacher of repentance who would win for us forgiveness.

So there it is in the life and work of Jesus: the marriage of the cross and the crown! It is amazing on so many different grounds. Jesus appears in glory to talk about his approaching humiliation. Jesus shines with the splendor of the sun and talks about the day when the sun will turn black as he suffers on the cross. Jesus appears as the almighty God at whose beck and call are even the long-dead-but-alive-in-heaven saints; and the only thing they want to talk about is his defeat at the hands of puny Jewish rulers and Roman soldiers. Jesus appears in glory as he prays to the Father he so perfectly loved and served to talk about the hour when that Father would forsake him. It's all just too much to take in. What mere human would ever behave that way? When we have a moment of triumph in our lives, we don't beam with gladness and talk about an impending death of shame and humiliation. Who would do such a thing?

Who indeed but our Jesus! He counts it his greatest glory to suffer shame, to be despised and rejected, to go down to defeat, to endure the torments of hell itself. And why? So that he could gain the honor, yes, the honor of bearing the name Savior! That's what St. Paul says about it (Philippians 2:6-11). That's what the writer to the Hebrews says about it too (Hebrews 12:2). It was a name, a title that he had to earn. And he could earn it only in the way prescribed: the way of the cross. What love beyond compare he had for us! The one who thinks his sins are little—let him think on how much love it took for God to accomplish his salvation. The one who thinks his sins are too great—let him ponder the perfect sacrifice that Jesus *looked forward* to making just to rescue and redeem the most unworthy among us. The one who thinks that God is far away and couldn't possibly be concerned with him—let him look on Jesus on that mountain who, in his glory, wanted nothing more than to get on with the humiliation that would gain for us salvation. Yes, and let the one who wonders if the cross Jesus has called us to bear is worth the pain it brings look on him who won the glory so beyond measure reflected on that transfiguration mountaintop.

> Lord Jesus, you are the center of the Scriptures. In them—from page to page and from age to age—I see your incomparable love and grace that wanted, yes, wanted to pay the full and

high price for my salvation. Oh, may your glory in winning the name "My Savior" at so great a cost fill my heart and mind and soul so that my only goal may be that you become my all in all, the center of my life, as you are its source. Hear my humble prayer, O most glorious Savior, as I look ahead to the day when the faith you have given me will be transformed into sight in heaven.

> How good, Lord, to be here! Your glory fills the night;
> Your face and garments, like the sun,
>   shine with unborrowed light.
> How good, Lord, to be here your beauty to behold,
> Where Moses and Elijah stand, your messengers of old.
> (CW 95:1,2)

II.

Luke 9:32,33 – Peter and his companions were very sleepy, but when they became fully awake, they saw his glory and the two men standing with him. As the men were leaving Jesus, Peter said to him, "Master, it is good for us to be here. Let us put up three shelters—one for you, one for Moses and one for Elijah." (He did not know what he was saying.)

While all of this majesty is unfolding before them, the disciples are fast asleep. We won't fault the disciples here too much for sleeping. After all, it was probably in the middle of the night. That Jesus had taken them especially to be with him as he prayed might well have suggested to them that it would be a good idea to stay awake, to watch and listen. But still, again, it was late at night. This would not be the last time that they would sleep when it would have been better to stay awake (Luke 22:45).

But at length they wake up. They wake up just in time to see their beloved Jesus in all his radiant splendor and to see Moses and Elijah with him. How it must have stunned them and taken their breath away. But then the moment when it would be best to listen, to watch, to worship and adore is broken by—guess who?—Peter, of course! Don't you just love Peter? He just can't help himself. He always has to say something, always has to give Jesus advice. Each time he shows himself a loving disciple, but is still foolish enough to think (the way we do so often!) that somehow God wouldn't know what to do if Peter didn't advise him. And, like so many of us so often, that he didn't know what he was talking about didn't slow him down in the least.

But this time, don't you have to call out, "Peter, you're right! If I were there, I would have done the same"? For it truly was good for them to be there and to see Jesus pull back the veil of lowliness and to reveal his glory as the eternal God. Indeed, the whole event had taken place not for Jesus' benefit but for theirs. It was sandwiched in between the heavy discourse about their taking up their own cross and the soon-to-be-accomplished sight of Jesus on his cross. The vision of Jesus in glory should serve to encourage them when the sight of his cross and later the experience of their own cross would seem too heavy to bear. The vision of Jesus in glory should comfort them and save them at such times from despair.

Who wouldn't want that moment to last? Haven't you had those moments something akin to the moment the disciples experienced here? Haven't you had those blessed moments given by God in his generosity when all was right with the world, with your place in it, and even with your conscience and your awareness of the love of God just for you? Maybe it was when you were confirmed or at your first Communion. Perhaps it was the day you were married. It might have been at the birth of a child. There could have been many such days and experiences in the course of a lifetime. Didn't you want to blurt out with Peter, "Oh, it's so good to be here; if only it would last!"

Indeed, Peter's outburst isn't really all that bad, is it? After all, besides just wanting the moment to last, he wants to do something good in return for being allowed to stay up on that mountaintop. He is willing to go to work and put up three—notice that, just three—dwellings. He doesn't even ask permission to put up one for himself or the other disciples. How thoughtful, how selfless! So what could possibly be wrong with Peter's advice, advice we would like to give Jesus too on the days when we have a mountaintop experience of peace and joy in faith and in life?

For starters, Peter has missed the point that we so often miss too. He has missed the point that the best way to worship and to serve God is, first of all, to listen to him! Moses and Elijah are there, one an author of five books in the Bible and the other one of the Bible's most famous preachers. Jesus is there, about whom they wrote and preached. This would be a good time to keep quiet and just to listen. For as always when God is speaking or showing us something out of his Word, it is for our benefit; it would be good then to listen and to receive what he has come to give when he speaks his Word, when he shows and gives himself in it.

Also, Peter has not yet learned a lesson that we too are often slow to learn. The lesson is hinted at just in the timing of this event. Again, it is in between a heavy discourse about cross-bearing and the beginning of Jesus' Lent of suffering and death to be followed by his glorious resurrection. The Transfiguration of our Lord—glory followed by suffering followed by still greater glory—serves as a pattern lived out by us during much of our lifetime here on earth. Does not life often seem to us like a roller coaster?

One day we are riding high; nothing is bothering us. We may even think we will never fall again, so strong and perhaps self-assured we are at the moment. But then the next day we are plunging down into the depths of despair; so great do the problems seem that we think we may never smile again or see a solution to the mess in which we find ourselves. That's life. It's even reflected in the liturgy with its rises and falls and its rising yet again: confession and its cry for God's mercy, followed by the exaltation of free grace and forgiveness, followed by the plea for mercy in the face of life's problems and difficulties beyond our capacity to bear, followed by a song of praise in anticipation of God's having it all figured out and that for our good and salvation. David spoke of his life in just these terms in Psalm 30.

So how does God manage all that for us, so that in days of peace and joy we do not become puffed up with pride and self-righteousness? How does he manage things so that in the darkest days we do not despair? He balances it all out! He gives days of peace and joy to prepare us for days of pain and sadness. And in days of pain and sadness, he reminds us that he has always in the past delivered us and that for the future he has promised us resurrection joy forever. The times of gladness get us ready for the labor ahead. And the labor ahead helps us appreciate the past undeserved joy and makes us look for its return in even greater measure than before.

> O God, you do all things well. You grant days of undeserved, even undiluted gladness; on such days you give me the joy of looking up into your face with delight and thanksgiving. Then you send me also days of sadness; on such days you teach me humility and remind me that on you and your gracious providence all my hope and help depends. O give me wisdom in it all to trust that in both, you intend only to bless me and bring me at last to the eternal joy that your Son has won for me by his holy cross and glorious resurrection.

> Fulfiller of the past, promise of things to be,
> We hail your body glorified and our redemption see.
> Before we taste of death, we see your kingdom come;
> We long to hold the vision bright and
>   make this hill our home. Amen. (CW 95:3,4)

III.

Luke 9:34-36 – While [Peter] was speaking, a cloud appeared and covered them, and they were afraid as they entered the cloud. A voice came from the cloud, saying, "This my Son, whom I have chosen;

listen to him." When the voice had spoken, they found that Jesus was alone.

What a perfect end to it all. Let Peter babble on with his well-intended but foolish advice. God gets the last word! And note how he does it. When God showed himself in the Old Testament, almost always he came in a cloud. He veils his majesty and his might. For who can endure his unveiled presence and live?! That was the clear understanding of those who experienced his presence in the Old Testament. And so now, the Father of grace and glory appears yet again as he had of old: he veils himself in a cloud to spare these poor men the consequences of their sin and their folly.

And what does he say? Oh, how beautiful! First he says what he always says: *Listen!* When Jesus is there, it is always time to listen before all else; your time to speak, whether in prayer to God or in loving service to one another, will come. But it will come best only if you listen first!

Listen to what, to whom? Why to Jesus of course! He is the Son of the majestic and all-consuming Father. He is the unveiled majesty of God, clothed not in a cloud but in our flesh and blood. He is the beloved emissary of the Father who longs not to destroy us but to save us and to do that by the gift of this: his beloved and only begotten Son. So if you want salvation from the majesty and all-consuming power of God, listen to his Son. So if you want some understanding of your roller-coaster life, listen to his Son. For he is the one who has come from God to save us. He is the one who brings heaven and earth together by his cross. He is the one who makes sense of our life by what he has done and by what he has said to us in his Word. Therefore, what could make more sense than this: Listen to him!

And then what happens? A perfect ending! The Father withdraws; he has summed up in one simple sentence what he wants from us in days of glory; he has summed up what he wants from us before and after days of sorrow. It is that we listen to Jesus. So it is that the disciples, terror-stricken by the presence of God and voice in the cloud, now look up. And what do they see? Jesus! Just Jesus! How perfect!

We are coming to the end of our Epiphany meditations. In these we have seen Jesus manifest his glory by what he did and by what he said. And now at its close, as the shadow of the cross begins to fall over us with the beginning of Lent, what is the sum and point of it all? It is that we should see Jesus our Savior in his Word. It is that we should find him and him alone as the real and lasting glory in our lives. For he has come to gain for us the only glory that is eternal. It is the glory of our status as saints because he has come to win forgiveness for us. It is the glory of those who bear the cross of suffering for his sake as we struggle against our own sinful flesh and its unending passions and lusts that would tear us away from Jesus. It is the glory of those who bear with the apostles and martyrs the dignity of enduring abuse and mockery because of loyalty to this Jesus and his saving Word. It is the glory of those who, clothed with lowliness in this life, know that they wear already the robe of righteousness given in Baptism and yet to be revealed fully in the resurrection.

That's how everything fits together. So then, we may join with Peter in babbling on our advice to God. But then when all is said and done: Listen! Look up, and see Jesus only. See him in his Word and in his sacraments. See him in the days of rich blessings he gives to wash away tears past. See him in the rich blessings he bestows to arm you against despair in sorrows yet to come. See him all along the road of your pilgrimage as you journey beneath the banner of his cross on the way to your resurrection!

> How good, Lord, to be here! Yet we may not remain;
> But since you bid us leave the mount,
>   come with us to the plain. Amen. (CW 95:5)

Lent

Up to Jerusalem

Mark 10:32 – They were on their way up to Jerusalem, with Jesus leading the way, and the disciples were astonished, while those who followed were afraid. Again he took the Twelve aside and told them what was going to happen to him.

So it begins: the solemn and holy season of Lent. And look at how it begins. Only One is eager for it to start. Only One has his heart set on all that will happen in Lent. Only One leads the way.

Jesus is the center of Lent. Who doesn't know that? But we are not absent from it. Quite the contrary is the case. As far as we are concerned, Lent is all about Jesus. But as far as Jesus is concerned, Lent is all about us.

See how it all begins: Jesus is on his last journey to Jerusalem. It is perhaps just a day before Palm Sunday. The procession of pilgrims on the way to Jerusalem to celebrate Passover has by this time grown to crowds of thousands. Everyone knows where Jesus is in that procession. Everyone knows that opposition to him has reached a fever pitch. It is no secret that the leaders of the Jews want to be rid of him. They have done everything they could to discredit him with the people, and they have failed. They have done everything they could to trick him into saying something that was either heretical or that could brand him a traitor to the Roman government, and they have failed. But no one is under any illusion that they have given up. In all of their efforts Jesus has shown them to be hypocrites and sinners. They will have none of that—there is certainly no repentance, no fleeing to Jesus for mercy. No, instead their hatred is only further enflamed.

Jesus knew it full well that day, as the procession drew near to Jerusalem. And he knew how it would end. In the verses immediately following he took the Twelve aside and spelled it all out for them again as he had before. He spelled it out in all its gruesome and ultimately glorious detail: betrayal, condemnation, mockery, spitting, flogging, and then execution and—three days later—resurrection!

See how it begins: Jesus is determined. Jesus leads the procession. Jesus can scarcely wait for it to begin and end. For to him it is all about us. He has no need to suffer for crimes. He committed none—no, not one. But for this hour he has come down from heaven so that he might suffer the torments of hell, for us, for us, for us. And he does it all so willingly. The sinners in desperate need of his saving work do not drive him on, do not push and shove him and insist, "Hurry up Lord! Get it all done for us! We can do none of it ourselves! So go, go quickly and accomplish the work of our salvation!"

No, the disciples are astonished that he is marching with such determination into that first Holy Week. And the rest of those following behind—they are afraid of what will happen. Just what is it that they are afraid of? No doubt some were afraid out of love for Jesus. But there were no doubt also many who were afraid of what would happen to them. Would there be a roundup of any and all who had anything to do with Jesus? After all, the authorities had already issued the order that anyone connected with Jesus or following him should be excommunicated from the synagogue (John 9:22). Or would there be some sort of riot, an uprising that perhaps Jesus or his disciples might lead (so little did many understand him!)? That would end in a bloodbath at the edge of Roman swords; for they were ever ready to end the least disturbance with a sword.

And so Lent begins for us. As we relive with the disciples and the crowds that first Lent, we too are astonished. How can it be that God is so eager for our salvation? How can it be that the Father does not spare his only begotten Son in whom he was always well pleased? How can it be that the Son does not balk when he considers the cost in the agony of his soul and the torment for his body? How can it be that the Holy Spirit is in full agreement with the love of the Father and the eagerness of the Son for our salvation, so eager that the Spirit will preserve the message and instill in it faith-creating power?

So as Lent begins—these dread and most blessed 40 days—we fix our eyes on Jesus, astonished every step of the way up to the cross. And our hearts are divided; our souls are ripped in two, like the curtain in the temple. A part cries out in love to Jesus: "Don't do it! I can't bear it to see you thus tormented. A glance at the cross pierces my heart and tears at my soul. Don't do it!" And then the other part of heart and soul cries out in like anguish: "Go, Lord Jesus! Go into suffering unequaled. Endure the shame, the spitting, the mockery, the false judgment, the hatred, the abuse, yes, the torments of the cross, even the unspeakable agony of being abandoned by your Father! Go, go quickly, and accomplish everything that I need for my salvation. For if you shrink from it, if you are unwilling to do it, then I am lost, lost forever. If you leave even the smallest shred of the work for me to do, then hell is my future and my present life a cruel wasted time in hell's waiting room. So then go, Lord Jesus, into Lent. Do it for me, even for me."

And so the soul is torn in two (Matthew 27:51) like the curtain in the temple that separated God and man. Separated they were and separated they would forever remain if Jesus would not go (and go willingly) to do for us all what none of us could do in the least for himself; and certainly we would not do anything even close to what he accomplished during Lent for someone else, even if we could. With the curtain torn and the soul ripped in two, we go through Lent. We await his anguished cries from the cross. And we long for its end in . . . *resurrection!* For there the torn soul at last will find its peace and rest. For there the victory of Christ for us will be confirmed. For there the soul is healed at last by the assurance that because he lives, we too shall live and live most blessedly forever with him in the heaven his cross has won for us.

Behold, he goes up to Jerusalem where all will be fulfilled. Behold, we follow with deepening anguish at what we caused and at the sight of what we should suffer. Behold, we will not leave him until he relieves us by the cry, "It is finished!" and the assurance that his resurrection gives, the assurance that what was all about him is all about us.

> See how deep his suffering
> > In his sacred Body
> > In his sinless Soul
> See how horrible its cause
> > In the sins of my body
> > In the sins of my soul
> See how perfect his love
> > For my body
> > For my soul.

We Would Like to See Jesus

I.

John 12:20-24 – There were some Greeks among those who went up to worship at the festival. They came to Philip, who was from Bethsaida in Galilee, with a request. "Sir," they said, "we would like to see Jesus." Philip went to tell Andrew; Andrew and Philip in turn told Jesus. Jesus replied, "The hour has come for the Son of Man to be glorified. Very truly I tell you, unless a kernel of wheat falls to the ground and dies, it remains only a single seed. But if it dies, it produces many seeds."

We have entered the holy season of Lent. Fitting devotions for any Christian in this holy season are the words that Jesus spoke as he entered upon the gruesome and so blessed task of our redemption. The gospel of

John is particularly rich in those words. A full two-thirds of that gospel is taken up with Jesus' words and works during Holy Week. As we enter this holy season, we want at its start to consider a section of his Holy Week discourses from John 12. As always, a complete consideration of any part of God's Word remains impossible for us; it is always so rich and so profound that on our best day, we can but scratch the surface. And with the passing of the years, his words become the more precious to us, never old or tiresome. That is true of all of his Word, but it is especially true of what Jesus has to say to us as he enters on the high point of his work for our salvation.

The high point? Do we really want to call Holy Week the high point of Jesus' life? Anyone looking at it in the way people ordinarily judge things would call this week the low point—yes, the lowest possible, given how this week will end. But look here at what happens in the middle of that week. So famous has Jesus become that even Greeks want to see him. So famous was he that they do not approach him directly but instead seek the help of one of his disciples, Philip. Philip was from Bethsaida in Galilee; Bethsaida was on the trade route that connected the northern and eastern Roman roads with the roads going south into Egypt. These Greeks who came to Philip were Jewish converts who might have known Philip from their travels for worship in Jerusalem or perhaps even from business trips that brought them to Bethsaida.

The point is that they want to see Jesus. He's famous. Philip was so impressed with the request that he did not at once take these Greeks to Jesus but went to consult a fellow disciple. "What does it all mean, that even Greeks want to see him? What should we do?" What indeed! Bring them to Jesus! But they are not quick to do that. Instead, they bring the request to Jesus.

And what is Jesus' reply? Does he say something like, "At last I'm getting the recognition that I deserve for all that I have said and done, even if it has to come from these foreigners"? Nothing of the sort. Instead, he takes his disciples aside and us with them to explain the meaning of all that is going on in this week. He speaks not as one who doesn't know what is about to happen but as the all-knowing Son of God, who knows exactly what is about to take place. Indeed, he has spoken of it often and in graphic detail.

Listen to how he describes it now. No one ever spoke as he does here. He pursues the theme we noted earlier that brings us to see that Lent is, in our view, all about him and in his view, all about us. With a smile of anticipation on his face he declares it: "This is now the hour that begins my glory. For the time has come for me to suffer and to die!"

In dogmatic theology we properly distinguish between Christ's state of humiliation and his state of exaltation. In the former, lasting from the moment of his conception until the moment of his resurrection, Jesus in his human nature veiled his power and glory and did not make full use of it. In the latter, lasting from the moment of his resurrection to all eternity, he in his human nature no longer hid his power and glory but makes regular and full use of it.

But here Jesus sees his glory as beginning with suffering and death! Again, who would ever think that way? Certainly no one else we have ever heard of in history would speak that way. Nor would we. But in Jesus' way of thinking—to say it yet again—it is all about us. For his death will be like the planting of a seed. The seed dies only to give birth to abundant fruit. See, here already is the beginning of it; these strangers from Greece want to see Jesus. Oh, how blessed will be that time when the message of the death of this seed and its rising again goes to Greece and beyond with the glad tidings of redemption! Philip and Andrew, together with the other apostles, will in due course be among those who plant the seed as a message of salvation. And they will have the joy of reaping its harvest in the souls who, by that message, spring to life and life eternal when they embrace the Savior in the Word as *their* Savior.

So it's Lent. It's the season of the year when we are most double-minded. We have good reason to weep and lament our role in his suffering and death. It is so tragic, that unbearable load of sin and guilt that we have heaped on him. So deep and complete is our guilt and shame that nothing less than the suffering and death of Jesus could rescue us. And in Lent we have occasion again and again to look at how willing, even eager, Jesus was to carry that load to the cross and to death. For that is why he came, just so that he could be a dying seed that would spring to life and bear abundant fruit. We would be the fruit that comes through the message of his grace and his work of suffering, death, and yes, of resurrection for our salvation. What love he had that in this discourse he was thinking of you, he was thinking of me. Would that there were a better word than *love* to describe it; for no human love has ever come near to that love which considers it nothing but glory to die for the object of his love—for you, for me! The deeper we go in our life and conscience judged on the basis of God's law, the more astonished we are at that love and the way he shows it to each of us in Lent.

> Lord Jesus, the Greeks came seeking you. In this holy season I also come seeking you. Let me each day of Lent both seek and find you in your Holy Word. Let me see my life as precious and holy because it is the harvest and the fruit of your suffering and death for me and for my salvation. Then when someone asks or even hints that they would like to see you, I with joy will bring that person to your Word, the seed that gives me life and can

give him or her life too. So may your death be glorious in my life and in my sharing of all that you have done for us and for our salvation. Amen.

II.

John 12:25,26 (ESV) – "Whoever loves his life loses it, and whoever hates his life in this world will keep it for eternal life. If anyone serves me, he must follow me; and where I am, there will my servant be also. If anyone serves me, the Father will honor him."

Again, awesome words! We can bear to hear them only if we have paid attention to the words of Jesus that precede these words. Jesus rejoices to be the seed that dies so that he may bear fruit by the message of his death and resurrection for us and for our salvation. That is his glory. That is the honor that he has from his Father—that by his work for us he should have the name above all others, a name none other may share, the name: *Savior!*

And now what is there for those who are the fruit of his suffering? They have honor too! As astonishing as is his description of his glory, the glory of a willing suffering and death, just so astonishing is his description of the honor and the glory that he has in mind for us. It is an honor and a glory bestowed by his Father on all those who serve Jesus, who serve him by hating "life in this world."

But again, we have to say it: Whoever heard of such a thing? We call someone who hates his life mentally ill, perhaps insane, someone who might even commit suicide. Such a person may indeed hate his life, but doesn't hate himself. In fact, his suicide is his ultimate act of love for himself; for by it he imagines that he will be freed from his suffering. For such a person love of self and hatred of life are one and the same thing.

What then does Jesus want from us when he bids us see our honor from God—really the only honor worth having—as consisting of a service to Jesus that has at its heart and core a hatred of one's own life? The suicidal person who hates life is filled with bitterness and despair. But the hating of one's own life that Jesus calls for from us is filled to the full. It has Jesus at its beginning and end and everything in between. Jesus' glory and honor from his Father are in his giving everything—in giving himself—willingly for us. Our honor and glory from his Father is the willing surrender of ourselves to Jesus our Savior in a life of service. It is a hatred of that life which has self at the center. "Listen to me!" gives way to listening to him. "I want . . ." yields to a longing for what Jesus wants. "Get out of my way!" gives place to "What can I do to help?" Such a life begins and has as its chief element listening to him. It consists of receiving his grace and salvation, forgiveness and eternal life full and free through such listening. And then it continues in a life of loving service to all around us; for he loves them and he died for them just as much as he loves us and died for us. That's how we follow him in Lent and in life. We listen to him and receive him and all he has by that listening. And then we imitate him by preferring him and service to him and to those around us—preferring that to life itself.

Such a life is the opposite of a life loved for its own sake. The goal of that kind of idolatrous love for one's own life is a happiness that is to be found in fleeting pleasure and self-satisfaction. Self is at the center. Such a person is happy and loves his life when he has the stuff he wants. He is happy and loves his life when those who get in his way or have somehow hurt him are pushed aside and are hurt in return. He is happy and loves life when people seem to love him, speak well of him, and are ready to do what he wants them to do. He is happy when he is successful in hiding his darker thoughts and wishes from those around him. He is happy when whatever good he does in the world is heartily appreciated and he gets the credit he thinks he deserves for it. Such a person wants to rule as much as possible the circumstances and people around him for his own benefit.

But wait a minute. That description of one who loves life with self at the center describes me some days! Indeed, there isn't a day that goes by during which at least some of that description doesn't haunt and tempt me. Ah, as Luther says so often, now you smell the roast! The words of Jesus that I should hate my self-centered life and instead imitate him in giving it in his service are a call to imitation. And he means it; that is indeed what he wants and intends for us. But at the same time his words are a call again to marvel at his love and grace. For only he could love his Father and love us that perfectly. So while we strive to imitate his love, we do it beneath his cross, always yearning for his pardon. And he unsparingly grants that pardon so that we will rise day after day from the foot of his cross to begin again hating our self-centered life by surrendering it to him and to his service—a service that first receives from him and then wants to give everything back to him in gratitude for his perfect love.

And yes, it is true that because of his love so perfect, it accomplished completely our redemption—because of that his Father honors us! He honors us as our service is washed and made perfect in the blood of his Son. He honors us as he adopts and makes us his own dear children for Jesus' sake in the Sacrament of Baptism. He honors us by promising us an eternity in his heavenly mansions in union with all the saints and angels, all because of the perfect love and work of Jesus.

What an amazing thing! Who can finish wrapping the mind and heart around it? We are called by Jesus, who counts it glory to suffer and die for us; we are called to hate all of our life apart from him and his work for our salvation. We are called to be honored by his Father as we serve him and those around us in a service made worthy and perfect by his forgiveness won for us during that first Lent. And as he said and promised, where there is such a life, there Jesus is; where he is, there his servants will be. What more could we want?

> Dearest Jesus, you loved me perfectly and gave your all for my salvation. What could be more reasonable than that I love you perfectly and give my all in your service? But I know from your Word and from experience that such is impossible for me—to love you as you have loved me. And still you continue to love and forgive, to shower me with grace and blessings beyond counting, beyond knowing. How I long for the day when, in the heaven you have won for me, I will at last love you completely! But for now, grant me still this grace that I grow in the virtue of hating all in life that is separated from you and contrary to your Word. Then I will surely grow in wonder and awe before the constant mercy and grace in Word and sacrament by which you still claim me as your own and one honored by your Father. Amen.

III.

John 12:27,28,30-33 – "Now my soul is troubled, and what shall I say? 'Father, save me from this hour'? No, it was for this very reason I came to this hour. Father, glorify your name!" Then a voice came from heaven, "I have glorified it, and will glorify it again." Jesus said, "This voice was for your benefit, not mine. Now is the time for judgment on this world; now the prince of this world will be driven out. And I, when I am lifted up from the earth, will draw all people to myself." He said this to show the kind of death he was going to die.

Jesus calls us in Lent to a love like his, a love that surrenders all of life in submission to his Word and in service to one another. But some have complained, "That's all easy for him to say. He is perfect God in the flesh. For him to be perfect in his love for his Father and perfect even in his service to us cannot have been all that difficult for him. His suffering could be easily endured and all temptations were as nothing to him compared to how difficult everything is for us."

But now in Lent Jesus sweeps away any such notions about him and what he did for us. He begins to do it with his words, "Now my soul is troubled." He will show us how troubled with greater emphasis and urgency in the

Garden of Gethsemane and in his cry from the cross. But he says it here already quite plainly. His heart is troubled. Deep within his soul as he contemplates all that is about to take place, he is stirred and disturbed. For though true God, he is also true man. His divine and eternal nature is clothed in a true human body with a human heart and soul. During his earthly life to this point he has not used all of the power that is his as true God, but has, as noted earlier concealed and veiled it in the lowliness of his human nature. He got hungry like any mortal. He became tired after a hard day and slept. And now, as he contemplates his approaching scourging, the mocking and spitting, the false judgment, the nails, and the hours on the cross, his human soul is troubled. As he considers what it will be like there on the cross—to be exposed to all the worst in humanity and then worst of all, to be abandoned by the Father he so perfectly loved and served—it all overwhelms him. For him to say that he is troubled is no small thing.

We at times are troubled too. We are afraid of things that we cannot control in our present and in our future. We may even have a dread of things in our past that might come back to haunt us. But our anxious thoughts are, for the most part, about uncertain things. Such is not the case with Jesus. He knows exactly and to the smallest detail what is about to happen to him. And he shows his true humanity when he gives this small glimpse into his soul: He is troubled.

So what should he do? Should he seek escape? Should he hide? That's what we would do. Should he take to himself at once the full exercise of his divine power and authority? Oh no, not that! Troubled he is and still more troubled will he become. But there will be no magic potion, no pill, no drug to still his troubled soul or relieve him of the anguish and pain yet to come. He clearly says so: this is what he came for. This is all and alone his desire, to glorify his Father. He will glorify his Father by doing perfectly his Father's will. And that will of his Father is centered on our salvation. That, therefore, will be his whole focus. Instead of fleeing from his troubled soul, he embraces all that troubles him for the glory of God and for our salvation.

So then Jesus does not call us to something that is difficult for us but altogether easy and simple for him. Quite the contrary is the case. His situation is, in fact, far more difficult than ours. We on our part owe God a life of surrender and loving obedience because he is our Maker. We owe him this debt of love even more so because, as our Redeemer, he has paid the debt in which our sins have drowned us—a debt we cannot begin to pay. But Jesus, what does he owe us by rights? Nothing at all. He pays in full a debt that is not his. What he does, he does purely out of love. And that love will not be cheap or easy for him.

And so his Father speaks from heaven to his beloved Son. He speaks of his good pleasure and of his satisfaction that his name will be glorified by the work his Son is about to do, painful and difficult as it will be. There would be no glory for the Father if the work was easy or simple and involved no effort from his Son. But the very fact that the glory of the Father will be so gruesome, so painful, so difficult to accomplish is what makes it all glorious in the eyes of the Father. This is how much the Father loves us. This is how perfect the love of Jesus was for his Father. It almost makes us shudder with this conclusion: If the Father loves us so much that he sees his own honor tied up with the terrible suffering of his beloved Son, then—can it be?—we shrink from even thinking it: The Father in a way loves us—no, we can barely get out the words!—more even than he loves his Son, at least during that one most holy week of recorded history!

So Jesus leads us into Lent. To the Father a fool might say, "No, don't let it happen to your Son, who so perfectly loves and obeys you. It isn't fair; it isn't right." To Jesus the self-centered might give the advice, "No, don't do it; it's not worth it. No one will deserve it and no one else would ever even think of acting as you do in Lent." The self-righteous might have this to say: "Leave me alone with this talk of your paying the price of my sins. I'll do it myself; I'm good enough—or close enough to good enough—to gain heaven on my own." The bold sinner might enter in, scoffing, "I love my life the way it is; I do as I please. I'm not interested in your suffering or what it is designed to accomplish; I just want to be happy and I deserve it. Go away, Jesus, and don't bother me with talk of surrender and loving service; that's just not my thing."

To all such and to us too in our weakness and in the recognition of our need so desperate and so great, Jesus answers, "The voice came from heaven to let you know that in spite of all that is wrong with you and all mankind, I go to win redemption for you with the anguish of my soul and the pain of my body. I go to do it willingly; I go because that's how much God loves you!"

> Jesus, let me now follow you in these holy days. Let me mark each day the greatness of the Father's love for me and your love for him that so benefits me. There are no words to express adequately the greatness of that love, just as there are no words that can fully express the greatness of my need for this your love that accomplished my salvation. Surely heaven must last forever for there to be enough time for me to worship and adore and give you thanks for your Lent and its saving benefit. Amen.

In the Upper Room

I.

1 Corinthians 11:23-26 – The Lord Jesus, on the night he was betrayed, took bread, and when he had given thanks, he broke it and said, "This is my body, which is for you; do this in remembrance of me." In the same way, after supper he took the cup saying, "This cup is the new covenant in my blood; do this, whenever you drink it, in remembrance of me." For whenever you eat this bread and drink this cup, you proclaim the Lord's death until he comes.

If ever there is a time when we should be loath to give advice to God, surely it must be in this most holy week of weeks. For in this week God redeemed us by his blood, and he did so willingly, did it for all, did it alone and without any help—much less advice—from us.

But still, even with a shudder and a chill running down our spine, we just can't help ourselves (and how well that sums everything up!); we just have to open our mouths and say something.

For starters, on this most holy night in which he gives us the Sacrament, there are a thousand things that we might want so say and ten thousand things worth thinking about. Here are just a few:

The Lord Jesus, on the night he was betrayed—really?! On that night of all nights you give this greatest gift? It is a night on which the disciples and all the world are at their absolute worst: the night he was betrayed, the night they all forsook him and fled, the night of denial with oaths and curses! It is the night when his church will curse and count him worthy of death for the sin of blasphemy. It is the night when the engines of the state will be set to call him innocent and then condemn him to death. Yes, it is the night on which only the icy arms of death and the hot breath from the jaws of hell itself are eager to welcome him.

Wouldn't it have been more fitting for you to give this great gift when the disciples, the church, and the state were at their best? How about giving it that day when so many went away from you but the disciples, with Peter as their spokesman, confessed, "Lord, to whom shall we go? You have the words of eternal life. We have come to believe and to know that you are the Holy One of God" (John 6:68,69)! What a beautiful confession. How fitting it might have been to reward it with the pledge of your abiding presence with them through this Sacrament. Or how about that time when you asked the disciples what they thought of you? Again, Peter, acting as spokesmen for the rest, boldly declared, "You are the Messiah, the Son of the living God" (Matthew 16:16)! Wouldn't it have been wonderful for you to confirm that confession of faith with the gift of yourself in the Sacrament?

But on this night? This night the disciples are at their worst. They are quarreling about which of them is greatest. Not one thought to wash your feet in reverent attention to common custom for an honored guest; you ended up washing their feet. And if that wasn't bad enough, when you speak of your coming suffering, not one expresses sympathy. Instead, all you get from them are empty promises of loyalty, which you know full well they are about to break. You know full well that in the Garden of Gethsemane, they will all abandon you at the first threat of danger.

On this night you give them the most precious of gifts, on a night when they deserve it least?

Yes—oh, most sublime truth! On this night—a night so heavy with the darkness of doubt and denial, of fear and failure, on this night when man is at his worst—you are at your best!!

And precisely because you picked just such a night as this, I come to you often to receive what you gave there and give us still. I will not delay until I am at my best—in any case, there is no such day for me. No, when I see myself stumbling after you, covered with shame, filled with the leprosy of my sin and crushed by my guilt, I come. When I begin to see again the horror of what I deserve, I will come for what I can never ever—not even in the slightest—deserve. I come not because I am holy but because you are. I come not because I merit anything but because you merit everything and that just for me. I come at my worst, a beggar about to become rich. I come with death in my bones and on my soul to receive life for now and forever. I come, in sum, aching in heart and soul as I make confession. And still I come with joy unbounded; for I am invited by your gracious Word and promise. So I come looking at you and away from myself to receive, to receive, to receive all that you are and all that you have done for my salvation.

> Lord Jesus, how kind and how considerate of you to institute this Holy Sacrament when the disciples were not at their best but at their worst! That simple fact, connected to all that you have said this night, emboldens me always to come at your invitation to receive you as they received you. It is not my strength that gives me courage to come, but your promise. It is not my merit that lets me dare to receive you here, but your inestimable kindness in calling and drawing me. And so, Lord Jesus, let me take the cup of salvation and worship and adore you forever for it. Amen.

II.

Matthew 26:26-28 – While they were eating, Jesus took bread, and when he had given thanks, he broke it and gave it to his disciples, saying, "Take and eat; this is my body." Then he took a cup, and when he had given thanks, he gave it to them, saying, "Drink from it, all of you. This is my blood of the covenant, which is poured out for many for the forgiveness of sins."

And so then, what is it that he gives us that makes us so glad on that night so filled with woe? He calls it the *blood of the covenant.* This particular covenant is his last will and testament before he dies. What does a last will and testament normally contain? It has in it the promise of a bequest, which will come to the "survivors" at the death of the one making it. Jesus is about to die. What does he have to leave behind to his loved ones? There are no palaces. Contrary to the oft hinted-at expectations of the disciples, there are no kingdoms or thrones. There is no hidden bank account or treasure trove with piled-up stores of gold and silver. There isn't even a little plot of land for them to use as a burial place for him once he dies.

And so, having nothing, he leaves them (and us!) himself! Having nothing, he gives them everything. Having nothing, he gives the endowment of the price of salvation.

For it is his true body that is there with the bread. It is his true blood that is there with the wine. It is the body and blood of the virgin-born Son of God. It is the humanity inseparably joined to the eternal God. It is the whole and entire person of the one about to be crucified and then rise again for our justification. That's it. That's all. That's everything!

He says it himself: It is for the forgiveness of sins. Indeed, how could it be otherwise? For if our bodies become the shrine and habitation of the Savior, then salvation is ours! God looks at us, and what does he see? Not our sin and shame. Not our guilt, not our death and hell. Not the eternal torment our sins have so richly merited and that from the moment of our conception. No, what he sees is Jesus! He sees the Son in whom he is well pleased. He sees the sacrifice for sinners slain. He sees the full and complete payment of the Lamb offered for the sins of the world. See how Jesus himself puts it: This is the "blood of the covenant." In the Old Testament it was blood poured out on the altar of sacrifice that sealed the promise of God to pardon. And now, here it is: the blood of the perfect Lamb making the perfect sacrifice to accomplish a perfect payment for sin and salvation!

So then, who could not but rejoice at hearing his call: *Take and eat. Take and drink. My body and my blood—the price of salvation given for you, yes, for you, yes, just for you!* On the night of woe what tears of joy we shed! On the night of suffering how we delight to hear him promise us deliverance from all suffering. On that night as his death draws near, when we might well despair, or for that matter on any day or night when we might think ourselves worthless, doomed, and damned—on such a night we sing hymns of praise and thanksgiving. For there he is, truly and really present, full of grace and truth and mercy and love for us. Because of him and in him and from him, we have worth and value beyond measure. The elderly man and aged woman, the young man and the maid, the highly gifted and the one who thinks he or she has accomplished nothing and has nothing to offer—to each he comes, to one no less than to the other. To each he declares it: *For you—for you I came! For you I give my body and my blood! For you I bring forgiveness and salvation! What you may think of yourself, be it much or little, matters not; what I think is what matters. And I claim you for my own. See how much I love you: I never want to be separated from you, not now, not tomorrow, not in the hour of death, and certainly not on the day of judgment. Here is my body. Here is my blood. Here is my promise for time and for eternity!*

So then on days of joy, may these words be your greatest joy: *Take and eat, take and drink my body and my blood, given for you for the forgiveness of sins.* On days dark with doubt and despair, may these words revive and sooth and be balm for the anguished soul: *Fear not! Take and eat, take and drink my body and my blood, given for you for the forgiveness of sins.* Yes, when the last hour has come and all human help is nothing, when strength and life drain away, may then these words enliven and open for you the gates of heaven: *Here I am! Come now to see what you have already enjoyed without sight when you lived with faith in these words: My body, my blood, given for you for the forgiveness of sins!*

> Dearest Jesus, there are no words adequate for your praise and our thanksgiving! Grant me still this grace that I never forget or take for granted your boundless love for me in this gift of yourself in Word and Sacrament. In days of pleasure let me call to mind this my greatest pleasure. In days of doubt or fear let me cherish you in Word and Sacrament as the unfailing pledge of salvation and the steadfast assurance of your constant presence with me and for me. In the hour of death console and strengthen me with this promise of life with you forever in heaven. In thanksgiving to your Father you instituted this holy Sacrament for me, even for me. In thanksgiving and joy unbounded let me ever receive it! Amen.

III.

Luke 22:23-30 – They began to question among themselves which of them it might be who would do this [i.e. betray Jesus]. A dispute also arose among them as to which of them was considered to be greatest. Jesus said to them, . . . "Who is greater, the one who is at the table or the one who serves? Is it not the one who is at the table? But I am among you as one who serves. You are those who have stood by me in my trials. And I confer on you a kingdom, just as my Father conferred one on me, so that you may eat and drink at my table in my kingdom and sit on thrones, judging the twelve tribes of Israel."

What kind of people are these disciples? It is almost beyond belief! Jesus has just given them an inheritance beyond measure. He has given forever the gift of himself in the Sacrament of his body and blood. And notice that it is on the night before his death that he gives the result of his death! That is to be for them a guarantee that he will finish the horrible work of their redemption that lies now so close at hand. Should there not now follow from these disciples at least a hymn of praise and adoration for this incomparable gift? Should they not be on their knees with faces to the ground and eyes filled with tears of joy for such an expression of his boundless love for them? Especially since he has made it clear all week long that this is his final meal with them before he suffers and dies, shouldn't we expect some sign of appreciation, some understanding from these men who have been with him now for almost three years? Yes, at the very least shouldn't we expect some sympathy for the one whose gift of himself will so soon and so painfully cost the shedding of blood and the sacrifice of his body as a lamb led to slaughter?

But oh, no! That's not what happens. Instead, according to Luke's chronology, right after they have received the Sacrament, there is not one word about the gift. There is not one word about how much the gift will soon cost. There is not the least expression of sympathy for the Lord who goes willingly to his suffering and death. The disciples start out with a quarrel about which one of them could possibly be the one who would betray him. And that quarrel brings them again to an argument they had had before. It probably went something like this: "I can't possibly be the one who will betray him; for I am the best of this sorry lot!" And then the next and the next, each following in his turn, berating his fellow disciples and exalting himself as the most important and the one fit to run things after Jesus has gone. And, again, they do this right after Jesus has given them himself in the Sacrament with the promise that he will give himself in the same way whenever they repeat this sacred act.

Jesus shouldn't need our advice here! For isn't it obvious? Can't they just—for five minutes—concentrate on him and his gifts so dearly won, instead of focusing on how great and valuable and important they think themselves to be? This is the time to really let them have it. The moment has come to tell them in no uncertain terms what ungrateful wretches they are and what they deserve because of it.

But listen! How astonishing is Jesus' response to their perverse self-absorption and that after such an amazing gift from him! Instead of the rant they deserve, he praises them! And his praise is so out of proportion to what they deserve. It is so much the opposite of what Jesus will shortly experience from them and what he indeed had already told them would shortly happen: they will all forsake him.

If you ever think your sins are too great to ever be forgiven, consider the disciples on this most holy night. If you ever think that you are so bad that God could not possibly love you, call to mind this text. While you may not be any better than they were, you couldn't be any worse either! Jesus' words here are really a commentary on the words that Jesus will speak to his saints at the last judgment recorded in Matthew 25:31-46. Recall that there Jesus has nothing but praise for sinners made saints by his grace, by his merit, by his forgiveness granted day by day in Word and sacraments. Not one word does he say there of all the failures, of all the faults, of all the foolish and perverse forgetting of Jesus in favor of service to self. Not a syllable does he utter there of the times when self-promotion won the day and contempt (spoken or not) for fellow believers found a comfortable place in the heart.

Instead of a well-deserved and disgusted rebuke from Jesus, Jesus looks ahead to the whole of their lives and to the end of their lives. He picks out what they will do that is right and in response to the gospel he will entrust to them at his ascension and at Pentecost. They had not in the past three years, in spite of everything, left him—though soon they will leave him. At least up to that point, they have stood by him while the leaders and the wise and the outwardly more holy have rejected and abused him and would soon kill him. And in the future, still plagued, no doubt, with weakness and faults aplenty, these disciples would stand by Jesus. They would stand by him in the face of persecution and death for themselves as his followers; they would stand by him in supporting those who believed their preaching and teaching about Jesus, the Savior. Yes, they would be the ones, for all their faults and weaknesses, who would carry that gospel throughout the world of their day.

That's how perfect the love of Jesus is in Lent. That's how complete the forgiveness is that he has gone to win for us there. It is so perfect that it completely covers all that is wrong with us—covers it so completely that it is as though nothing wrong ever happened. It's so kind and generous that it looks only on the good accomplished by these in whom he will continue to live by his Word and this Sacrament. Luther reminds us in his catechism explanation of the Eight Commandment that we should think well of our neighbor and always put what he does in the best possible light. How perfectly Jesus does that here! All Jesus wants to talk about is the fruit of his suffering, as that fruit had already been seen, however faintly, in his disciples and would be seen in the future. For again, to Jesus, Lent is all about us.

> Lord Jesus, in that first Lent you fixed your eyes on me and made it all about me as you went to win my salvation. As I follow you in your passion this day of Lent, may I fix my heart and mind on you and the greatness of your love for me. Oh, may then the fruit of your love and of your suffering become ever more evident as I cling to your forgiving grace so dearly won and then as I strive to serve more nearly as you have served me. Hear me for the sake of that same forgiving grace. Amen.

In Gethsemane

I.

Luke 22:39-46 – Jesus went out as usual to the Mount of Olives, and his disciples followed him. On reaching the place, he said to them, "Pray that you will not fall into temptation." He withdrew about a stone's throw beyond them, knelt down and prayed, "Father, if you are willing, take this cup from me; yet not my will, but yours be done." An angel from heaven appeared to him and strengthened him. And being in anguish, he prayed more earnestly, and his sweat was like drops of blood falling to the ground. When he rose from prayer and went back to the disciples, he found them asleep, exhausted from sorrow. "Why are you sleeping?" he asked them. "Get up and pray so that you will not fall into temptation."

There are so many things here that make us draw back in awe and amazement. Consider first of all Jesus' instructions to the disciples: "Pray that *you* will not fall into temptation." Wouldn't a more fitting instruction have been: "Pray that *I* will not fall into temptation"? After all, it's not the disciples who will soon be arrested, falsely condemned, and all the rest of what will shortly follow. If anyone might be tempted to give up on this whole endeavor, wouldn't it be Jesus himself?

But no; there is no possibility that Jesus will fall and sin. For though he was tempted most severely (Hebrews 4:15), he is the eternal God and therefore never could, never would, never would even want to sin. But the disciples, well, we have already seen how weak they are and how prone to falling. They should pray so that when the temptation to despair comes, as it surely would come, they would not fall. They should pray that in that hour they would remember all that Jesus had said and done, especially the transfiguration, especially the promise of his coming resurrection.

But still, what follows? It is not the disciples but Jesus who prays. Jesus prays as no one has ever prayed before. With loud cries and tears (Hebrews 5:7) he calls to the God he alone can address fully and rightly as "Father." He sees all that is ahead of him: each blow, each humiliation. He sees the quick flight of these very disciples as soon as he gives them the chance to run. He sees the tears of his mother at the foot of the cross. He sees and feels already in his soul the horror beyond description of being abandoned by this same Father. Yes, he sees himself covered from head to toe—body and soul—with the only thing he could not stand: sin, the sin of the whole world. And so just as he does not need to pray that he will not fall into sin because he is God, so we see that he is true man; as true man he recoils before the burden so soon to be heaped upon him. And he pleads for rescue from it, if it is possible to accomplish the mission of *your* salvation and *mine* in some other way. We know how it is to break out in a cold sweat when we dread something we know is about to happen to us that will be painful or unpleasant. Just a trip to a doctor's office can evoke that response in us. But to shed, as it were, great drops of blood in an anguish like Jesus' anguish here? No, that is impossible for us to imagine. See how he shows his humanity just as surely as he had shown his deity.

And now yet again, proof of his deity: The angels come to serve him. The Father does not answer his prayer at once. Oh, to be sure, he will answer it, but not until the work is finished, not completely until the third day—the day of resurrection. So the angels come to serve him. What an amazing thing! The angels worshiped and adored him before he became man. They sang—but not to him—at his birth. They appear to him now to strengthen him for the journey soon to begin. It is already an amazing thing that they do not come to tell him to give up on the task before him, given how miserable and ungrateful these are for whom he came to die. It is doubly amazing that there was a way for these heavenly creatures to strengthen their Creator and Lord. Who can begin to fathom it? We can but marvel at the evidence of these two natures: the human and divine joined perfectly in the one person. We can but marvel that God in the flesh was served and strengthened by those he created. We can but marvel that the Father did not intervene and rescue his beloved Son at once but waited until the cup of sorrow had been emptied completely on the cross.

Oh, let all who doubt the love of God their Savior behold the God-man in Gethsemane. Let all who cry to him for help and are ready to despair because it does not come immediately remember the prayers and cries of the Savior who waited for the Father's answer. Let all who struggle under the weight of their own temptations pay heed to the call of Jesus, who bids us pray that we will not fall—a call the disciples to their own hurt did not heed. Let all who fear any distress or pain consider that the angels who served the Savior serve us no less with their mighty protection. Let all who are baffled by the mysteries of life and have questions they cannot answer go with Jesus to Gethsemane. There let them hold their breath and cover their mouths in amazement; let them utter only the confession:

> O my God and Savior, I understand so little and so often nothing; give me grace, therefore, to surrender myself completely to your understanding; to your hidden purposes; and to your promise of rescue, of redemption, of resurrection! And then let me sleep the sleep of the safe and secure, the sleep of the exhausted who yet have nothing to fear because you are ever near. Amen.

II.

Matthew 26:47-50 – While [Jesus] was still speaking, Judas, one of the Twelve, arrived. With him was a large crowd armed with swords and clubs, sent from the chief priests and the elders of the people. Now the betrayer had arranged a signal with them: "The one I kiss is the man; arrest him." Going at once to Jesus, Judas said, "Greetings, Rabbi!" and kissed him. Jesus replied, "Do what you came for, friend."

John 18:7,8 – [Jesus asked the crowd,] "Who is it you want?" "Jesus of Nazareth," they said. Jesus answered, "I told you that I am he. If you are looking for me, then let these men go."

Do you marvel at the depth and extent of Jesus' love for his disciples and for us as you have seen it so far in Lent? Marvel still more! It is not possible for us ever to exhaust our useful consideration of the grace that makes our Lent all about him and his Lent all about us. Pause for a moment to ponder yet again the love of Jesus for his disciples, a love no different than the love he has for us, in these two texts.

Judas has sold him out for 30 pieces of silver, the price of a slave in those days. And here he comes to earn his pay. Astonishing as is his act of betrayal, more astonishing still by far are Jesus' words to Judas. Jesus has known all along what Judas was up to. He knows that all of his teaching has been wasted on Judas. He knows that all of his proof of a desire to save all and thus to save Judas too are here repaid with treachery of the worst imaginable sort: Judas greets Jesus and kisses his cheek! How could he betray his Savior in such a way? How could he show such a despicable hypocrisy?

And what does Jesus say to him? He asks him a question for which Jesus fully knows the answer. He introduces the question with a Greek word that is used only three times in the gospels. He calls him "friend." That particular word is used only for a friend who has received friendship but not returned it, who has, rather, shown himself utterly unworthy of friendship (Matthew 20:13; 22:12). Is that not an amazing thing? Just with that word, Jesus lets Judas know that he is fully aware of what Judas is doing. At the same time the use of that word is a most powerful call to Judas to repent and return; it holds within it the assurance that on Jesus' side, for his part, he is still a friend. In effect at this very hour of betrayal, when it is impossible for Judas to undo what he has done, Jesus holds before him the offer of forgiveness! The words *love* and *friend* seem altogether inadequate to express what Jesus expresses in that one word of address to the betrayer. But there are no words that could ever be adequate to fully express Jesus' love for Judas—and for us.

And then there's the next evidence of his love and his friendship so impossible to grasp fully, so beyond compare. Jesus performed the miracle of causing those who have come to seize him to fall to the ground when first he asked them, "Who are you looking for?" He gave proof by that miracle that they could not take him without his consent—without his willing it. The miracle did not cause them to repent; they got up and came at him again, and again he asked them who they wanted. As always when Jesus asks a question, he is not looking for information; rather, he is setting the stage for what he intends to do. And what does he intend to do here? Another miracle!

After he answers, in effect, "Well, here I am; now you can do what you came for!" he adds a command: "Let these men go!" The about-to-be-arrested gives a command to those who have come with clubs and swords in order to seize him! Who ever heard of such a thing? That Jesus uses his almighty power here not to spare himself in the least but to spare his disciples—that's no small miracle.

"Let these men go"! Now that is astonishing indeed! Consider that the disciples had not to that point abandoned him. In fact, Peter even at this moment was ready to fight with the sword to save Jesus. Peter and the rest, for at least a moment, had kept their word that they would not forsake him. But now Jesus gives a command to those who have come to seize him, and by that very command he gives the disciples permission to go and to leave him alone. No, more than that: He all but commands them to leave!

And all obey! The soldiers do not lay a hand on the disciples—no, not even on Peter, who had drawn his sword to strike off the ear of the high priest's servant. And the disciples for their part? They are not slow to take advantage of the opportunity; their courage vanishes in an instant and so do they.

Yes, how amazing Lent is! Jesus makes it all about us. See how he does everything to prevent anyone from imagining that they are somehow in control here. The soldiers fall to the ground and then obey him when he commands them to let the disciples go. See how he makes it sure and certain that no one will help him, none will comfort him, not one single soul will share in the work of our redemption. He does it all. He does it all alone. And he does it for all. He does it for all, none excepted—not Judas, not the soldiers, not any of the disciples, not any of us! When it comes to the work of our salvation, our whole concentration is on Jesus alone. When it comes to the work of our salvation, his whole concentration is on us and our salvation.

> Even so, Lord Jesus, I call to mind those things in myself that make me shudder. How could you possibly have come into Lent for someone like me? Satan holds before me my sins when I was at my worst. And when he isn't doing that, he tempts me to think that somehow I might contribute a little something towards my own salvation or perhaps deserve it at least more than some others I could mention. What folly! How foolish! Let me fix my eyes on you and all that you have said and done in Lent. In seeing you alone, let my sins disappear because of the pardon you won for me there. And then replace all self-righteous nonsense with gratitude that you have done it all, done it all alone, done it all for me. Amen.

In the High Priest's Courtyard

I.

Luke 22:59-62 – About an hour later another asserted, "Certainly this fellow was with him, for he is a Galilean." Peter replied, "Man, I don't know what you're talking about!" Just as he was speaking, the rooster crowed. The Lord turned and looked straight at Peter. Then Peter remembered the word the Lord had spoken to him: "Before the rooster crows today, you will disown me three times." And he went outside and wept bitterly.

What a complete mess Peter has made of things. Surely Jesus could have found a better lead apostle than this one. Jesus had warned him. Peter didn't listen. Jesus had told him to watch and pray, lest he fall into temptation. Peter didn't watch, and he didn't pray. And now when the hour of temptation has come, he falls and falls and falls again. He had a chance to boldly confess what he had confessed earlier under more favorable circumstances: "You are the Messiah, the Son of the living God" (Matthew 16:16). He had a chance to do some real mission work by repeating what he had said so well on yet another occasion when so many were leaving Jesus; Jesus had asked his disciples if they too would go away. Peter had boldly and beautifully confessed his faith: "Lord, to whom shall we go? You have the words of eternal life. We have come to believe and to know that you are the Holy One of God" (John 6:68,69).

What an opportunity to share that faith now in this critical hour! There may even have been some there in the courtyard who either shared that conviction or were close to it; Peter could have strengthened them. But that's not what happens. Instead, Peter makes a complete mess of things. Even when the rooster crows the first time, Peter does not come to his senses and remember Jesus' earlier warning.

Now all the damage is done. Jesus has in his lead apostle no bold defender, but one who with oaths and curses has denied him. Jesus has no missionary, but one who is an offense to any who might have believed and an obstacle to any who could have been turned by a bold confession of the truth. Jesus has no faithful follower, but one who has done incredible damage to his own soul as well by his denial of the author and sustainer of faith. Now when all the damage is done, the rooster crows yet again.

And then this: "The Lord turned and looked straight at Peter." What a look that must have been! The crowing rooster captures Peter's ears. The look of Jesus bores into his heart, into his conscience. He whom the priests and their servants mocked, struck, and spat upon looked at Peter. Peter is safe from ridicule and arrest, safe from mockery, beating and spitting; for he has denied any connection with Jesus. And the condemned, the humiliated, the spit-covered Jesus looked at him. The innocent One looked at one so guilty, one so cowardly, one so shameful.

The preaching of the rooster and the look of Jesus has its proper effect. Peter does not say within himself, "Good thing I didn't confess my faith; if I had, I could end up in the same terrible condition as Jesus is now in." No, at least that didn't happen. Instead, Peter is crushed. He is devastated. He is filled with shame and remorse. He goes out and weeps bitter tears of repentance.

> Lord Jesus, let me hear the sermon of the rooster. You warned me not to play with sin. You warned me not to hang around with

scoffers and mockers unless I was there to confess your name. You even promised me that even if I should endure ridicule because of my faithful confession, you would stand by me. Yes, you promised that your Word purely and boldly confessed would sometimes have the blessed fruit of strengthening the weak or even turning a foe to a friend. But so often I think that I know everything better. I too stumble and fall when I should stand firm. I too hide in the crowd and hope no one will notice that I have been with you. I too have had times when I behaved little or no better than those who mock you.

Lord Jesus, turn and look at me! Look not in the anger I deserve. Look not with the disappointment or the disgust that I know and feel in myself. Look at me as you looked at Peter. Look at me with pity, with eyes bloodshot with your tears of longing for my redemption. Look at me with the promise of pardon that you gave to Peter when earlier you had told him that you would pray for him, that his faith fail not. Look at me with eyes that move me in this holy season to join Peter in shedding my own river of tears in sorrow and repentance. Then by the rooster's sermon and your look, perform still this miracle in my heart that still I cling to all that you have done for my salvation; let my tears be not only those of sorrow over what I have done; let them be at the same time tears of thanksgiving for what you have done in winning my pardon, my restoration, my peace. Amen.

II.

But wait! There is still one more thing to note. Did you catch it? Peter, even in his repentance, is still a loaf half-baked. He did not go back and attempt to undo the damage he had done by his denial. Shouldn't he have done that? After all, if your child steals something, don't you insist that he go back and not only apologize but also return what he has stolen? Peter has robbed Christ of his honor by his refusal to defend him with his words— that's all, just with his words. And in the process he has put a rock in front of any hearts that might have been turned by a faithful confession. Peter has become a rock of offense to any who might have had at least some respect for or maybe even faith in Jesus. Doesn't genuine repentance prove itself at least by an attempt to undo the damage my earlier sins have done?

But Peter isn't ready for that yet. It will have to do that the rooster's sermon and the Savior's look have brought him back to the essence of faith, to sorrow over what he has done, and to renewed trust in what Jesus is doing for his salvation—no matter how stumbling that trust may be. Peter's soul is exhausted. All confidence in himself is shattered, as indeed it should be. It will take the words of the risen Savior to restore in Peter the bold confession of his faith that will occupy the rest of his life.

We too perhaps on this day in Lent are exhausted and spent. We too still stay for so long half-baked loaves like Peter was on that fateful night. We just cannot bring ourselves to go back—at least not right at this moment—to those we have offended by our silence and make instead a bold confession. Our tears of repentance are not always all that deep or profound; if they were perfect and complete, we would run to undo the damage we have done. But sadly, sometimes that takes time, more time than it should. And so we are always left with this: Looking at ourselves, we can only break out in confession—"Oh, God, be merciful to me, a sinner!" Then looking at Jesus we can but sink to our knees before him and melt with thanksgiving that he looks at us, looks still at us, looks at us and speaks words of pardon and peace as he would to the disciples on Easter Sunday.

Aren't you glad that Jesus picked someone like Peter? For if Jesus did not spurn him, I can draw comfort and encouragement from that: he will not spurn me either. If his grace was big enough for Peter, it will be big enough for me too! For he who does not lie has promised it: "Whoever comes to me I will never drive away" (John 6:37). It is the look of Jesus so deeply embedded in that promise that moves us to come and then to come again and again. Once again we have to note it: Every time Jesus does something that to our fallen eyes and reason makes no sense at all, he does it for our comfort and benefit.

> Dearest Savior, forgive me, forgive me; then strengthen me against myself and my fears so that I do not again deny you. Strengthen me in love for you so that in my confession to you, I not only pour out my need for your pardon so undeserved but also that I embrace your merits and your promise to forgive. Then embolden me to take advantage of those opportunities you give me to confess you as Lord and as my only Savior. And, yes, even this grant me: that I find in you the strength to do the hardest work of all—the work of laboring to undo damage that I have done by earlier denials of my faith either by my wrong words, by my silence, or by deeds that contradict the faith I profess. In it all, O Jesus, look on me still with pity and pardon in your Word and sacrament. Amen.

The Lesson of Judas

Matthew 27:3-5 – When Judas, who had betrayed him, saw that Jesus was condemned, he was seized with remorse and returned the thirty pieces of silver to the chief priests and the elders. "I have sinned," he said, "for I have betrayed innocent blood." "What is that to us?" they replied. "That's your responsibility." So Judas threw the money into the temple and left. Then he went away and hanged himself.

What a tragic business all this is! Judas, how did you come to such a pass? He was among the chosen Twelve. He had followed Jesus for the better part of three years. He had seen the miracles and heard the beautiful message of the gospel so many times. And, yes, he believed it. But with all that, Judas—like all the rest of us!—had flaws in his character. His was a temptation to greed that passed into secret theft from the small treasury of the apostolic band. The temptation to steal snuck up on him. He doubtless resisted it for a time. But then he toyed with it. Then he yielded to it—*oh, just this once; I won't do it again; I'll repent and repay when things are a little better with me.* We know the story, do we not? Ours may not be Judas' fatal flaw; but we all have one. How many times have we acted on our fatal flaw as Judas did on his? How many of us have lived it, lived it more than once? Most of us? In one way or another, all of us?

How long did it take Judas to get to this point that he went in the dark of night to sell out his Savior? Was it after the third time that he stole something? Was it after the tenth, the twentieth? How often did he repent—but not return what he had stolen? How often did he toss sleepless in the night in guilt and shame over what he had done, only to return and do it yet again?

Now the damage is done. The Savior had to be betrayed as it was prophesied of him. But the one who betrayed him was not predestined to do the dread deed. That was Judas' choice and his responsibility alone. Perhaps Judas thought that Jesus would somehow rescue himself, in spite of what Jesus had said about his coming suffering and death.

But now look at the sorry state of things once Judas realizes that Jesus will not save himself. He is seized with remorse. His conscience with the devil laughing at him drives him back to the temple in a desperate and futile attempt to undo the damage he has done. Notice the differences between Judas and Peter at this juncture. Peter too was seized with remorse. But Peter made no attempt to undo the damage he had done. Judas at least wanted to do that much. But Judas' efforts are too little, too late.

No better than Judas are the chief priests and elders who were supposed to be the pastors of God's people. Fine pastors, these! They are determined to be rid of their true pastor. And as for consoling a despairing soul who helped them succeed in their murderous plot, well, nothing could have been further from their minds. Judas has a conscience wracked with despair. These men have no conscience at all.

Still, however, there was hope for Judas. Jesus had called him "friend" with that special word that held in it the underlying offer of pardon. Did Judas miss that? Was his heart so cold that in that moment, it could not hear Jesus' offer of grace? Or having heard it, did his conscience block out its significance so that he could only conclude, "Friend? Me? No, that is just not possible. It is out of the question. My sin is too great, my guilt beyond measure, my possibility of redemption forever lost."

"Then he went away and hanged himself." That short sentence spells out the bottom line of Judas' remorse. While, unlike Peter, he tried to undo the damage he had done, his remorse was nevertheless different from Peter's. Peter's grief did not end in a despair that would reject the Savior's grace and work for his salvation. Judas' remorse was not one that led to a yearning for forgiveness, but rather a rejection of it. Judas properly looked at himself in despair, but then he refused to look outside of himself to the only source of pardon and peace. He made Lent all about himself instead of all about Jesus and what Jesus had come to do, even for him. And so in despair he lost grace by his own choice. In despair, a pain that he could not endure, he went to a pain far worse and a torment that will never end.

As horrible as this account in the Lenten history is, it is still a very useful one for us. Faith in the Savior's work for our redemption is always a miracle worked by the gospel, a pure gift from God without either our merit or our cooperation. But it is not an irresistible work of the gospel. God has left to us the ability to turn our backs on his incomparable love in Christ and to reject the gift so precious that flowed from his holy cross and passion. That such a rejection is beyond all reason and wicked beyond all conceivable wickedness has not prevented Judas and countless others from committing this monstrous crime of rejecting the forgiveness so dearly won.

We do well to ponder how Judas, once a faithful follower, ended up as he did. We do well to consider that the plunge into the crime of betrayal and then the ultimate crime of rejecting the Savior's work did not happen overnight. He didn't just get up on Thursday morning of Holy Week and decide to cast aside the gospel as he had already cast aside the law. No, it all took time. It took repeated embraces of his fatal flaw of greed. It took who knows how many thefts from the treasury that did not end in repentance. It took how much toying with the idea that perhaps his sin wasn't really all that bad and that, in any case, he would eventually repent. The day came when he had so completely clutched his sins to his bosom and so tightly wrapped his heart in guilt that he would not—no never—repent.

Could it be held before us with greater clarity or emphasis than it is here? Sin has its consequences. Sometimes in the case of open sins committed before the world, the consequences are likewise open, painful, and obvious to all. But sometimes the sin in secret has no apparent outward consequences; its consequence may lie hidden deep in the anguish of the soul wracked by guilt. In some, those consequences are far worse than an outward punishment would have been. Peter's sin ground him down to the ground in tears of guilt and anguish. It may well be that for the rest of his life, that guilt stung him and pierced his heart, even after the same heart had embraced again Jesus' forgiving grace. Judas' sin ground him down all the way to hell; an eternity of sorrow will never get him out of there. For us the warning is clear: Toy with your own tragic character flaws at your peril. Whether it be Peter's overconfidence in himself that led him to ignore Jesus' word and warning or secret greed or vice as in Judas that finally ended in faith-and-forgiveness-rejecting despair—take heed! Lent isn't all about us and how much we can get away with because of the great love of Jesus and all that he did to accomplish our salvation; that's a sure road ending in the despair of Judas. It's all about Jesus who looks at us in his suffering and calls us "friend," inviting us to the tears of Peter that long again for the Savior's word of pardon. Indeed, if Lent kept Peter's and our eyes focused on Jesus, we wouldn't have fallen into the temptations that brought Peter so much misery. And as well, if our eyes were focused on Jesus, we likewise would not fall prey to the faith-killing despair of Judas. Oh, that Lent and life might be for us all about Jesus, just as for Jesus, Lent was all about us!

> O dearest Savior, hold ever before me that so expensive love and grace which brought you to the cross for my sake. Oh, preserve me from the arrogance of Peter and from the hard heart of Judas. Look on me with pity and call me with the gospel that shows me your friendship and your eagerness to forgive me. Yes, make my Lent and my life all about you, as you made your Lent, your life, your bitter sufferings and death all about me. Amen.

The Seven Words of Christ From the Cross

Let us go then to the altar of the cross. Let us watch with him there. Stand at a respectful distance, not too close as if to help him. He does not want your help. He wants to do it all and all alone. For only if he does it all will our rescue, our ransom, and our salvation be sure and secure. As we watch, the watchword will be as it always is: *listen!* For in listening he will give us what he earned there for us.

Look, my soul, and consider it well! See here the greatness of your need. See here the greatness of his love!

"Father, forgive them, for they know not what they do." (Luke 23:34 ESV)

What a commentary on the Eighth Commandment! Luther tells us in his explanation to the Eighth Commandment that we should construe the actions of others in the best possible way. But this? How can it be that you pray for them with words such as these: "They know not what they do"? Who do you mean by "they"? Do you mean the chief priests and the other members of the Sanhedrin who have brought you to this end? They knew that their accusations against you were lies prompted by self-righteousness, greed, and envy. They even knowingly put up false witnesses to accuse you. They knew. Or do you mean Pilate, who ordered your crucifixion? He knew. He said it repeatedly that you were innocent, even washed his hands to try to rid himself of guilt for this dread deed. He knew. Do you mean the soldiers? They heard the false accusations of the Jews. They heard and saw the trial before Pilate. They too knew you were innocent. Do you mean the people who came along the way of sorrows and the women who wept? They all knew. They all did nothing. Do you mean your relatives, do you mean the disciples, do you mean the thousands you fed in the wilderness, the lame you caused to walk, the dead you raised, the blind and the deaf to whom you gave sight and hearing? They all knew. They all said nothing. They all did nothing.

Or—oh, dread thought!—do you mean . . . me? After all, it is a recurring theme all through Lent, in sermons and readings and hymns, that it is my sin that brought you to this shame and pain. And I cannot deny it or hide it: I knew! I knew your Word and ignored it. I knew that the law requires me to love God above all things, but I preferred so often his gifts over him. For them I had time always, love in abundance, and trust that they would give my life purpose and meaning. I knew that that was idolatry. At the very least, I had no excuse for it if I did not know it. You said that I shouldn't lie or cheat or think evil of my neighbor. You said that I should serve them out of love for you and always count myself as last in preferring their good to my own. You said that I shouldn't complain about my lot in life, my times of loss of wealth or health or honor or even family and friends. But I looked at you in anger when you took back what I didn't deserve in the first place. I knew.

Like a worm on a hook, I squirm when I hear you pray for those who bring you to this pain. For I stand beside them all as one who knew.

But still you pray! You pray for them! You pray for me! What is it, then, that they did not know that I, in every moment when I have turned away from you, did not know? What is it? It is just this: The real cost, the real penalty for what I took so lightly is what you feel and endure in these dread hours. I did not know that I deserved the spitting, the beating, the crown of thorns, the nails. I did not know that those were just the outward tortures of the devil and the damned in hell that lasts forever. I did not know how horrible sin really is in its dread consequences under the eternal wrath of God. Only you know that. You go to taste the wrath of God against my sin. You go to bear the penalty of my guilt. You know! Only you know the depths of the Father's wrath against my sin. Only you know what I have deserved. And you know not from afar. You know it because even as this dread drama begins, you enter into that terror.

Had I known, would I have turned away from my sin to God in love? Or would I rather have melted away in the heat of the flames and dissolve in the horror of that dread abyss of hell. But you spared me all of that. And now you pray: Father, forgive!

Yes, and still you pray thus. Still at the right hand of your Father, you hold before him this your dread cross and passion. Still with your perfect merit in your wounded hands and feet, you enter into the Holy of Holies in heaven with your blood to cover me and all my sins. And still your Father hears your prayer for me—and because of it, he forgives.

I'll never get over it, dearest Jesus. You begin these dread hours thinking even of me, praying even for me. Let me watch with you now. Let me watch with eyes of wonder, with mouth wide open, with gasps of amazement. So great is my need. So much greater is your love.

"Woman, here is your son." [And to John:]
"Here is your mother." (John 19:26,27)

What an astonishing thing! The pain in his body will shortly reach its peak, if it has not already. His humiliation from the mouths of the really important people who came to his execution to ridicule him is in full sway. The grief caused by most of his relatives and disciples who have abandoned him is beyond calculation. And most horrible of all: Very soon he will make the dread cry that speaks of his entrance into the torments of hell itself as he calls out to God, his Father, who has abandoned him; and he knows that it is coming, is immanent, and is beyond all the torment that he had already endured. But now, in the midst of all this horror, he does this. He thinks of his mother. He thinks of his friend.

He has no earthly wealth to bequeath to his mother. He has no property to give her. He has no earthly way of providing for her welfare. But couldn't her other relatives have done that? She had others, and they were not all poverty stricken. Isn't it their turn now? And as for his friend, the apostle

John, well, what can we say? At least he showed up! What reward will there be for at least that, even though the night before he had been among those who forsook Jesus and fled? The grief of John, who always in his gospel is identified as the disciple whom Jesus loved, must have been great indeed. How could it be otherwise, given his own guilt mixed in with the love he had for his suffering friend? But what can Jesus do now to assuage John's grief and dry his tears? Indeed, given the greatness of his own suffering, how can Jesus really even think about the sorrow of his friend and the needs of his mother?

But did you notice it in the gospel accounts of Jesus' dealings with those who suffer? He never shunned them. Indeed, he did not merely deal with their obvious need but attended to needs they never expressed, down to the smallest detail. He touched the leper who had been deprived of human touch for as long as he had his leprosy. He called the woman who was treated as an outcast because she had a blood disease "Daughter!" And after he raised Jairus' daughter, he told her parents to give her something to eat—they certainly could have figured that out for themselves. But Jesus always paid attention. He was never in a hurry to get rid of anybody. He always took care of those in need down to the last detail, even beyond what they either asked or expected or had thought of themselves.

Now he provides, in the midst of his agony, for his mother and his friend. Oh, how beyond kind! How more than loving to both of them, that he should give each into the care of the other. The gospel tells us that John took Mary into his own care from that moment on. And in the honor of caring for Jesus' mother, John has the consolation that he served Jesus in a way befitting the love each had for the other. How grateful John and Mary must have been for this gift as the years went on. How they too must have marveled that Jesus so thought of them in this dread moment of his own profound loss on the cross. We might have advised him to deal with this matter before the hour of his own great anguish. But had he followed our advice, neither Mary nor John would have grasped the greatness of his gift. And we, for our part, would have missed this further sublime, incomparable, inconceivable proof of the extent of his loving concern for them.

Now we stand at the foot of that cross. In his agony did he have time to think of me too? In his hour of torment did my needs, the ones I recognize and the ones I don't, rest on his heart? In the impending moment of his tortured cry as he suffers all the torments of hell compressed into these hours on the cross, did he even then remember me?

Oh, yes, a thousand times yes! Far more deeply than I have ever thought of him, he thought of me. He thought of me in eternity when he planned to come to save sinners. He thought of me at the hour of his incarnation when he began the work of my salvation promised already in the Garden of

Eden at the time of my first parents' fall. And now, especially in this hour, he does not sneer at my weakness. He does not curse me for my failures. He does not cast me off because of my sin. As he said earlier in the week, it was for this that he came—namely, to glorify his Father by redeeming me. Not for a nameless, faceless blob of humanity did he so suffer and die, but for people—for sinners, for the lost and condemned—one at a time with each engraved on his mind and heart.

The thought of it is too much for me. I sink at his feet and look at myself with disgust for my weakness of faith and my boldness to sin. But then I hear his words to his mother and to his friend. And I remember what he said—that those who hear his Word and keep it are his mother, his brother, his sister (Mark 3:34). And his Word does its work; it takes me out of myself to look at Jesus, only Jesus. Wordless—at least for now—in wonder and awe, in gratitude too great at the moment for expression, I want just to watch, to wait, to listen, and to receive from him in his hour of sacrifice grace and mercy heaped on grace and mercy.

"I tell you the truth, today you will be with me in paradise." (Luke 23:43 NIV 1984)

Consider, O my soul! How great the power of the gospel, and how vast the love of Jesus. Here he hangs, stripped naked and impotent. The state has condemned him to death. The church has cursed him. His disciples, if they are even there, stand in despair at a distance; only John is nearby supporting the desolate mother. Even the wretched thieves hanging beside him mock him. Was ever a man more helpless, more useless than Jesus in this hour?

But see what happens! One of those two miserable convicts calls out in his last hour, calls out even after he himself had earlier mocked the impotent Christ: *"Jesus, remember me when you come into your kingdom"* (Luke 23:42). Can it be? How can it be? On this dread day, only one looks to the cross for rescue! And that one does it when there is not a shred of evidence left to see that Jesus could help anyone. Had not his tormentors cried out rightly: *If you are the Son of God, come down from the cross. Others he helped; himself he cannot help.* And had not both criminals agreed and joined the cry: *If you are the Son of God, help yourself—and at least as important—help us!* But now, when no help was forthcoming—not from God, not from men, not from any hidden power in Jesus himself—now in this moment of Jesus' apparent helplessness, this wretched creature calls out for rescue in the hour of death. He has no small request to make. What he wants is everything! He wants entrance into the kingdom of heaven. And he wants it from one who at that very moment is himself suffering the torments of the damned.

Oh, wondrous gospel! Such power has God given it that even at this moment, it can overcome misspent years. Even at this moment it can triumph over all the evidence of its own apparent weakness in the Christ who suffers. Even in this moment it can create faith, certain trust that Jesus is indeed the Son of God; even in this moment it can convince at least one that Jesus is the Savior to whom alone belongs life and life eternal and in whose power and gift alone is the kingdom of heaven! Dark is the hour and black as night. And still the gospel message shines in the saving Word. Did the thief perhaps hear Jesus' first cry from his cross, the prayer of forgiveness for his tormenters? Hearing it, was that what pierced through the iron gate of unbelief that had earlier blocked his heart? How little we trust that saving Word of the gospel and think it as weak as its heart and core appears on the cross. How ready we are to despair of preaching it in all its simplicity for fear that no one will listen to such a seemingly foolish Word. How tempted we are to gussy it up with our own cleverness so foolish and our own compromises so wicked in order to make it more palatable to those who might mock it. But there it is—all shabby and weak, all bruised and bloodied. And it works! In the anguish of ultimate need, pounding on the door of hell and at the gates of death, the thief cries out—in faith!

O wondrous love of Jesus! He does not say to the thief, "Where have you been all your life? Where have you been these last hours when you joined in mockery? If I am the Son of God, you can be sure that in this last hour you receive in your anguish just a small down payment of what awaits you when death and the devil finally take you to where you richly deserve to go!" No, there is not a bit of that. Instead, Jesus gives him everything. Not just a remembrance and the possibility that he will intercede for him. Not just the small comfort that perhaps in his kingdom Jesus will find a way to lighten this wretched man's suffering in hell. No, more than the man dared ask, Jesus promises him heaven!

And so ponder it, O my soul, on this most holy day of days, in the presence of the one who alone is holy. Will you still doubt the power of the gospel to save even you? Will you, in the anguish of your own conscience and guilt, despair of the love of Jesus even for you? Here is the answer of the suffering Savior to whom you call this day, *Jesus, remember me, me too, even me, when you come into your kingdom.* Into his kingdom he has come. And his words to the dying thief so guilty and so wretched spring to life in my own anguished soul. That one, he remembered. And so he has not forgotten me. On the cross he thought of that totally undeserving thief and willingly died for him. On the cross my sins too he bore. My name too was engraved on his heart. For me he entered into his kingdom that I might enter it too!

Who, then, will say that the gospel cannot create and preserve faith even in the hour of death? No, there is none into whose heart the gospel cannot break. Then, O my soul, look from your guilt and shame so great. Look up to him who hangs on the cross. As great as your need, still greater is his love. As much as you remember of your worst misdeeds, so much better he remembers them all—and then dies to cover them and you in his blood. As much as the devil and hell have every right to claim you, so much more has his cross the merit to redeem you and his Word the power to save you.

Yes, ponder it, O my soul! Ponder it well! Ponder it with tears overflowing as you look inside yourself. Ponder it with tears of joy exultant as you look to him who dries them all with his promise of paradise won here this day.

"My God, my God, why have you forsaken me?" (Mark 15:34)

And now, there it is! It is the most anguished cry possible. It is the most horrible suffering—suffering beyond imagination. Note it well!

Jesus calls out, saying, "*My* God." He doesn't address him as Father this time as he had before, and will again later. For now the loving bond has been shattered. But still God remains God—his God to whom he owes perfect love and uncomplaining obedience. Any curse at his own treatment by God, any complaint that it just isn't fair would be rebellion, would be sin.

And he will not rebel. He will not complain. Instead, he cries out the first verse of Psalm 22, to let us know just exactly what is happening here. He is fulfilling the Scriptures. But there is nothing mechanical about that. Oh, no, not که. Instead, we hear in these words from the cross the most profound mystery mingled with the most horrible suffering. It is a mystery how God can abandon God when the two persons of the Trinity are one in essence. It is a mystery altogether beyond and above us how both Father and Son could agree to and will this horror of the Son being forsaken by the Father. The Father loved the Son of his own essence. The Son loved the Father and did so in his human nature every moment consciously, yes, consciously; and he obeyed him and submitted perfectly to God's law—did so lovingly, eagerly, most happily. Not a thought, not a word, not a deed ever had the slightest fault or flaw.

But now, there it is: He is abandoned by the God who had loved him and whom he had loved and served perfectly. He is, in fact, suffering the torments of hell and suffering them in a worse way than anyone will ever suffer them. To be abandoned by God, to lose all of his mercy and kindness—that is the essence of hell. And that is horrible indeed. But at least those in hell have to admit that they deserve every bit of it. Not so for Jesus. He deserves not one shred of it. More than that, those in hell suffer only for their own sins and unbelief. But Jesus in this anguish suffers not just innocently; he suffers for the sins of the whole world—all of it is pressed on him, and he cries out in the agony of that dread punishment from *my God!* He is, as he says in the psalm, like a worm on a hook, crushed on the outside and ripped apart within.

We will never exhaust the absolute nature of his suffering in this anguished cry. For the moment, however, we have one more thing to notice. His cry is in the form of a question. Why a question? Doesn't he know why he suffers thus? Of course he knows; he had expressed the reason for it in all the prophecies of the Old Testament and in all that he had said about his coming passion during the three years of his earthly ministry. As with so many of the questions that God asks, beginning with the questions to Adam and Eve in the garden, God is not looking for information. And so Jesus here is waiting not for an answer from God. He is waiting for an answer from you, from me.

What, then, will we answer him in this hour so dreadful, so full of agony and mystery? The answer can only be this: I know, Lord Jesus, I know why you have been abandoned. It is because your Father loves me and does not want me to perish forever in hell as I deserve. I know, Lord Jesus, I know why you have been abandoned. It is because you loved me before the foundation of the world, and you love me still in this dread hour as you endure the torments of hell itself. I know, Lord Jesus, I know why you have been abandoned. It is because the Holy Spirit too loves me, even me, and he has planned to proclaim that love in the Word and sacraments in such a powerful way that I will believe it. I know, Lord Jesus, I know why you have been abandoned. It is so that the Holy Trinity might love me until death and beyond. It is so that the debt I owe and which I in a thousand hells could never pay would be paid for in full. It is so that the filth of all my sins would be washed in the blood of this sacrificial Lamb who has come to take away the sin of the world.

Even with the little that I can understand of the terror of this cry from the cross, I might be tempted to blurt out, *No, no, Lord Jesus! Don't do it! Come down from the cross. You merit it not; I merit it all.* But no, I won't blurt that out. Rather, I put my hand over my mouth and whisper (for who would dare to say such a thing out loud?!): Yes, Lord Jesus! Suffer thus! Suffer the torments of the damned. Suffer it all. Suffer it for me so that I will not have to. And I, for my part, will eagerly and thankfully and, yes, joyfully receive all the benefit. I claim no merit. I worship and adore you for this: you willed and wanted to suffer for me and are pleased when the message of the cross brings me to trust in your perfect, all-sufficient, and saving merit. Here indeed is miracle upon miracle, wonder multiplied by wonder, amazement that knows no bounds: God is abandoned by God. God wills it for God and does it all for me, and because of the power of his Word,

I believe it; I receive it. I trust it all in accord with his saving purpose, his redeeming love for me, his rule over time and tide that I might have his promise now and eternally.

"I am thirsty." (John 19:28)

Now yet another wonder! In the catechism we confess on the basis of the Word of God that "Jesus Christ [is] true God, begotten of the Father from eternity and also true man, born of the virgin Mary." All through the events of his passion and, most wondrously of all, in his crucifixion we have seen that he is indeed true God. For who but true God could pray as he did for his tormentors as he is lifted up on the cross? Who but true God could be so forgetful of self, of his own anguish and pain, to think of his mother and his friend and then to provide for them by giving each into the care of the other? Who but true God could turn and look at a miserable, contemptible criminal worthy of death, a criminal who only moments before had joined his fellow malefactor in mocking the Son of God—I say, who but true God could turn to such a one and promise him paradise before that very day ended? And yes, what is more, who but true God could by his own suffering pay for all the crimes that wretch had committed in his wasted life and thus earn forgiveness and life eternal for him? And then there is that awe-filled cry from the depths of hell: the cry of the damned, of the forsaken not just by men but by God. Who would not burn up and turn to ash in such a moment? Only the Son of God could in the midst of life endure such a death of abandonment by God on high!

But now this: "I am thirsty"! How can we fathom that? The Son of God is thirsty? Yes, the Son of God who is Mary's son, the Son of God who has taken to himself a complete human nature, human flesh and blood, a human soul—he is thirsty. It is the Son of God who, from the moment of his conception to this moment on the cross, has now humbled himself so completely that he is thirsty. He has hung there exposed to the elements for hours. God does not come to his aid. Nor does nature rush to relieve his body of human need. The angels who sang at his birth and who served him in the wilderness and in Gethsemane are nowhere to be seen. For hours before this moment he had been subjected to beating and to bleeding. Parched and exhausted, he says that he is thirsty. How could it be otherwise?

But tarry a bit in the presence of his implied prayer to his tormentors for something at least to wet his tongue and moisten his bleeding lips. Over all that Jesus said and did during his lifetime, in all that he said and did to this very moment on the cross, there is written the bold superscription: *Pro nobis, pro me! For us, for me.* Is this his human thirst also for me? Is this humiliation that he has to ask his executioners for something to relieve his thirst, is this too *for us, for me?* Yes, even this is evidence of his love and grace for us and for our salvation. For the gospels tell us that as soon as he had received just the smallest sip of vinegar, he cried out *with a loud voice* the last two words from the cross that we have yet to hear. They are words so important, so vital, and so saving that he does not want to whisper them. He wants us all to hear them. He wants the whole world to hear them. He wants them to echo down through the ages and resound in the halls of heaven itself. Exhausted as he is, as full of pain and woe incomparable and impossible for us to imagine, he thinks of us and wants each of us to know what it all means for us, for time and for eternity.

But before we consider those last two words that he can cry out with a loud voice, we consider still this in his "I am thirsty": Jesus in his humiliation as a man knew what it was like to be in need. He knew what it was like to have to depend on someone else to give him even the least little drop of moisture—vinegar at that, not water. So the holy writer tells us that we do not have a high priest in Jesus who cannot be touched by our needs and our weaknesses; for he was touched by them all (Hebrews 4:15).

Oh, what sweet comfort we draw from the agony of his thirst! Ah, Lord Jesus, you asked for human help in your agony, asked it even of your tormenters! How humiliating! Ah, Lord Jesus, you received not wine or water but vinegar in your agony. And you did it for me, even for me, so that I might hear your final cries from the cross. You did it for me, even for me, so that I might know that you understand all my needs, even the simplest but most necessary of them: the need for more than a drop of water and earthly refreshment. Yes, and for me you purchased it all by this your dying thirst. For apart from your sacrifice how could I ever pray with confidence the petition you have taught me to pray: "Give us this day our daily bread"? But now I do pray it. And you answer it, but not as you were answered; you answer by giving in abundance all and more than I need for this body and life. For whether I have a lot or a little, it is more, so much more, than those drops of vinegar you received in this your hour of greatest need. Oh, dearest Jesus, by all that you have purchased for my earthly good, grant me this: Grant that I use it ever more and more to satisfy your need for hands and feet, for minds and mouths to show with words and deeds your redeeming love to those around me—at home, at work, in church, and in the world.

"It is finished." (John 19:30)

What, then, are those words that he was so anxious for us to hear that he was willing to humiliate himself with the call to his tormenters for something to drink? This word, the one before his last, is a word that causes us again to stop, to put our hands over our mouths, to fall backward in wonder and in awe. *It is finished!* He cries out these words, we are told, with a loud voice. And by so doing, his divine and human nature combine to tell us all that we need to know. He can speak now, and with a loud voice, since his tongue and his lips have been moistened by the vinegar given to him from a sponge extended to his mouth by his tormenters. But what he cries out from his pain-wracked human body is the verdict of the Son of God most holy.

For *it is finished!* And just what is it that is finished? His life here on earth, to be sure, but that isn't really what he wants us to hear in these words. Indeed, that he cries out with a loud voice already tells us that he is not merely referring to his life; that wouldn't be necessary—it's obvious. But more than that, were he simply speaking as Mary's son, even with a drop of moisture for his tongue and his lips, he would not have been able to cry with a *loud* voice.

No, this "It is finished" is the verdict of the Son of God and Mary's son—true God and true man—over all of his work, over the work of our redemption. For the gospels tell us that thus he cried in connection with his thirst that the Scriptures might all be fulfilled. So here it is: The promise is finished and fulfilled, the promise of the seed of the woman given in the Garden of Eden at the damnable fall of our first parents. The promise of Isaiah 53 of the One who would bear our sins and heal us by his stripes is finished and fulfilled. The promise of David in Psalm 22 that after suffering the torments of the damned, David's son and David's Lord would proclaim his righteousness; yes, and in its proclamation he would promise to give his righteousness to generations yet unborn—that promise is finished and fulfilled. All the promises that God made in his Word, the promise of the sacrificial lamb at Passover and of the sacrifices on the Day of Atonement— they are all finished, they are all fulfilled in this triumphant and loud cry from the cross: "It is finished"!

Will you not weep at the word, weep in anguish over your sins that caused all this misery? Who cannot help but hide his face in his hands at the sound of them? See how horrible your sin and how great the price demanded by the law. Will you not weep still more and at the same time in thanksgiving for the result of this unequaled woe? Behold how great is the love of the Father that he sent his Son to suffer the penalty of our guilt fully, perfectly, and completely! Behold how beyond measure is the love of the Son that he willingly came and endured it all for me, even for me, and for you, even for you! Behold the love so above all understanding that he sent and sends still the Holy Spirit in Word and sacraments so that—are you ready for it?—we actually believe this message so beyond human reason, so utterly past human love or sentiment.

It is finished! My penalty hanging over me is paid for in full. *It is finished!* The devil's chains on me are shattered and hell's claim to my guilty body and soul is cancelled. *It is finished!* All the righteous wrath of God is gone! *It is finished!* The fear of his anger when I suffer in this life and the fear of death as I approach the next life, all of it is done for. *It is finished!* The dread thought that I must do something to earn God's favor and the dread that comes from the knowledge that nothing in me can undo what I have done, all that is gone. For *it is finished!* Jesus, and Jesus alone—the Son of God and Mary's son—has done it all, fulfilled it all, finished it all! For God—Father, Son, and Holy Spirit—this solemn declaration from the throne and altar of the cross is all about me! For me this guarantee of salvation from God on high is all about Jesus!

Ah, Lord Jesus, let my ears ever be open to your anguished and triumphant cry! As I smite upon my breast in anguished confession of my sins that brought you to this place, at the same time with deep thanksgiving I hear it: these words that spell life and salvation for me in time and for eternity. Now forgiveness is won. Now the heart of God is assuredly open to my cries for pardon. Now heaven is unlocked as hell's gates are slammed shut for all who trust in you and in the Word of your all-sufficient and saving fulfillment of the Scriptures. The message is never old; for there is not a day, not an hour, not a moment when I do not need your finished work for me, even for me. Therefore, give me still this grace that I may ever hear these words and cry out with the church of every generation: Thee we adore, O Savior, because by your holy cross and passion you have redeemed the world—and therefore have redeemed me, even me.

"Father, into your hands I commit my spirit." (Luke 23:46)

Now in the last word before he dies, consider in wonder and awe the peace in his dying words. There is no angry cry, such as might have come from our lips had we suffered as he did, so innocently and so terribly. There is no anger, no rage against God and man at the injustice of it all. There is no whining of complaint, no, "It's too much; I can't stand it anymore!" There is no, "These wretches are not worth half my pain, not a one of them; my coming has all been a mistake. Send now the angels of death to visit them with what they deserve, instead of dumping it all on me! Open wide the gates of hell and pour them all into it once and for all!" No, none of that, not a bit of it!

Instead, Jesus points us back again to the Scriptures, something he always did and does still. For his dying word is from Psalm 31. He calls in peace to God and addresses him again as "Father." It was his Father who sent him; and the Father sent his Son for us in love so ardent that he would spare his Son no agony, no torment, to accomplish our redemption. He sent him as well with the loving goal of giving his Son the honor only he could win and that only by the cross, the honor of being the Savior of the world (Philippians 2:9-11). And now quoting from the psalm of God's own inspiration, Jesus dies not in defeat but in triumph. For *it is finished!* He has accomplished all that his Father sent him to do. He has gained for us salvation and for himself the honor of being alone the one who could save us and did. Just think of it: When we look for honors, we do it for our own benefit, but Jesus gives up all comfort and all that he deserved in order to win honor—every benefit—for us. Thus he has fulfilled the promise made in Genesis 3 and the promise made at his holy and sinless incarnation: "You are to give him the name Jesus, because he will save his people from their sins" (Matthew 1:21).

So most gladly he can commit his soul into the hands of his loving Father—he who is the Son of God and Mary's son, true God and true man. He has not let his Father down. He can return to him not a failure, not ashamed, but in triumph. Oh, how the angels must have sung for joy! Oh, how the Holy Trinity must have exalted in this unique and all-important work now successfully completed, as promised, as planned. In peace he prays. In peace at the moment of his choosing, when all was accomplished, he dies. And his death is not a reason for mourning, but for rejoicing, for thanksgiving.

Because he dies in peace, his dying prayer can become our own at the end of this day and at the end of all our days. We too can pray the psalm with our Savior: "Father, into your hands I commit my spirit." That's why he came—to put his own prayer into our hearts and souls, to pray as we fall asleep tonight and as we fall asleep in the hour of death. What a relief! Our suffering he has suffered. Our sin he bore. Our hell he endured. Our death he died. And because of it, God is now my Father who will welcome me into paradise as he welcomed the dying thief—yes, as he welcomed his only begotten Son, now our Savior. Our breath at the end of day is not one of fear. Our last breath at the end of days is like his, one of rejoicing and thanksgiving, as we go to be with him and his Father into the eternal blessedness so dearly won by his cross.

So we end this day so filled with anguish for our souls, so filled with peace at the same time. So we end this most holy day of days with a sigh and with the quiet and confident prayer:

> O good Jesus, hear me;
> Within your wounds hide me;
> Suffer me not to be separated from you;
> In the hour of my death call me,
> And bid me come to you,
> That with your saints I may praise you for all eternity. Amen.

Holy Saturday

John 19:38,39 – Later, Joseph of Arimathea asked Pilate for the body of Jesus. Now Joseph was a disciple of Jesus, but secretly because he feared the Jewish leaders. With Pilate's permission, he came and took the body away. He was accompanied by Nicodemus, the man who earlier had visited Jesus at night.

Here is another one of those special comforts for us lying just beneath the surface of all the great events that occupy us as we prepare for the great event of early tomorrow morning.

Consider who these two men are that attend Jesus' funeral and even conduct as much of it as they could. There is Joseph of Arimathea. He was rich and obviously well connected politically or he would not have been able so easily to procure the body of Jesus from Pilate. Nicodemus too was a man of some wealth and position. He was a member of the very council that had condemned Jesus to death, as was Joseph.

But it is not their wealth and power for which they are most easily remembered. It is for two things. The first: They were weak before Jesus' death. Though members of the Sanhedrin, we know only that they did not consent in the verdict that condemned Jesus. But couldn't they have done more to defend Jesus, at least before Pilate? So that's one thing we know: they were weak, and apparently ineffective.

The other thing that we know? They were bold confessors! Isn't it interesting? The disciples, who the night before were so strong that they said they were ready to die with Jesus, do not even attend his funeral! They are in hiding—as fearful as Joseph and Nicodemus had been when the disciples were making their proud boasts of faithfulness unto death. What an odd thing! The moment of truth came for Joseph and Nicodemus after they could no longer do Jesus any good at all—good they might have done the night before and early in the morning during the trials before the Jewish and Roman courts. But now, when all others are in fear, in hiding, and in despair, these two come forward, really forward. Gone is their fear of the Jews. Gone is any timidity before the Roman governor and King Herod. The only ones who are their equals in courage are the women who stayed at the cross and now observed Jesus' funeral. The women in a short while will be richly blessed for this their courage and faithfulness—they will be the first to hear the Easter gospel. One of them will be the first to see Jesus and hear him. They will be the first after the angel at the tomb to share the gospel message. But of these two, Joseph and Nicodemus—we hear nothing more of them.

We may well wonder what these two men were thinking when they became bold confessors at Jesus' funeral. We may wonder what the content of their faith was as they buried Jesus. How much of what happened on the cross for their salvation did they understand? How much of Jesus' promise to rise again flickers in their hearts in the dark of the approaching night? However weak and confused their hearts and minds were, nevertheless they retained still a deep devotion to Jesus that they just had to express in their service to him in his burial. Their love was no doubt mixed with profound grief; it had perhaps just a glimmer of hope mingled with despair or something close to it. But still there it was: love and devotion that had been kindled by the words and deeds of the Savior. There it was: love and devotion that the cross and death could not kill. There it was: love and devotion that came out into the open at the most unexpected and inopportune time. There it was: love and devotion that human reason and the hatred shown by both their friends on the Jewish court and acquaintances at Pilate's court could not extinguish.

How comforting to know that Jesus used these men who earlier had been such weak cowards at such a moment. For I know how weak and how cowardly I have been. Still Jesus has not cast me off. Still Jesus finds uses even for me and perhaps will in some future time grant me the grace to be a more bold confessor than I am today. For it is still true that sometimes the strong fail and unexpectedly give way to the weak who take their place. After all, St. Paul warns us that the one who thinks he is standing strong should be careful, lest in his self-confidence he fall the way the self-confident disciples fell (1 Corinthians 10:12). And he reminds us as well that God shows his strength not in our strength but often in our weakness (2 Corinthians 12:9; 1 Corinthians 1:26-30).

But perhaps at least as important in the account of these two men and with them the timid women observing from a distance at the funeral is this: How many times and how easily we dismiss from our minds this little child, this timid lady, this seemingly uninterested (even dozing) man, as people so weak in faith as to be useless in the service of the Savior—as though we could read what Jesus has done and yet will do in their hearts by his Word and sacraments! Yet often those so lightly dismissed as weak and unimportant come forward and, so to speak, "save the day," while the seemingly most blessed and the strongest prove to be a disappointment.

We know so little of what God accomplishes in our own hearts by his Word. His message of forgiveness and salvation so often lies hidden deep within, like the yeast or the seed in his parables. We know even less of how that Word sprouts and grows in the hearts of those next to us, even those we think we really know well.

So then, as we await the joyous message of the angels tomorrow morning, we may do well to ponder in wonder and in awe how the message of Jesus' cross and resurrection works hidden in hearts and minds, in souls and lives.

In which people does it work and how much? I don't know. But still in some, sometimes in many. But still even in me. Just as for Joseph and Nicodemus, the moments perhaps have come and still will come in the future when the message of Jesus' love and grace wins victories over my fear, my timidity. May it be that I too make a bold confession, even if the strong are hiding out. Until then, O Jesus, speak to me still and assure me that even for me you have died and risen—risen indeed—so that with heart and soul and then more and more with mouth and life, I may call out, *"Credo!* I believe!"

> *Ruht wohl, Ruht wohl,* Rest well, Rest well,
> *Ihr heiligen Gebeine* Thou sacred limbs.
> *Und bringt mich auch zur Ruh!* And bring me also to rest!
> *Amen.* Amen.
> (J. S. Bach, *St. John's Passion*)

Romans 6:1-4 – What shall we say, then? Shall we go on sinning so that grace may increase? By no means! We are those who have died to sin; how can we live in it any longer? Or don't you know that all of us who were baptized into Christ Jesus were baptized into his death? We were therefore buried with him through baptism into death in order that, just as Christ was raised from the dead through the glory of the Father, we too may live a new life.

It's time to take a deep breath. The ghastly drama is finished. He has died. His tormenters have gone home. The funeral so poorly attended is over. Nicodemus and Joseph of Arimathea have gone home, no doubt both grief-ridden and confused. The women are left to weep and the disciples to hide out.

And now we wait. On the night of preparation for the glad news of tomorrow morning, what should occupy our minds? Our baptism! That's what makes this night so different for us than it was for Nicodemus and Joseph, for the weeping women, and for the hiding disciples.

To be sure, we, like them, have enough things in life to be confused about. We often have been too much like Nicodemus and Joseph, timid when it counted and bold when it didn't make any difference. We have been like the women and wept for the wrong reasons. We know what it is to hide out like the disciples to avoid ridicule for defending the truth of God's Word, worried more about what people would think than about what God thinks. Certainly in the great drama of his passion, we have had reason to weep rivers of tears for our role in its cause.

But now, on the night before the great rising of the sun, let us go and hide differently than did the disciples. We will not hide as the disciples who, in fear, shunned his tomb. No, rather (Are you ready for it?) we want to hide in it. Let us go into his tomb and wait there a while.

It is dark in his tomb. Only the eyes of faith can see anything at all there. And what do they see? They see Jesus. He is wrapped in a white linen shroud. But in that shroud there is not just a dead body. In that shroud are hidden all the sins of the world. Under that shroud, everything—absolutely everything that is wrong with me—lies buried. All the filth of the sin in which I was conceived and born is there. Every denial of him by word and work is there. The pain I inflicted on him by the pain I have inflicted on those around me when I wouldn't help them—there it lies. My harsh words, my loveless indifference, the idolatrous "me first" attitude that has haunted me every step of the way—it's all there.

Still and quiet is the tomb. No anguished cry comes from my lips. No despairing groan rises from my soul. For it is as Paul says to us in the reading: I too have died there. All that I was and am by nature was sin and guilt; and there in the tomb I, it, is dead. And what's left?

If I with my sin and guilt am dead, what's left for me, even for me, in the quiet stillness of Jesus' tomb? Jesus is wrapped in white linen. For me too there is a covering of white linen. The linen that covers me is Jesus' innocence. It is Jesus' righteousness. It is Jesus' sinless perfection! How so? I was buried with him in Baptism, and in my baptism, he covered me with that white linen of full pardon and forgiveness. As his body was washed before he was wrapped in the linen shroud, so I too was washed clean in Baptism, and the white robe of righteousness was wrapped around me there. All that was washed from me he carried with him to the cross and buried it forever in his tomb. And now there we are, we two: Jesus, the sin-bearer, and I, the sinner, the one washed clean, so that—wonder of all wonders!—buried with him by baptism I am more alive than ever! Death can no longer touch me. The grave will not be my home nor hell my eternal abode. For I have died with Christ to live again with him—I can hardly wait to shout it tomorrow at the break of day!

But still, what a blessed moment it is to rest a while with him in his tomb. Oh, how blessed in its quiet stillness and in the dark to see clearly "all my sins on Jesus laid." How good it is to wait with him for what I know is coming in just a few short hours. But for now:

> Blessed be God for the linen robe I wear from my baptism!
> Blessed be my dear Savior for granting me the death in Baptism
> that gives me life and life eternal in his resurrection! Amen.

Easter

Romans 6:8-12 – If we died with Christ, we believe that we will also live with him. For we know that since Christ was raised from the dead, he cannot die again; death no longer has mastery over him. The death he died, *he died to sin once for all;* **but the life he lives, he lives to God. In the same way, count yourselves dead to sin but alive to God in Christ Jesus. Therefore do not let sin reign in your mortal body so that you obey its evil desires [emphasis added].**

Oh, blessed death! Oh, most glorious life. It's Easter! He has burst forth from the grip of death. He has triumphed over all the hosts of hell. And now he lives—lives ever more. He died to sin *once for all*—that means for me too, even for me. And now he takes me with him out of the cold, clammy grip of death, out of the grave, out of that house of the dead, and into the bright sunshine of Easter Sunday morning.

As he died and now lives to the glory of God, so he takes me too into a new life with him. It is a life delivered from sin, a life washed with forgiveness brought by his Word and sacraments. What, then, will be my answer to this most holy day of days, this most holy event of all the events in history and in my own history? Shall I chase the Easter Bunny, running aimlessly across the lawn? Shall I stuff myself with brightly colored eggs (while forgetting that they are just symbols of the resurrection)? Shall I dress myself in Easter finery for a parade designed to impress people with my good taste?

How silly it would be, if that's what Easter was all about. No, even before I head off to church, I will bask in the sunshine of his grace in the new life that is mine from his resurrection. Oh, I know that I am still weighed down with my nature. I know that I will still be tempted even today to put myself first. I know that at day's end I will still have confession to make, pardon to crave, grace to seek. Ah, but—and that's the joy of this day—from God's point of view my sins have all been left behind in Jesus' empty grave. Instead of sin, I have pardon; in place of guilt, there is grace heaped upon grace. For Christ is risen! The debts of yesterday have been paid for. So too have the debts of today and tomorrow! They're all paid for. And Jesus' resurrection is the proof of it, the proof that God is not only satisfied with Jesus. Wonder of wonders—he is satisfied with me too! For after all, it is for me that Jesus came. For me he died. For me he has risen.

So then, will I wallow in guilt? No, not that! Will I resign myself to my sins, my weaknesses, my faults, my failings, my shame? Oh no, not that either. Rather, buried with Jesus through Baptism and now risen with him anew on Easter Sunday, I will strive and strain and struggle with joy all the more eagerly to be what I already am in God's eyes: one risen with Christ, one washed and redeemed by his blood, one over whom death and hell no more have a claim because of everything that Jesus has done in his death and resurrection for me, even for me. He lives and I count myself alive, really alive, in him. Oh, most blessed, most happy day! The last thing I want is for sin to continue to rule over me; the only longing I have is for Christ to live ever more fully in me.

Join in the apostle Paul's exultant hymn: *I am alive to God in Christ Jesus!* If Christ Jesus is alive and I am in him, then I can never die; for Christ died once and dies no more. His life is mine and mine is his. We are by the message of his death and resurrection bound together with the ties of his love and grace that not death, not the devil, not hell itself can break. For they lie vanquished, smashed, broken, and defeated by our triumphant Savior. And his triumph is ours. That's why he came. That's why he died. That's the fruit for us of his rising again. It is all for me; it is all for you.

> Dearest Jesus, the tomb is empty! Not just your tomb but mine as well can collect mold and must. For I am not there. I am risen with you into the bright sunshine of your Father's grace and favor. Oh, joy beyond all earthly gladness! Write it, O God, on my heart and mind: Christ is risen! He is risen indeed! Hallelujah!

Mark 16:6 – "Don't be alarmed," he said. "You are looking for Jesus the Nazarene, who was crucified. He has risen! He is not here. See the place where they laid him."

Oh, joy beyond all measure! *He is risen! He is risen indeed!* That was the angel's message to the women who had come to complete what had been left undone (the anointing of his body) on Friday in the burial of Jesus. But he is not there! *He is risen! He is risen indeed!* Let the mountains rejoice and bow down before him! Let the valleys leap for joy! Let the sun that was so dark on Friday shine with never greater splendor! Let all creation shout in exaltation! See! He is not there, cold in the grave. *He is risen! He is risen indeed!* All our sadness is turned to songs of praise and thanksgiving. For now our salvation is assured. The promise in his word from the cross ("It is finished!") has been confirmed. The Father has accepted his sacrifice for us and for our salvation. Every sin has been paid for—paid for in full. Death has been conquered by him and for us. For if he could keep the promise of laying down his life and then taking it up again, he will have no difficulty in keeping his further promise that since he lives, we too shall live. We shall live forever—live in blessed and forgiven fellowship with him, with his Father, with the Holy Spirit, with the saints who have gone before us, and with all the holy angels! For look! It is an angel who announces it—an angel sent from heaven itself who rejoices in the resurrection that restores our fellowship with God and with all the holy angels of God in heaven!

So then, don't be alarmed! Don't be alarmed because you cannot see him in the grave. Don't be alarmed by the troubles of the moment in your life. Don't be alarmed by sins of the past, whose consequence you indeed may bear in the present. Don't be alarmed by the fear of troubles or sickness or death in the future. For all of that is to be fixated on the grave: the grave that holds him no more, the grave in which is buried all that is wrong with us. To be sure, there are troubles enough left for us to face before we join him and the holy angels in heaven. But the troubles of this time are not to be compared to the glory he has won for us. Besides that, those momentary troubles keep us from fixing our focus on this world and its perishing pleasures so that we focus on the eternal things purchased for us by his death and resurrection. So, as the angel said, Don't be alarmed! For he lives. He rules and reigns. He governs and guides. Death can never again claim him, and because he is risen, it can't claim us either! *For he is risen! He is risen indeed!*

And then there is this: Our first thought at the message of his resurrection might well have been, "Now I really have reason to be afraid! For my sins caused his suffering, my ingratitude his loneliness there on the cross, my indifference his anguish of soul and body. Now that he is risen, I'm going to get from him what I deserve." It is exactly because such thoughts might reasonably have come to us that the angel cuts them off before we have a chance to think them: no, not to punish, not to torment, but to take away *all* fear and sadness. *He is risen! Don't be afraid!*

So then, leave behind the sins and the fear that he has conquered. Leave it behind in the cold dark tomb from which he has burst forth. And then get out of there! Get out into the bright sunshine of the grace that he has lavished on you by his death and then doubled by his resurrection. If you are, as you should be, overwhelmed by his love for you in his death and resurrection, then there will be less and less room for the things that you have left behind in his empty tomb. Oh, may we on this most holy and joyful day of days come to see it as true: Our greed is so foolish when we have a Savior who gives us all and more than we need for this body and life. Our obsession with avenging hurts inflicted on us by others is likewise so foolish, when he has so fully and freely forgiven all of our hurts inflicted on him. Our fears of death and judgment are so foolish, given the ransom paid for us and the verdict already pronounced in the gospel of his death and resurrection.

So then, rejoice this day with joy unbounded. For what can compare or what can dim the luster of these words: *He is risen! He is risen indeed!*

> Thousand, thousand thanks to you, Lord Jesus! My sins you have paid for on the cross, and my fully justified fear of God's wrath you have vanquished by your resurrection greetings from the mouth of the angel! Let me this day bask in this bright sunshine of your incomparable grace. Let me from this day on be eager to reflect the joy of your rising and all that it means for me in life and in eternity still more and more to the glory of your name and the benefit of all around me. Amen.

---

1 Peter 3:18-20 (ESV) – For Christ also suffered once for sins, the righteous for the unrighteous, that he might bring us to God, being put to death in the flesh but made alive in the spirit, in which he went and proclaimed to the spirits in prison, because they formerly did not obey, when God's patience waited in the days of Noah, while the ark was being prepared.

Well then, if he isn't in the grave, where is he? For starters, on Easter Sunday he rose from the dead and then, as we confess in the Apostles' Creed on the basis of what St. Peter tells us in his epistle, Jesus "went and proclaimed to the spirits in prison."

There is the beginning of his glory—a real glory that we have so long wanted to see in our risen Lord. Of course, we only get to see it through the eyes of faith because of this verse. Nevertheless, our mind boggles at the prospect laid out for us in this verse. Jesus, triumphant over all his foes on Easter Sunday, went down to the dwelling place of his enemies. He went to the hell of those who had already died and who suffer with Satan himself and his hosts. He didn't go down there to suffer; his suffering was finished on the cross. He went down there to proclaim his victory over death and hell. He went down to show to the doomed that he was indeed serious about all of his Word. Satan had rejected that Word already in heaven and was in hell because of his rebellion. And those who followed Satan's example in rejecting the Word and the Savior in unbelief share in Satan's torment. So much for the silly notion of some ancient Gnostic sects, who taught that all of creation exists in a constant state of flux between good and evil. No! Satan and his hosts are beaten and suffer in hell forever. They thought they had a great victory on Good Friday. But see here: He is risen! He proclaims his victory even in hell—a victory won for us!—as a first work of his triumph!

What a sight that must have been! How hell must have shaken and its inhabitants shrieked at the sight of him whom they had despised and rejected. How the sounds of church bells and trumpets must have pierced their ears in agony at the triumphant preaching of the victor. They are in hell, but not because God wanted them there. No, as in the days of Noah, God showed great patience; Noah preached for 120 years. But only eight souls listened to the Word of the Lord calling them to repentance and forgiveness. And so God, who always takes his Word seriously, sent the flood; those who did not listen perished and then were cast into the eternal torment originally intended only for Satan and his angels. And now their torment is made worse—if such a thing is possible—by the appearance and the victorious message of the forgiver they had spurned.

But where is there joy in that for us as we continue our celebration of Easter? It is in the words of St. Peter that reveal that Jesus has, by his death and resurrection, rescued us from the fate of those in hell. He has won the pardon and peace which was offered to the thousands upon thousands in the days of Noah and thereafter, but which they had rejected. It is offered to us now in the gospel of Good Friday and Easter Sunday.

Oh, may none among us be found following the doomed lead of those who spurned the preaching of Noah. Rather, as we confess that we deserve the fate of eternal doom no less than they do, let us rejoice in Jesus' triumphant victory for us and for our salvation from Satan and from hell. Jesus went to the cross to win the triumph promised by Noah. Jesus rose and went to hell to proclaim his victory that he has won for us so that we would not end up in torment with the devil and all who follow him. Hell could not lock him out and prevent his victory preaching; hell has likewise no power to claim us as its own and lock us away forever in torment. For Jesus has defeated hell and its dread claim over us—a claim it could only exercise if our sins had not been fully paid for.

But he died! But he rose! But he preached victory even in hell itself! And now in the Easter message he continues that preaching to us. Thanks be to God for our victorious and risen Savior! Thanks be to God for the rescue he has won for us from hell's torments! Thanks be to God for the heaven of the saints and angels, of which he has made us heirs by his resurrection!

> O risen Savior, you tasted death and spit it back out. You endured on the cross the torments of hell and then went there

to proclaim your triumph. When I am tempted to follow in the footsteps of those in hell by turning aside from your Word, let me call to mind the end that comes to those who despise your Word. Even more, let me with joy turn away from the stench of the doomed and damned as I cling to the rescue you have won for me by your death, your resurrection, and your triumphant victory for me over hell and all its torments. Hear me, I pray, for the sake of all that you have done for my salvation. Amen.

Mark 16:7,8 – "Go, tell his disciples and Peter, 'He is going ahead of you into Galilee. There you will see him, just as he told you.'" Trembling and bewildered, the women went out and fled from the tomb. They said nothing to anyone, because they were afraid.

Oh dear! What a sorry note even the best of his followers can put on the Easter message. And such were the women who first heard the glad tidings of the resurrection, and that from an angel no less. These women had been at the cross while the great disciples, for the most part, were in hiding. They had attended the funeral conducted by Nicodemus and Joseph of Arimathea while everyone else just went home from the cross in despair.

But now, when all that Jesus has promised for their salvation has come to pass, now when by the message of the angel they are most richly rewarded for their earlier devotion, now of all times when they should listen with rapt attention and unbounded joy, this is how they respond. They hear nothing; they are terrified; they flee; at least for a while, they tell no one.

Well, we just have to say it: If we were arranging events on Easter Sunday, things would have gone much better. To be sure, to some extent we can hardly blame these poor women. After all, the resurrection had happened in secret. That, for starters, seems to us a mistake. They had not seen his triumphant bursting forth from the sealed tomb. And of course they were neither witnesses to his triumphant appearance in hell, nor had they heard his victory proclamation there. It was quite bad enough that the crucifixion took place in plain sight of all. It was quite bad enough that any and all could see Jesus' disgrace and humiliation. But now, this seems almost worse: the most glorious event in the whole history of the world—his rising from dead—no one sees! Shouldn't that be the event that takes place most publicly and in the open? Shouldn't trumpets be blaring from the temple mount? Should we not hear choirs of angels singing Handel's "Hallelujah Chorus" in the sky for all to hear? Instead, just one angel talks to these women from inside the cold and empty tomb?

Shouldn't the soldiers guarding the tomb, instead of being struck dumb, be standing at attention before the spectacle of the risen Lord? Shouldn't they be kneeling in worship and adoration? Shouldn't Pilate and Herod be running to the tomb to beg for pardon? Shouldn't the leaders and the mob that had cried out, "Crucify him! Crucify him!"—shouldn't they be cowering in dread of the horrible judgment awaiting them for their monstrous and unrepented crimes?

But none of that happened. Instead, these poor women, now torn by grief and confusion, are left—left with what? Only, at least so far, with the Word! Ah, there it is! The Word that Jesus had preached also to them, and in which he promised his resurrection, is all they have. The Word rejected by the scoffers from Noah's day down to our day is the power of God for the creation and the sustaining of faith in his saving work for us on the cross and on Easter Sunday. But oh, what obstacles that Word must triumph over. It has to conquer sight; we would rather see him than hear him. It has to conquer reason; we prefer to hang on to our own thoughts rather than on to him in his Word. It has to conquer experience; death and despair is what we experience in our conscience, in our memory.

But there it is: the Word: Don't be afraid! He is not here! He is risen! Jesus is getting the women and us ready for this basic reality of our Christian life: We walk by faith and not by sight. We live by the living Word of the risen Christ. In all of the remaining events of Easter, leading up to and including his ascension, Jesus prepares us all to rejoice in the event of his death and resurrection, but not because we have seen it. He prepares us by his Word to rejoice now and to the day of our own death in his living presence, his powerful and convincing presence. That presence is not only revealed in his Word, but it is given to us by that same Word! In heaven there will be time for sight, for fully converted reason, for eternally bliss-filled experience. For now the risen Christ comes to you in the Word when you read it and when you hear it from his faithful messengers in church. Rejoice! It is still as sure and certain as it was when first preached by the angel to the women at the tomb. It took them a while to gain the conviction and the strength to share it. But it worked in them, and as we see from the rest of the Easter account, later in the day they did share the glad tidings of the resurrection with the disciples (Luke 24:9,10). May it thus work in us as well, growing from a seed to a plant that bears the fruit of firm conviction—ever greater joy—and then a zeal to share the message as the Lord gives us opportunity to share it!

> Lord Jesus, there is so much in my life that causes me to be like the women at your empty tomb: bewildered, confused, and afraid. So little of life is under my own control. The power of nature, the will of others, my own ignorance sometimes, and

sometimes my own foolishness cause me to want to just run away and hide. But you have risen! Because you have risen, I no longer even want to control everything; nor will I fear the seeming control of nature and of other people. For you have risen, you have risen indeed. My life and my times I most gladly leave in your hands. By the assurance of your victory, restore and renew my courage to live in you by living with your Word close to my heart. For by that Word your victory is mine. With renewed confidence in you, give me still the grace to share your victory with those around me. For whether I see it or not they are in as much need of it as I am; without the message of your resurrection victory they will remain bewildered today, confused tomorrow, and afraid at your last appearance on judgment day. So, Lord Jesus, grant me the honor of sharing in the work of the angel who proclaimed your resurrection on Easter Sunday. Some may hear and rejoice today, others may tomorrow. And what greater honor could there be for me than bringing that joy to any and to all? Amen.

John 20:15-18 – He asked her, "Woman, why are you crying? Who is it you are looking for?" Thinking he was the gardener, she said, "Sir, if you have carried him away, tell me where you have put him, and I will get him." Jesus said to her, "Mary." She turned toward him and cried out in Aramaic, "Rabboni!" (which means "Teacher"). Jesus said, "Do not hold on to me, for I have not yet ascended to the Father. Go instead to my brothers and tell them, 'I am ascending to my Father and your Father, to my God and your God.'" Mary Magdalene went to the disciples with the news: "I have seen the Lord!" And she told them that he had said these things to her.

The Easter appearances of Jesus are amazing and so rich in comfort on so many different levels. As during his three years of serving before his ultimate service on the cross, so in his resurrection Jesus knows exactly what each one needs and supplies their need and more by what he says and by what he does.

And so it is here in his appearance to Mary Magdalene. What an interesting woman she was. Jesus had freed her from demon possession (Luke 8:2). But unlike so many helped by Jesus, she together with a number of other women followed Jesus and served him and the disciples in ways appropriate to their position in life. Like the other women, she was devoted to him and showed that devotion in ways that sometimes put the disciples to shame by comparison. She was there on Good Friday when most of them were in hiding. And she was there at the tomb early on Easter Sunday with the other women when, again, the disciples were not. And Jesus had blessed their devotion and faithfulness by making them the first to hear the message of his resurrection.

But now here is Mary, still at the tomb. What the angel had announced had not really taken hold in her and had not taken root in the minds and hearts of the other women either. What was going on in her mind and theirs? How did they track the events of Good Friday? Why did she and the other women remain so devoted to Jesus that they would come early in the morning to finish what had been left undone at his quick funeral on Friday? Weren't they disappointed? Didn't they feel cheated by a Jesus they had loved and served, who had now abandoned them in death? So many things there are that we would like to ask them, questions that will have to wait for an answer until we meet them in heaven.

But this much is clear and certain about Mary's state of mind and soul even after the first announcement by the angel of Jesus' resurrection: Mary does not yet know or grasp that Jesus has truly risen from the dead. And so long as there is no certainty of Jesus' resurrection, there can be nothing else in her soul—or in ours—but the most profound and incurable sorrow. She shows it in a way that the disciples didn't. They had a different chief need and problem (of which there is more in due course). They, one may suppose, like many men think themselves just too "manly" to weep uncontrollably and that right there in the open. But not Mary. She is inconsolable. Her Jesus is gone. All she wants to do is serve him. But she can't. He's gone. There is nothing for it but tears.

That is, there is nothing for it until Jesus appears—no, until Jesus not only appears but also speaks! He sees her need and fully meets it. That's just the way he always is! Do you get it? She wants to serve him. But that's not the way it works with him. First and foremost he wants to serve us! He did it preeminently on the cross. But he did it on Easter Sunday too. First he serves, and then our greatest "work" is to receive him as he comes to us on Easter Sunday in his Word. He calls us by name and assures us that he is still our Jesus! He died for us! He rose for us! He comes and comes again for us! How quickly Mary's tears are dried when he speaks to her and she cries out, "Teacher!" That's the title she most likely used in the days before his death; so, though it doesn't express even half of the reality, it's the word that springs quickest to her mind and mouth.

Mary's one most pressing and obvious need has been met. Sorrow has been replaced with joy, and the tears that blinded her eyes have been dried so that she can see Jesus now in his glory. That's why we celebrate Easter, whether we tend to cry in public or tend not to. For all alike there is nothing but tears and inconsolable sorrow if Jesus has not risen. We may wish as she did to serve God, but if Jesus is dead, what's the point? We are still, as St. Paul reminds us (1 Corinthians 15), in our sins; death and hell are still what we ultimately deserve. But Jesus has risen! His appearance to us in his Word with its assurance of his grace wipes away all tears of sadness! He is risen indeed! He is with us still, yes, even to and then through the hour and the gates of death.

So what is there to cry about? Will we cry at the death of a loved one who died in faith? We may cry perhaps because we will miss them. But we will not cry as those who despair over a corpse that proves the ultimate futility of life. Oh no, not that! For Jesus has called by name our loved one who died trusting in Jesus' merit and has now dried all of his or her tears. That person is now safe in his arms forever, and we rejoice at the entry of another saint into the company of the apostles and prophets and all the holy angels. Yes, and we look forward to that blessed day when he will call us too by name and finally wipe away all tears from our eyes. Then we will see him as he is and rejoice to join our loved ones who have gone before us in perfect joy and adoration before the throne of the Lamb who was slain and who lives—lives forever, our Jesus, still the same!

But having appeared to Mary and having dried her tears by his calling her by name, Jesus is not yet done blessing her. She had come to serve but first had to be served by his assuring words. Now Jesus satisfies her longing to serve him by filling her with still more joy and certainty in his resurrection and then by giving her a most sacred and important assignment. She who was once possessed by demons gets the honor of proclaiming the resurrection to the disciples. How backward that seems to us. But that is so often Jesus' way. The pastor gets to preach and teach. And little children sing in his hearing that "Jesus loves me, this I know; for the Bible tells me so." And the pastor hears. The pastor has his own faith restored and reassured from the songs of little children. The pastor tells the sick or the dying or the otherwise suffering of the mercy and grace of the risen Savior. In his own heart he wonders if, in their pain, they hear him. And then when he is finished he hears this suffering soul say, "Yes, Pastor; thank you for reminding me." Not infrequently the confession of faith is mingled with tears of joy. The one who came to strengthen is strengthened by one whose confidence in the gospel was at that moment greater than his had been! Yes, that's the way Jesus does things still.

So Jesus tells Mary not to grab hold of him or to try and hang on to him. That's not how he wants her to serve. Rather, he tells her to serve by telling—telling the good news to the ones who should have known it better than she did but who were still hiding in fear. May all those—young and old, high and low—rejoice to be served by the Savior's appearance in his Word; may all those who rejoice then delight in sounding forth the joy of his resurrection in words and in life to the glory of the Savior and the joy of those who hear them!

> O risen Savior, with the message of your resurrection, you wipe away all of my tears in this life. Indeed, such tears as I have bring me again before your empty tomb where you meet me and call me by name. Let me hear your voice in the message of your resurrection and be assured by that message that you still do all things well for me. And then make me, like Mary Magdalene, a messenger of your resurrection to the glory of your name and the joy of those who hear me. Amen.

Luke 24:30-32 – When he was at the table with them, he took bread, gave thanks, broke it and began to give it to them. Then their eyes were opened and they recognized him, and he disappeared from their sight. They asked each other, "Were not our hearts burning within us while he talked with us on the road and opened the Scriptures to us?"

Read the entire account of Luke 24:13-35 for yourself. Jesus spent hours with these two disciples on the road to Emmaus. And again we are tempted to ask this: Wasn't that really a waste of valuable time? After all, they were not even apostles, much less anyone that the rest of the world would consider worth noticing. Wouldn't the time be better spent with, let's say, Pontius Pilate? Or how about the soldier at the crucifixion who said, "Surely, this was the Son of God"? Why not come instead to Nicodemus and Joseph of Arimathea? Why waste time with these relative nobodies who, in spite of the time they had spent with Jesus, still understood so little? And now they have left the company of the apostles in Jerusalem and that even after reports of Jesus' resurrection have been coming in. That too doesn't put these two in a very good light. Shouldn't they have stayed in Jerusalem with the apostles to see what was yet to happen? After all, even the chief priests and elders remembered that Jesus had promised to rise again. But no. They've had enough. It's time to go home, unsatisfied, confused, depressed.

Oh, how beyond measure the patient love of Jesus! He didn't waste his time after his resurrection. He spent it in consoling the desperate and the despairing. He spent it coming to those who should have known better than to despair or to be depressed, given all that he had done to show himself to them as the Son of God and their Savior. He spent it confirming his promise of his own resurrection and therefore his promise of their redemption. He comes to the weak and the lowly—those whose hearts were troubled precisely because they had listened to his Word but had difficulty believing it.

And how does he deal with them? First and foremost, he fixes their attention yet again on his Word! Now in the depths of the confusion and despair, which they endured because they had not listened to that Word well enough earlier, he does not first show himself; he first preaches his Word. And this time they listen. And this time it has its blessed effect. "Were not our hearts burning within us while he . . . opened the Scriptures to us?" Did you get that? They didn't exult over the fact that they saw Jesus, though that too certainly filled them with joy. They rejoiced over what they heard, over his Word!

Who of us hasn't been in the company of these two Emmaus disciples? We remember those times when we too have spoken with one another of our confusion and perhaps our despair. We had heard the words and promises of Jesus so often. When all was well, we thought we understood it and believed his Word. We may even have quietly muttered, *Why do they keep telling me things I already know?!* But then came the times when Jesus hid himself. Then came the anguish of dark nights filled with doubt. Then came the questions: *I thought he loved me; I thought he promised always to be with me, but look what has happened. How can it be that he died for me and rose for me and lives for me when he permits this temptation, this weakness, this trouble, this trial? Could it be that I have believed in vain? Could it be that these reports of Jesus as my Savior are not really true, or at least not true for me?*

What's the cure for such anguish in the soul? It's so simple that many turn away and refuse it. It's the cure that Jesus gave the disciples on the road to Emmaus. It's hearing again his Word and its promises. That's always—yes, always—the way that Jesus restores the broken spirit and raises up the crushed heart and restores reason run amuck.

The disciples on the road to Emmaus had not listened well enough in those earlier years with Jesus. When they fell as a result into confusion or despair, Jesus cured them with his Word. Only after that did he reveal himself. And so it is with us. Jesus creates our faith in the first place by his Word. When our faith is broken, he repairs it with his Word. Then, when all is done, he will appear to us as well. No, not now. No, not yet. But in the hour of our death and on the day of judgment, there he will be in all his glory. What will we say as we bow down to worship and adore? Will it not be the glad confession of these two disciples: "Were not our hearts burning within us while he . . . opened the Scriptures to us?" Oh, how we long for that day!

Lord Jesus, my risen Savior and Lord, forgive me all those times when I was so foolish as to think that I didn't need to hear your Word anymore because I imagined that I already knew it all. Forgive me those times when I was so weak that in days of trial and sorrow, I doubted your love and watchful care. Now receive my thanks for your patience with me. Receive my hymns of praise that you came to me again in all such times with that precious Word. Receive my adoration for your power and presence in that Word, which brings me again and again to trust you, no matter how much my reason or circumstance may rage against your promises. Yes, Lord Jesus, let my heart too burn within me with grateful joy as you open to me again and again the sacred Scriptures for my strengthening, for my salvation. Amen.

John 20:19,20 – On the evening of that first day of the week, when the disciples were together, with the doors locked for fear of the Jewish leaders, Jesus came and stood among them and said, "Peace be with you!" After he said this, he showed them his hands and side. The disciples were overjoyed when they saw the Lord.

We noted earlier that in his Easter appearances, Jesus meets the particular needs of those to whom he came on Easter Sunday. Mary Magdalene was overwhelmed with sorrow and her eyes so filled with tears that she could see nothing, not even Jesus—until he not only appeared but spoke to her. Her sadness, if Jesus was still dead, would have been fully justified. Without his resurrection, sadness and despair are all she could have and all we could have too.

The disciples certainly were filled with sorrow too. But that is not the need that they present on that first Easter evening. Their most obvious problem is not sorrow but fear. And it too is utterly reasonable and an altogether appropriate response if Jesus has not risen. They may well consider themselves marked as dead men. Surely with Jesus dead, the Jews and the soldiers of Pilate must be out looking for them to finish ridding the world of this pretender Messiah/King.

Even more than that, how must God look at them now, given the way they had behaved towards Jesus? Whatever they have left of faith in him, in their confusion they still know that at the very least he was a prophet, indeed the greatest of the prophets. But they had denied him. They had abandoned him. They had neither loved him enough to stand by him nor trusted him enough to consider any loss for his sake anything but an honor for them. Yes, on Easter Sunday they are hiding from fear of the Jews. But if their conscience is at work, they must have been hiding as well in fear of God. But look at how Jesus deals with their need and does so much more than they could have expected.

Jesus appears! Luke tells us that, even at first sight of him, they still had trouble believing that it was really Jesus. Luke says that "they still did not believe it because of joy and amazement" (Luke 24:41). It just seems too good to be true.

The disciples are so like us. They have heard the reports from the women and still do not believe or rejoice. They have heard the report from the two disciples just returned from Emmaus. And yet they remain in terror behind closed doors. Indeed, Peter and John had themselves been to the tomb and had seen for themselves that Jesus was not there. But still the absence of his body and all these reports did not fully convince them. Without the conviction that Jesus has risen from the dead, fear is altogether warranted—in them and in us too! Their fear and all of our fears testify to our doubt and sometimes to blatant unbelief. If Jesus has not risen, then we must face our past, our present, and our future alone. If Jesus has not risen, we must die in dread of what will become of us in that hour. If Jesus has not risen, then the voice of conscience that damns us and the verdict that the devil himself laughingly shouts in our ears is correct. Fear in this life and even greater fear of the life to come is altogether reasonable, if Jesus has not risen.

Oh, to be sure, there are those who think otherwise. There are those who, altogether apart from God's Word—indeed, contrary to it—live in a fool's paradise of unreality. They are like those who whistle when they walk past a cemetery in the vain delusion that it will not one day claim them. They decide for themselves that if there is any life after this one, it will be heaven for them and not hell. And why? Simply because they think so, without any basis for the thought in what God has said. That's not faith; it's superstition. And so it is with such people whenever they talk about the mercy and love of God or about the hope of heaven: it is without Jesus, without his resurrection, apart from his presence in and with his Word.

The disciples in the upper room on that Easter Sunday were much more realistic: separated from Jesus, with his Word and promise out of their hearts and minds, they are afraid. That's reasonable. That's realistic.

Oh, the mercy and patience, the grace and goodness of the risen Lord! There is in us, as in his disciples that first Easter, so often doubt about God's love or his rule over all things for our benefit or about his promise of his gracious presence with us. Sometimes even when we hear the good news of grace and mercy because of his resurrection, we still find ourselves wondering how it could possibly be true. And that doubt begets fear, the fear that when all is said and done, we are really all alone. Both the doubt and the fear are there because we have neglected or forgotten his Word.

But there he is this Easter again. He is risen! He is risen indeed! See how he shows the disciples and us the nail prints in his hands and feet and the spear wound in his side. It's really Jesus! Yes, and isn't that a wondrous thing all by itself: He doesn't come to them and say, "Look here! I have a halo around my head and a golden crown on it! See here! Angels sing above me and dance around me!" Oh no, not that! Instead, he shows them the very wounds he received to redeem them! Let that sink in for a moment! His wounds were most painful. His wounds were most gruesome. His wounds—those are marks of the wrath of God against sin and unbelief. That's what he shows us. For those wounds are to him—and to us—most glorious. Even in heaven we will see them. For by his wounds our sin was paid for. By his wounds our guilt was covered. By his wounds our death was defeated. By his wounds heaven was opened for us. By his wounds God has become our dear Father instead of the angry judge that he was to his Son on the cross.

After showing them those precious wounds, Jesus opens to the disciples the Scriptures. He repeats what he had said so often about his death and resurrection. They—and we with them—have heard it all before. Ah, but how sweet it is as he binds us to his Word, which amid all the changes in our lives, does not and cannot change.

The disciples were finally convinced that he had risen indeed when they saw his wounds and then ate with him. We are finally convinced too after he opens to us the Scriptures and tells us what he has told us a thousand times before. In times of trial we began to doubt it or maybe didn't believe it anymore. Fear replaced confidence, and the darkness of Good Friday supplanted the sunshine of Easter Sunday. Then to our heart locked behind the closed doors of fear, Jesus comes. He repeats it in his loving patience with us: "See here! My hands and my feet and my side! See here what those wounds mean, why I suffered them! See here! I have risen for you, just as I died for you!" And by his Word he performs again that miracle; he brings us again from doubt to certainty. His Word again brings us from unbelief to faith. His Word again brings us from fear to joy.

> Lord Jesus, remember that I am dust. The winds of change and the storms of temptations blow over me, and I am moved from certainty to doubt and from confidence in your promises to despair over my own weakness. Be patient with me, Lord Jesus. Speak to me still in your Word. Show me the wounds that prove your love and pay for all that is wrong with me. Show me in your Word that empty tomb, which guarantees not only

your resurrection but my own as well. And then let me rejoice with the disciples that, in hearing your Word, I have seen you and again received you as my only Savior and my God. Amen.

I.

John 20:20-23 – The disciples were overjoyed when they saw the Lord. Again Jesus said, "Peace be with you!" . . . And with that he breathed on them and said, "Receive the Holy Spirit. If you forgive anyone's sins, their sins are forgiven; if you do not forgive them, they are not forgiven."

Consider the difference that faith makes once Jesus is risen from the dead and convinces us of it in his Word: the outward circumstance changes not one wit. Ah, but for the soul and the heart and the mind, what a difference it makes that Jesus has risen! The disciples still know very well that those whose blood lust was poured out on Jesus just days before would not be satisfied until the disciples too have been arrested and tried and crucified. But with Jesus' resurrection that really doesn't matter. For he has risen and so they too will rise. To be sure, they still have their sinful nature within. With that nature, temptations will never cease until their own hour of departure for their heavenly homeland. But they will live in repentance. In a stumbling struggle against ever-present sin and temptation, they will live in the Word of promise, the Word of grace and forgiveness fully won by Jesus' death and assured by his resurrection.

But there's more. Jesus gives them on Easter Sunday a most holy and glorious assignment: *As the Father has sent me, I am sending you!* He spells out just what that work was which his Father sent him to do and which he is now trusting them to do. It is the work of forgiving sins. That's the work that the Father had given Jesus to do. And he did that work completely and perfectly by his sacrifice on Good Friday and by his resurrection on Easter Sunday and now by his gift from his Word, the gift of peace that comes from sins forgiven. But soon he will remove his visible presence from this world. Someone will have to go and tell all who will listen that peace is theirs too because of the forgiveness Jesus has won. Someone will have to announce: "Yes, for you too he died; for you too he rose; for you too there is peace and pardon." Someone will even have to declare with all boldness and certainty: "Those who reject the won forgiveness forfeit it, even though it was won for them. Ultimately, if they die in such rejection they will face for all eternity the wrath of God for their ungrateful, their pernicious unbelief. Their sins will fall on them with all the dreadful punishment that Jesus died to remove."

Of course we're ready here to give Jesus some advice: "These you're going to send? You can't be serious! They all abandoned you. They were slow even to believe that you had risen from the dead. And now you want to entrust to them a work like your own, the work your Father sent you to do? Surely you could find better emissaries than these."

To be sure, these men are unfit for the task. Yes, and no one else is fit for it either. Therefore Jesus "breathed on them and said, 'Receive the Holy Spirit.'" Just what that meant will not become fully evident until Pentecost. But the point is clear already on Easter Sunday. It is just as St. Paul would say later of this same assignment that had been entrusted to him: "Who is equal to such a task? . . . Our competence comes from God" (2 Corinthians 2:16–3:5). It is the Holy Spirit who will make them fit.

The Holy Spirit likewise will work through their preaching and teaching to accomplish the miracle of faith that trusts in Jesus' completed work—just as by his Word he worked and would sustain that same miracle in their own hearts. Are the apostles he sends unfit in themselves? Of course! Are we who follow in union with the church in their footsteps unfit? Of course, we are just as unfit. But still the assignment is the same; it is a holy assignment, a saving assignment. Yes, it is an assignment to do in preaching and teaching what the Father sent the Son to do in suffering and dying and rising again. What an amazing thing! Our assignment from Jesus is the same as his assignment from his Father. He alone earned and won what we have to offer. But he elevates that offering of his forgiveness and sets it alongside his own unique work of winning it. Could we imagine a greater honor?

How good that Jesus would not have taken our advice to find better people than the disciples to do this saving work! How good it is that he still doesn't look for better than they were to do it now; he looks for us to do it. And then he equips and makes us fit by forgiving us as he forgave them. He equips us and makes the work a success because his own Holy Spirit is present and active in the work. Oh, how thankful we are to God that he did not find anyone better than those disciples—that he did not find anyone who was already fit. That spurs us on as likewise forgiven ones to also give what we have received and to do the work that he has done.

> O Lord Jesus, make still the same difference in my heart and mind as I receive again the glad tidings of your resurrection. No matter what burdens I bear or what worries afflict my soul, let me rejoice in the peace you have brought by your rising again. By that same peace of forgiveness daily offered and

received in your Word, may your Holy Spirit make me fit to share the good news of redemption won, peace obtained, and eternal life granted by all that you have done. Amen.

II.

But there is another point that we do not want to miss. What is it that they are to proclaim? Peace and forgiveness. That means that the day will never come when peace is not needed. That means that the day will never come on this side of eternity when there are no more sins to forgive. So then, to what is he sending them? To what is he sending us? He sends them and us to a world torn by strife caused by sin. He sends them and us to a world in which people are just like us: fallen by nature, doomed and damned by merit. He sends them and us to a world where the fallen sinful nature is evident on every hand in the suffering that people cause themselves and inflict on one another by their hatred, their lust for revenge, the passion for pleasure, and their unquenchable greed. And the tragic truth is that the message will not be welcomed by one and by all. Jesus has already said that when he tells them and us that he is sending us like the Father sent him. Did the Father send him into a welcoming world? Hardly! The events of the past week proved that, if there were indeed any doubt about it before Holy Week.

It is to that same hostile world that he sends the apostles. Their deaths for the sake of the gospel and the whole history of the church demonstrate both: the desperate need of the world for peace and forgiveness that comes alone from Christ in the gospel; and as well it demonstrates the price of suffering that must often be paid by those who bring that Savior and his saving peace and forgiveness.

How will they find the strength, even the desire, to persevere when the message is received only by some and rejected by most? The apostles and those who listened knew well that they themselves would never lose their own need for washing in the blood of the Lamb. That they received his washing, his peace, his forgiveness over and over again is what kept them from losing heart when their precious gift of the gospel was despised and rejected. They would learn to imitate the loving patience of the Savior that they experienced every day. Preserved by the Word they preached, they would follow in the way of the cross to their own resurrection.

And so there it is: "The disciples were overjoyed when they saw the Lord. Again Jesus said, 'Peace be with you!'" The assignment changes neither the joy at seeing him nor the peace received in hearing him! Of course the disciples still had a lot to learn about the full implications of

Jesus' gift of peace and as well about the cost of his sending them. It also takes us a lifetime to learn it and then to realize it perfectly in our own resurrection. Would there be for them and will there be for us sorrow over earthly loss, pain in sickness, and even a measure of fear at the approach of death? Yes, that's unavoidable. But Jesus uses it all to separate us from the worship of the things of this life. He uses it all to remind us of our constant dependence on him for help and rescue. Will there be times when the conscience gets burned by temptations that just never go away? The answer to that question is writ large in the conscience of each of us. But Jesus uses even this to bring us back and bind us still closer to his Word, to his cross and resurrection. For not in our victories but in his is salvation; not in our works—even the best of them—is our hope of heaven but in his pardon is our peace.

Just think what an excellent preparation all of the disciples' weaknesses and failures were for the very work that Jesus was about to give them. We know about that too, don't we? We see it all around us in coworkers and friends, in parents and children, and—most of all—in the mirror. Not a one of us is perfect. Many in their turn may hurt or disappoint us. But we call it to mind: Even if we—and that is highly unlikely—have never hurt or disappointed them, we nevertheless have to come again and again, each Sunday in confession and each day in the Lord's Prayer, to the Savior for pardon. We have hurt and disappointed him more times than we know or can count. And what has been his answer? *Peace be to you!* And besides filling us with joy, that message of peace gets us ready for this: "As the Father has sent me, I am sending you!" To do what? To bring peace. To show his patience. To forgive as we have been forgiven. To strengthen the weak. To encourage the strong. To serve as we have been served. To share the gift of the gospel with those who like us have not and could never deserve it. To call to faithfulness to the Word those who like us have sometimes doubted, sometimes wanted to pick and choose only what suits us. Impatience with others is always a sign that we haven't looked deeply enough into the mirror of our own weakness, our own need. It is a sign as well that we need to look still more into the patience of Jesus with us so that from it, we may grow in patience. We demonstrate that patience when we give to those around us what he has so generously given to us: that same peace, that same pardon.

> Even so, Lord Jesus, I rejoice in seeing you again in the Easter gospel. Bring me also in the enjoyment of your peace and forgiveness a zeal to follow in the footsteps of the apostles. Let me see in all of my life's trials, temptations, and weaknesses the training wheels of service that keep me going with patience

and love to share as I have daily received the same from you. Hear me for the glory of your name as Savior. Amen.

I.

John 20:25-28 – [Thomas] said to them, "Unless I see the nail marks in his hands and put my finger where the nails were, and put my hand into his side, I will not believe." A week later his disciples were in the house again, and Thomas was with them. Though the doors were locked, Jesus came and stood among them and said, "Peace be with you!" Then he said to Thomas, "Put your finger here; see my hands. Reach out your hand and put it into my side. Stop doubting and believe." Thomas said to him, "My Lord and my God!"

We notice it in all that Jesus did and said during the days of his visible presence on earth that he always had in mind the specific needs of people. While what he said always had a universal application, he still kept in mind the very individual needs of those with whom he came into contact. Now, even after his resurrection, he shows that special love for his own that he had demonstrated so consistently before his suffering and death.

As amazing as it is that Jesus had time for each individual, here in this text it is especially surprising. Poor Thomas! Through his own fault he is in misery. He should have been with the disciples that first Easter Sunday. Where was he? What did he have to do that was more important than to be with his fellow disciples who were in mourning over the death of Jesus, in guilt over their own role in his death, in fear of those who had killed him, and yes, in confusion early on Easter Sunday over reports that Jesus had risen from the dead? Look at what Thomas missed! Jesus showed himself to the others! He was there, in the flesh. He spoke to them. He spoke words not of scolding, not of rejection, but words of peace that included an implied forgiveness. What joy! Their joy was in his words no less than in his appearance. Indeed, the words gave a lasting joy while the appearance provided a confirmation of the joy and then a memory.

But Thomas was not where Jesus might be expected, namely, with those to whom he had for so long shared himself and his Word. And so he missed out on the joy of Easter. But now he compounds his misery by clinging to it. The Word for him was just not good enough. That Word had not been brought to him by gullible and easily fooled men. It was brought by men who themselves needed convincing and were not convinced until they had seen the risen Savior. So Thomas, in a way, isn't much worse than the other disciples had been a week earlier. Still we can't help but shake our heads. For a week the others insist that Jesus has indeed risen. But Thomas just grows in stubborn unbelief—not just doubt, but rank unbelief. He insists that he won't be satisfied like the others were with just an appearance of Jesus. He demands more: a crude thrusting of his fingers into the nail prints and a jabbing of his hand into the spear wound on Jesus' side. Apparently by the end of the week, Thomas had at least advanced from rank unbelief to doubt; for after all, now he is at least back with his fellow disciples. More significantly, Jesus' first words to Thomas rebuke not rank unbelief, but doubt. Still, the greatest insult to God is a refusal to believe his Word; not far behind is the crime of doubting it.

Surely, Jesus, you should not accommodate such stubborn unbelief or his persisting doubt either! Surely now would be the time to declare Thomas as much an outcast as Judas had become by his despairing suicide.

But wonder of wonders! Jesus now exalted in his resurrection still humbles himself. No longer limiting himself to space and time, he appears when and where he wants to. Here in the upper room without bothering to knock on the door or even to just pass through it, he just is there. And listen to what he says; it's the same thing he had said the week before: "Peace be with you!" To be sure that was a common greeting in those days. But when it comes from the lips of the risen Savior, there is nothing common about it. It is filled with grace and power, the grace to assure the fallen and the power to conquer unbelief and doubt and to instill joy-filled trust instead. This time that grace and power is for all the disciples, but especially for Thomas.

Then comes the astonishing offer and invitation: "Thomas, here are the nail-imprinted hands and here is the wounded side. Go ahead! Thrust in your fingers and jab me with your hand! Put away the unbelief that you preferred to faith and the doubt you preferred to certainty; for now you have seen what you refused to hear!"

Yes, it's indeed astonishing on so many levels that Jesus would accommodate Thomas' unbelief and doubt in this way. We marvel at it not least because that is not the usual way for Jesus. He always exalts his Word over sight, hearing over seeing. Even when there is something to see, as was the case with his miracles, they are always first and foremost signs that point to what he said—to his Word.

Why, then, does Jesus satisfy Thomas' rejection of his Word and grant him sight and even the offer of touch to overcome his doubts? That certainly was an act of supreme and extraordinary love on Jesus' part. And it had its intended result. Thomas cries out, "My Lord and my God!" The word *Lord* is a synonym for "Savior." The word *God* contains all of the great and almighty attributes that belong to God alone. With that simple exclamation

Thomas returns to an embrace of all that Jesus had taught in his Word. Thomas, all unworthy, a sinner and a stubborn one at that, is acknowledging his own desperate need of a savior. He is claiming this Jesus as his own and only Savior. He is confessing that this, his Savior, is also his God, a God who has shown such amazing grace by becoming Savior—Savior even for such a one as Thomas. In sum, Jesus' appearance that night and especially for Thomas did not only convince Thomas that Jesus had risen. It convinced him of much more than that; it convinced him that all of Jesus' Word is true, that Jesus was the God-man, made flesh for him and for his salvation. And that confession to the truth of Jesus' Word and the reason of all that Jesus had done now became for Thomas the center, the heart and core of the rest of his life.

But really we still haven't answered the question of why Jesus let Thomas have this special accommodation to his doubts. After all, Jesus doesn't do that for us. He doesn't come to the scoffer and stand before him and invite him to touch his wounds so that the unbeliever will come to believe what he had earlier rejected from Jesus' Word. Nor does he make a personal, visible appearance to us either when the shadow of doubt is cast over our soul because of our own failure to listen enough to his Word.

Thomas had a special need but no special merit that entitled him to this unique manifestation of love from the risen Lord. So why, then, did Jesus appear this way for Thomas? The benefit of this appearance of Jesus was not intended just for Thomas. It's intended for us too. After all, there are so many who refuse to believe that Jesus rose from the dead. There are, most tragically, so many who even want to call themselves Christians but who insist that Jesus' resurrection wasn't real, wasn't physical. They imagine that his resurrection only takes place in the heart of the believer.

Jesus' appearances, especially this one, should put all such to shame. The disciples, and here especially Thomas, were not stupid or foolish, easily deceived bumpkins. They did not invent a resurrection story to fit what they wished would have happened but in reality never did. Quite the contrary, they were skeptics and in the case of Thomas, wavering between doubt and unbelief. The appearance of Jesus, and this one especially, was necessary to overcome such doubts and unbelief. We are the beneficiaries of these proofs of his resurrection. Those who refuse to believe these proofs, that is, those who reject the eyewitnesses and God's own Word, will be as Jesus said in his reproof of all doubt and unbelief: "If they do not listen to Moses and the Prophets, they will not be convinced even if someone rises from the dead" (Luke 16:31). The leaders of Jesus' own day were certainly examples of that; they could not deny that Jesus had really risen. Nevertheless, they refused to confess with Thomas, "My Lord and my God!"

So then, we are glad in a way that the disciples were not so easy to convince. We are even glad that Thomas started out so bold in his unbelief. For by his so gracious appearances, Jesus confirmed all of his Word and brought them back to that Word. He even made them bold confessors of the truth that Jesus came to seek and to save the lost and did exactly that in his suffering, his death, and, yes, his true and glorious and bodily resurrection. They themselves were the first to experience just how truly great his love and grace is. For he embraced them even after they doubted.

> Jesus, my Savior and my God, by the power of your Word keep me from doubt and unbelief, and preserve to me your embrace, the embrace of my Lord and my God. Amen.

II.

John 20:29-31 – Then Jesus told him, "Because you have seen me, you have believed; blessed are those who have not seen and yet have believed." Jesus performed many other signs in the presence of his disciples, which are not recorded in this book. But these are written that you may believe that Jesus is the Messiah, the Son of God, and that by believing you may have life in his name.

What a perfect conclusion to the incident of Jesus' appearance to the disciples and his restoration of the faith of Thomas! "Blessed are those who have not seen and yet have believed." The sentence is packed with significance for us. For we have not seen, nor will we see until Jesus takes us to himself in heaven. But we are blessed! Jesus says so! We are blessed, that is, we have the enjoyment of the peace that Jesus gave to his disciples in his Word in his Easter appearances. For look! We do believe the witness of the disciples. We believe it not because we are better than they were or more deserving. We believe the Easter message because the risen Jesus is in that Word. We believe it because he has overcome our native and inborn unbelief with his gracious words: "Peace be with you!" We believe it and confess with Thomas, "My Lord and my God!" And so Jesus—himself the content of our faith, its author, its giver, its preserver by means of Word and sacraments—pronounces us "blessed"! What an amazing thing that is: that Jesus so praises faith, which is ours by his gift alone.

Yes, and we don't want to miss it: In his blessing he is once again and as always urging us to listen to his Word. For it is by that Word alone that the miracle of faith in his saving work for our salvation is accomplished and preserved in us. Worthy of praise and adoration is he alone; his incarnation was a miracle; the love that moved him to it is beyond reason; his work on the cross is positive proof of an ardor beyond compare for our rescue from all that sin deserves; his resurrection confirms it once and for all; and the miracle of faith places the last seal on it. He alone is Lord and God; he alone is Savior.

Still there is another point we don't dare miss in all of this. It is the other side of the coin: If those are blessed who have not seen and yet have believed, then what of those who have not seen and have refused to believe? St. John answers the question: All that is written in the gospel and the events following Jesus' bodily resurrection have that glorious goal in mind; it is the goal that Jesus had in all he said and did, namely, that we should believe him. It is the goal that we should trust that he is Savior, as we have said and noted so often. But those who refuse him as Savior refuse also this blessedness so dearly won also for them. For while faith is always and alone a gift of God given in the powerful gospel, it is not a gift that God forces on anyone. Those who refuse Jesus refuse the gift of blessedness; they do so through their own fault, not the fault of the gospel. We notice it already with Thomas. How miserable he was apart from the Word. How blessed he became when by means of that one appearance, the Word again became dominant, as we see from his confession of faith in Jesus as both Savior and God.

Is it not clear? It is God's good and gracious will that we believe the gospel. And he has given that gospel the power to overcome doubt and unbelief. God's intent and the gospel's power is evident as it overcomes the doubt of the disciples and even the unbelief of Thomas. They had only God to thank both for their redemption and for their faith in Jesus as their Savior and God. Judas, on the other hand, and all who reject the witness of the disciples in that powerful Word have only themselves to blame for their loss of blessedness and their eternal doom.

That serves as both an encouragement to us and also as a warning. We are encouraged by the obvious fact that the disciples were unworthy of so great a grace and blessing. So too are we. But the promise of God's favor and his intent that we be rescued by Jesus' redeeming work and saving Word extends to us no less than to them. How deep and how often have we fallen? Here is Jesus, Savior and God! How often have we doubted or even perversely rejected our dear Jesus? Here he is still, our Savior and our God. But the warning remains: Do not perversely cling to doubt and wallow in a rejection of Jesus, our only Savior and God. When doubt assails and unbelief threatens, fly to the Word, listen to it. For there is the power of God to restore trust in Jesus again. When self-righteousness pushes away the confession of unworthiness and the embrace of Jesus— Jesus alone as Savior—then it's back to the Word. For there God will still crush our foolish pride and bring us again to the foot of the cross and to the empty tomb of our dear Redeemer. There we again will cry for pardon and for peace.

And Jesus will not cast us aside, but still will speak peace to us as he did to the disciples in the upper room. When despair comes from the shrill cry of the devil reminding us of our unworthiness, then too, listen; then too, it is back to the Word. See how he loved those disciples. See how he loved Thomas. See how he even extended to Judas a call to repentance in the Garden of Gethsemane. To you he comes no less with the same burning zeal for your redemption, a redemption already fully accomplished on Good Friday and confirmed on Easter Sunday. His embrace of his disciples and, not least, of Thomas is his embrace of you too. For as St. John tells us by inspiration of the Holy Spirit, all these things happened and have been written just so that you too would believe that Jesus is your Savior, and that by believing you should have life—life eternal through his name, his work, his Word.

> Lord Jesus, my Savior and my God, there are no words that can sufficiently express my thankfulness to you for all you are to me. You are the Savior who won my peace. You are the God who is present in your Word to defeat unbelief and overcome doubt. You are the all in all, my joy, my life here and hereafter. I have to say it again: Heaven has to last forever; for that's how long it will take for me to adequately express my thanks. Just let me make a sort of down payment on that worship now by a life that more and more reflects the faith created and sustained by listening to your Word. Amen.

I.

John 21:15-17 – **When they had finished eating, Jesus said to Simon Peter, "Simon son of John, do you love me more than these?" "Yes, Lord," he said, "you know that I love you." Jesus said, "Feed my lambs." Again Jesus said, "Simon son of John, do you love me?" He answered, "Yes, Lord, you know that I love you." Jesus said, "Take care of my sheep." The third time he said to him, "Simon son of John, do you love me?" Peter was hurt because Jesus asked him the third time, "Do you love me?" He said, "Lord, you know all things; you know that I love you." Jesus said, "Feed my sheep."**

Again we note it: Jesus always has time for the specific, individual needs of his disciples. And again we note as well that whenever Jesus asks a question, it isn't because he doesn't know the answer; it's because the one being questioned needs to consider and learn something more about himself and then, still more important, about Jesus' love and grace.

But was there ever a more anguished and yet still love-filled question and answer session than this one that Jesus has with Peter? Each line leaves us breathless before Jesus' grace and at the same time almost heartbroken in pity for Peter.

Peter needed this unique session with Jesus. What is it especially that the Lord knew about Peter that made this heart-rending conversation necessary? It is the condition of Peter's own heart and soul, a condition that Peter might have shared with no one. But Jesus knew. We remember well what Peter had done, and so too did Peter. After declaring so boldly his devotion to Jesus and even his willingness to die with and for him, Peter, with equal boldness—even with oaths and curses—had denied that he even knew Jesus. We remember too how at Peter's final denial, the already bruised and spat-upon Jesus turned and looked at Peter while Jesus was passing from one court to the other. That look, so painful and pathetic, had stirred in Peter a deep anguish of soul; he went out and wept bitter tears of repentance.

Since that time Jesus has appeared to all of the disciples more than once and restored their faith in him and in his redeeming work by that repeated greeting: "Peace be with you." Peter expressed no outward doubts that he was included in the greeting. Nevertheless, there may well have been some troubling things still going on in his heart and soul. Did you catch it even on Easter Sunday? The angel at the tomb told the women, "Go, tell his disciples *and Peter* . . ." Why this singling out of Peter? If the women reported exactly the words of the angel, what might Peter conclude from that special mention? Should he conclude that he was special because of the mention of his name? Or might he have been more likely to wonder if he was no longer considered a disciple since his name was mentioned separately? This discourse with Jesus inclines us to the second opinion.

Now consider the discourse itself. If Peter nurtured in his soul doubts about the continuing love of Jesus for him, then these questions must have pierced deep into his heart. Three times Jesus takes Peter's own earlier words into his questions. Jesus asks three times, the same number of times that Peter had denied him. Even more than that, Jesus trims the question each time he asks it: (1) Do you love me more than these?—that had been proud Peter's boast; (2) Do you love me?—be it more or less; (3) And then the third time Jesus changes the Greek verb for love to a word that means really nothing more than the love of friends—so much as to ask him, "Are we friends?" That's why Peter was so grieved by this third question, not just because it was the third time that Jesus asked, but because of the change in the very nature of the love that Jesus was questioning.

Note too that Jesus does not address Peter with that name, Peter; that was the name Jesus had given him after Peter's earlier bold and correct confession of faith that Jesus was the Christ, the Son of the living God (Matthew 16:13-19). With Jesus not calling him by that name and then with the form that these questions took, it is a wonder that Peter did not collapse and dissolve in tears not just at the questions but at the way each one was put.

Given that, as Peter himself says, Jesus knows all things, why did Jesus put Peter through this ordeal? That Jesus always takes special care to meet the specific needs of those he loves may provide the answer. We may well understand it too if we have memories of some things we did in our past that we consider all but unforgivable. It may haunt us for years, perhaps all the way to the grave: How could I have done such a thing? Such things!? How can God love such a person? How can he forgive me when I cannot forgive myself?

We note it yet again, as we did with Jesus' very special consideration for Thomas the week after Easter: What Jesus did for Thomas and what he here does with Peter is not only for the benefit of Thomas and Peter. It is for our benefit too when we find our souls in the condition of one or the other. When doubt plagues us and unbelief threatens—those greatest sins of all—we have the example of Jesus' dealing with Thomas for our comfort and encouragement. When we have a past that haunts us and always threatens to push us into the abyss of despair, we have this exchange with Peter to pull us out of the abyss and back again to trust in the Savior's unfailing love and grace.

For it is out of love that Jesus deals here with Peter as he does. He needs to cure any lingering or hidden despair in Peter's soul. He wants to give Peter the antidote for when, in the future, the recollection of his sin might yet again threaten Peter with despair.

In our next meditation we will consider Peter's answers and Jesus' reply. For now it is enough to focus on this so important truth about ourselves and about our Savior. The devil's spiciest temptations usually come with the suggestion that the sin really isn't all that bad. And sometimes, as was the case with Peter in the high priest's courtyard, the temptation comes so quickly and with such force that we don't even think about it; we just fall! And then when we have fallen for the devil's lie, whether from a sudden or from a prolonged attack, he follows up with, "You did what!? And you think you can play God for a fool and expect his pardon? Don't be ridiculous! There is nothing for you but the doom of Judas, a doom you richly deserve! You might just as well continue in your sins; you are lost anyway!"

If you have not been down that path, thank God for it! But you perhaps know someone who has traveled that despair-paved road. Even if you do not know someone like that, you can be sure that, like Peter, there are those around you who carry just such a burden hidden deep within; they share the burden with no one and that makes the load all the more crushing.

What, then, shall we say to ourselves if we totter on the brink of such despair? What shall we say to those we know who we might suspect suffer those deep wounds and scars in the memory and on the soul? Go back to the way that Jesus was with Peter. Jesus knew the ache in his heart. Jesus knew the sin that caused it. Jesus had that all in mind as he hung on the cross, as he suffered willingly—and for what? For the sins of the world, yes, even for the sin whose weight crushes the soul of the sinner long after the dread deed was done. That sin did not crush the Savior! In love he bore it. In grace he paid its penalty. And now, still today, he draws near to the sinner. He shows us the nail prints and the wounded side. And now, still today, there is for us as there was for Peter the question, *Do you love me?* Our answer:

> O Lord Jesus, you confront me in my sins and in my guilt and ask if I love you. Clearly I have not loved you as much as you love me. For I am dust, worthy of being trampled underfoot. I am guilty, deserving of the penalty of all my sin and shame. I am without excuse, without, therefore, any claim on your love and pardon. Nevertheless, you have loved me more than I loved you. You have loved me to death on the cross. You have loved me in the preservation of your powerful Word and sacraments so that from them I may learn of your love and in faith embrace your forgiving grace. And so, not on my love for you do I rely but solely and alone on your love for me so perfectly proven on the cross and given in the gospel. Risen Savior, trusting in your work and Word, I rise from my sorry state and rejoice in your resurrection and its promise of my own. Love me still in my need until that day in heaven when I will finally love you perfectly. Amen.

II.

We noted earlier that the first two times that Jesus asked Peter if Peter loved him, Jesus used that sublime word for love so often used in the Bible to express God's love for us; it is a word that in Jesus' question means, "Do you have a love for me like mine for you, a love that always and alone seeks what's best for you?" Peter had been so bold in his expressions of that first kind of love early on Thursday, as we noted before. He had a love that was willing, he said, to give up everything—life itself—for Jesus. Sadly, all that boldness disappeared in the courtyard of the high priest's palace. The third time Jesus asked Peter, Jesus used a word for love that is used for the love of friendship. And again, as noted, Peter was grieved by the third question and the form it took.

But now, what about Peter's answers to these three questions? In all three answers Peter uses the word for love that Jesus used in his third question, not the word that Jesus used in the first two! He answers, in effect, "Lord, I will not say that I love you more than the rest; no, and I will not boast that I love you with the love that you have had for me. The best I can do, as I have proven by my denial, is to claim a love for you far less than your love for me, only love like that of friends."

Oh, how painful that must have been for Peter! To be sure, the love of friends is a beautiful thing; but when compared to the love and devotion that Jesus deserves, a love like his own, it is a sorry substitute. Peter's choice of words has within it an anguished confession. He has learned that, as the saying goes, talk is cheap. It's easy to boast of my devotion to Jesus and to his Word on Sunday morning or when all is going well. How deep that devotion goes, however, may prove to be shallow indeed in the hour of testing, when Jesus' Word is mocked. Then there comes a strange silence when bold defense is called for. Or the love may be shown as rather cheap when the devil, the world, and the flesh come on with full force and say, "Just do this and you will be happy, fulfilled, satisfied. Forget what Jesus said to the contrary; don't even think about it."

Then comes Jesus' question: Do you love me? Do you love me more than the rest? How the question pains us and strikes us deep in the soul. I thought I did. I said I did. But now I know the truth of the matter. The best I have managed, the best I can muster is all too often: "Well, Lord Jesus, I sort of love you. We're friends, aren't we? But are you my all in all? Are you the reason I live and the one I live for? I thought so. I said so. But . . ."

But Jesus keeps on asking the question, even when he knows that the answer he will get on those days when we are most honest with him is not the answer he wants! The answer he wants is an answer in which our love for him and our devotion to him matches his love for us and his devotion to the cause of our salvation. That, after all, is the essence of what the First Commandment requires. But when he does not get the answer he wants, he does not leave. Instead, he assures that his love continues, even when the answer he gets is imperfect; for he keeps on asking the same question. Is that not astonishing in Peter's case, in yours, and in mine?

It is true that as he continues to show the perfection of his love for us, our love for him and our devotion to his Word will increase and grow. But, and we know it well, it will never match his love for us. But still he loves us. Still he keeps on coming to us in his Word and sacraments to declare it. Still he keeps on blessing us even in earthly things to demonstrate his faithfulness to his promises to bless and keep us.

As with Peter and Thomas, he does it all on an individual basis, never forgetting our specific, very personal needs and conditions. When I think I am so strong that I can get along for a moment without him, he lets me fall. When I am so confident of my wealth and health that I don't really need his health and wealth so much, he takes some of it away so that I am afraid. When I am so sure that I know everything, he lets me prove that I am a fool so that I am ashamed. And then he comes with his question: Do you love me? Do you love more than these? One by one he deals with us. And by his question he brings us again to a recognition of our need. Then in his Word he still forgives and restores joy and thanksgiving. For yes, he does still love us and so much more than we have loved him. Year in and year out he teaches us that we cannot out-love him or out-serve him.

Is that not an amazing thing? Does not the mind stumble to contemplate it? Will not the heart melt in the presence of Jesus' incomparable grace and mercy? Who would ever behave as he does toward another person? Perhaps the closest we come to it is in the love of a husband and wife in a good marriage. Little wonder, then, that so often in the Bible Christ is the Bridegroom and we his bride. Perhaps the closest we come to it is in the devotion of parents for their children. Little wonder, then, that so often in the Bible a favorite picture of our relationship to God is that of children to a kind and loving Father. But even those comparisons of marriage and parenting are but dim reflections of Jesus' love so perfectly proven on the cross and then so often demonstrated in the lives of each one of us. The reflections, however dim in marriage and in parenting, serve best when they point us to and remind us of that reality.

> Even so, Lord Jesus, keep asking me if I love you. And then overwhelm me with the reality that however much I may love you, you have loved me more and still love me more. Yes, by the perfection of your love increase my own. Bring me to that joy of growing in love as I draw ever closer to the day when you will finally perfect it in heaven. There I will finally have my goal in life eternal, the goal of praying as in Psalm 73:25, "Whom have I in heaven but you? And earth has nothing I desire besides you." For today and tomorrow, O Lord, grant

that my love for you may increase and spill over in abundance in loving, selfless service to those around me. Amen.

III.

John 21:17-19 – Jesus said, "Feed my sheep. Very truly I tell you, when you were younger you dressed yourself and went where you wanted; but when you are old you will stretch out your hands, and someone else will dress you and lead you where you do not want to go." Jesus said this to indicate the kind of death by which Peter would glorify God. Then he said to him, "Follow me!"

And now there it is: the spillover! Even as Peter is confessing that his love is neither what it should be nor what he would want it to be, Jesus heaps grace on top of grace. Each time Peter answers Jesus' question with, "I do love you, but not as much as I should and not as much as I thought I did and said I did, and certainly not as much as you love me." And how does Jesus respond, even as he repeats the question? We might be foolish enough to rush to Jesus' side and give him advice: "Now would be a good time, Lord, to tell Peter, 'All right, if that's the best you can do, from now on I'll match your devotion and no more than that will I give you; from now on we'll just be friends.' " But just the opposite is what Jesus does and says.

He responds to Peter's confession of an inadequate, imperfect love with an incomparable blessing: "Feed my lambs. Take care of my sheep." Jesus' lambs are so weak and helpless. Jesus' sheep are so prone to straying away from the pasture; they so easily wander off into thorns and thickets to their own destruction. These poor little lambs, these sheep so needy—these you want to entrust to someone like Peter, who himself was a poor little lamb, himself an ever needy sheep? Jesus, you are the only good Shepherd, as you yourself have said (John 10); you love those little helpless lambs and you wash them clean and pure in Baptism; you love those sheep and lay down your life for them. Are you sure you want to hand them over to the likes of Peter?

Jesus is insistent. He repeats himself for emphasis. That's exactly what he wants to do. That is remarkable indeed. It is Jesus' way of saying to Peter in his special need and circumstance that he forgives Peter. He could just have said that, and that would have been wonderful. But Peter was a disciple. Jesus had told him three years before that Peter would one day be a fisher of men for Jesus. Had Jesus just said that he forgave Peter, Peter would have been left in doubt about how far that forgiveness extended. Did it extend to a restoration of Peter's place as an apostle? Did Jesus no longer want to trust him in that position and for that work so vital, so holy? To overcome any such thought in Peter's mind, Jesus forgives Peter without ever using the word; he forgives him by restoring him to his high and holy position.

But there is still more. In the rest of what Jesus says to Peter, he gives Peter a very special and most beautiful promise. Peter had said that he would die for Jesus and then had denied that he ever knew him. But now Jesus promises him that the day will come when again he will be tested and face the temptation to deny his Savior. But when that day comes, Jesus assures Peter, there will be no denial. On the contrary, Peter will prove his love and his devotion. He will die the death of a martyr, and by his death, he will glorify God!

To us that might sound like a punishment. But it didn't sound that way to Peter! It is a promise that his love and devotion will grow to such a great degree that death for Jesus' sake will be an honor. It will be Peter's way at the end of his life of declaring, "All that Jesus has said is true; he died for us and rose again; he redeemed us by his blood; nothing in life matters more in comparison; life itself is but a temporary gift on the way to the full enjoyment of all that he won for us and all that he has promised to us. To die a martyr's death just proves that my love has grown and is now about to become complete forever in his blessed presence in heaven!"

Peter had years ahead of him to think of these things and to put them into their proper perspective. The epistles that he wrote under the direct inspiration of the Holy Spirit prove that he got the point. He rejoiced to be a shepherd of Jesus' lambs and a provider for Jesus' sheep. His life was devoted to caring for those lambs and sheep and to bringing them always and again to the abundant pasture and living water of Jesus' Word. Nothing would matter to him more than the wounds of the Good Shepherd who laid down his life for the sheep. For that Good Shepherd had proven so beautifully his love for Peter himself by these gifts of restoration and the promise that Peter would be faithful in that ultimate hour of trial at the end of his life.

Then to complete the picture, Jesus ends with the words that he had spoken to Peter when he called him three years before: "Follow me!" How perfect is that? What could better assure Peter of forgiveness than those words by which Peter had become a disciple in the first place? As at the first, those words are filled with power. They contain within them the power that works in Peter's following from that day on. For the rest of his life and in the hour of his death, that would be Peter's goal—just to follow Jesus.

What a great way to come almost to the close of our Easter observance! We noted in Lent that for us, Lent is all about Jesus and what he did. We noted in Lent that for Jesus, Lent is all about us and what he did for us. It's the same in Easter. Eyes overflowing with tears of grief on Good Friday become eyes overflowing with tears of joy on Easter Sunday. For see how

Jesus does it all, does it perfectly. See how Jesus does it all for us, for each of us. With such tenderness he came to the women early in the morning. With such attentiveness to their individual weaknesses, cares, and concerns he met the disciples on the road to Emmaus, the apostles in the upper room, Thomas a week later, and then Peter beside the Sea of Galilee.

"Jesus Christ is the same yesterday and today and forever" (Hebrews 13:8). As he was with them, so he is with you and with me. For all these things have been written not as just nice stories with a happy ending. They have been written for our learning, our comfort, our encouragement, our instruction. He loved the confused and the weak and loves them still. He loved the doubting and the foolish and he loves them still. He loved the fallen and the despairing and he loves them still. Which are you? Today this one. Tomorrow that one. We may change. We may stumble and fall along the uphill road of our pilgrimage. But he remains the same. Our love may falter, even as it grows. His love and care for us never grows, for it is always perfect and changeless.

And so he loves us and even trusts us with his Word to both enjoy it and to share it. And his assurance to us remains that he will not leave or forsake us. He will remain our Jesus, our Savior to the end. Oh, cling then with joy to your dear Redeemer as he comes to you and abides with you by means of his Word and sacraments! For such love as his is nowhere else to be found. In the Word and the Sacrament, his love keeps forgiving. It keeps on restoring. It promises renewed strength for the next round of temptations. It grants even a growing love for him whose love is perfect. It affords the blessing of being able to share his love in greater measure with always new opportunities. And finally in the hour of death, in just that same love, Jesus reaches out with his nail-imprinted hands and takes us up to his spear-wounded side to enjoy forever and perfectly his love and grace.

What more could you want than all of that? Indeed, what more could there ever be than all of that?

> Dearest Jesus, I can never love you as much as you love me. Nevertheless, I dare to trust in your grace and mercy; for you earned full pardon even for me by your cross, and you assure me by your resurrection that you want me to enjoy your blessed presence forever. Oh, grant that I may still grow in my devotion to you and to your Holy Word until at last I gain in heaven all that you won for me in Lent and Easter. Amen.

John 17:6,9,10 – "I have revealed you to those whom you gave me out of the world. They were yours; you gave them to me and they have

obeyed your word. I pray for them. I am not praying for the world, but for those you have given me, for they are yours. All I have is yours, and all you have is mine. And glory has come to me through them."

We are almost at the end of our Easter meditations. It is difficult to leave our consideration of Easter, so filled is this festival with joy, with comfort and encouragement. But as we come to its close, let us bring it to an end with a consideration of at least a small portion from Jesus' great High Priestly Prayer. It ranks alongside the Lord's Prayer as the greatest prayer ever spoken. In just a few verses from it, we will consider how Jesus ties together Christmas and Easter and, by implication, Pentecost, the whole history of Christianity with us in it, and ultimately the Last Day and heaven itself.

We eavesdrop on Jesus' prayer to his Father. It is a prayer filled with joy and confidence about his own work and ours too. That is astonishing, given that he prays it just moments before his march to Gethsemane and then to the cross.

For starters, we might call to mind that at Christmastime we had a lot to say about God's gift to us of a Savior. And we memorialize the importance of that gift at Christmastime by giving gifts to one another. But did you notice? We made no mention of any gift from the Father to Jesus, his Son. Nor was there any mention of Jesus' gift to his Father. That had to wait until this prayer that inaugurates Jesus' suffering and death! That's when an exchange of gifts is considered.

What, then, are the gifts that Jesus and his Father exchange? *We* are the gifts! Our mouths drop open in amazement. Just before he goes to the cross because of our sin, Jesus lets us eavesdrop on his great joy—his joy and full pleasure in the gifts that God gave him, the gifts of those who trust him as their Savior. Have you ever thought of yourself as God's gift to Jesus? What an amazing thought that is! To be sure, Jesus found those gifts not all pretty and pure and tied up with a bow under a Christmas tree; he found them—he found us—full of leprosy and warts, of sin and guilt. But he was delighted!

He shows his delight in the gifts (each one of us) by the fact that he wants nothing more than to give us back to his Father. When he got us, these gifts from his Father, we were like an old bicycle recycled by a father at Christmas for his child; the bicycle needs to be cleaned up and put together before it can be of any use. But the cleaning up and putting back together, so to speak, is Jesus' work, the work he has come to do in Lent and Easter. He will give us back fully assembled and made useful. He will give us back healed of our leprosy and with all the warts removed. He will give us back sinless and free of all guilt. For the sin and guilt he will pay for; all the filth he will wash away in Baptism. That's how he makes us a gift to his

Father. That's a thought even more mind-boggling than the first thought, that we are the Father's gift to Jesus.

In the proclamation of all that he will do for us, he will unite us with the Father and with one another by a living and loving faith that trusts and rejoices in nothing more than in that status as the gift of Jesus to his Father. Could there be a better or more beautiful way of summing up the gospel and the Christian faith and life than how Jesus does here in his beautiful and great High Priestly Prayer?

Look how he concludes this brief section of his prayer: "All I have is yours, and all you have is mine. And glory has come to me through them." He's talking about us! He's talking about our faith! He's talking about our life! We are the Father's gifts to him. We are his gifts to the Father. And as a result of all that he has done for us in Easter and Lent, by his Word and sacraments, glory comes to him from and through us. There are ways too numerous to mention by which glory comes to Jesus from and through us. We can just skim over a few of them.

First and foremost, glory comes to Jesus because through us, he gets the name so glorious, the name "Savior"! How backward that all seems. Glory should come to him through what we do for him, but he considers the most important glory for himself this name of Savior. His highest honor is not what we do for him, but what he has done for us! St. Paul makes such a point of that in Philippians 2:9-11. Jesus considers that his highest honor and glory, that he should be our Savior—a title that could be his only through his coming at Christmas, his work in Lent and Easter, and then through the faith-creating power of the gospel in his Word and sacraments.

Second, glory comes to Jesus because we believe him. It is not as though that were a great accomplishment on our part. For our faith too is altogether his gift, as we confess with Luther in his explanation of the Third Article of the Apostles' Creed. Nevertheless, Jesus considers it a great thing that though it is altogether his gift, it is still our believing! He counts it a glory, this faith that he has given and that we receive.

Then glory comes to Jesus as we confess that faith, share it, and live it in union with him, with his church, and with one another. Down through the ages that glory will be multiplied, will grow, and will increase as from one generation to another, the gospel is preserved and proclaimed. Glory comes to Jesus on a mother's knee as she teaches her children the story of Jesus' love. Glory comes to Jesus as a father brings his family to church and prays with them at home. Glory comes to Jesus as men and women and children love and serve one another as Jesus has loved and served them. Glory comes to Jesus as the faithful support the spreading of the gospel in church, at home, at work, in the neighborhood, among friends and other family members.

Not least of all, glory comes to Jesus in the effort to live a chaste and decent life because that's what Jesus has called us to. Glory comes to Jesus when we labor to overcome our nagging temptations, especially those either to self-righteousness or to despair. Glory comes to Jesus in our tears of repentance on Good Friday and our tears of joy on Easter Sunday. Glory comes to Jesus in our final sigh in the hour of death: "Even so, come, Lord Jesus!"

Yes, how reluctant we are to leave our formal celebration of Easter! But as we move through the seasons of the year, we of course never really leave it, do we? No, in each breath we take, in each moment that we recall all he is for us and to us, in each instant when we are moved to pray or to give or to serve, we do it all with Easter joy. Heaven itself will be one never-ending celebration of Jesus' resurrection and of the resurrection he has won for us by his own. If that didn't last forever, it just wouldn't last long enough!

> So, Lord Jesus, let this be my prayer, let this be my life: Christ has died; Christ is risen; Christ will come again! To you, O Jesus, be all praise, all glory, all adoration in my faith, my life, and finally in my life with you forever in heaven. Help me in life and in death to remember and treasure this wonderful truth: I am the Father's gift to you; I am your gift to your Father. Amen.

The Ascension of Our Lord

I.

Matthew 28:18,20 – "All authority in heaven and on earth has been given to me.... And surely I am with you always, to the very end of the age."

We have come now to the close of the festival half of the church year. From Advent to the great festival of our Lord's ascension, we have considered with wonder and awe the love of God for us and the astonishing, always amazing ways that he has had of proving that love. For behold, God became man for us. God lived among us for some 33 years; concealing his almighty power and glory, he walked among sinners, looking like any mere mortal. He was tempted. He suffered abuse and rejection from those he came to save. He endured misunderstanding from relatives and friends who should have known better. Church and state conspired to kill him and then crucified him. He was betrayed, he was denied, he was abandoned in his suffering. Even God forsook him as he hung on the cross to redeem our guilty and thankless race.

And now his earthly pilgrimage has come to a glorious conclusion. He has risen victorious from the dead. He is ready to ascend into heaven with his human and divine natures still perfectly and forever joined. The man who is God is, as the psalmist had prophesied, ascending amid shouts of joy in heaven, rising to heaven amid the sound of trumpets (Psalm 47:5).

Aren't you happy for him? At last he will receive there his due. His human nature will share in the glory that his divine had before the beginning of time. He himself says it in his final words to us: "All authority in heaven and on earth has been given to me." St. Paul sings of this his glory so beautifully in Ephesians 1 and so often elsewhere in his epistles. Jesus has gone to the right hand of the Father. No more will he be subjected in his body to abuse and torture. Never again will he hang exposed on that dreadful cross. Now instead of ridicule and mockery he will forever enjoy the chants and praises of saints and angels. Yes, aren't you happy for him on this his coronation day?

And yet—the day for us may be tinged with sadness. The disciples on Thursday of Holy Week felt that sadness when Jesus spoke of his soon to be finished work and his return to the Father (John 16:5,6). On one side of our soul we can say, "Good for you, Lord Jesus! You will finally be rid of all that the sinful world did to you! After all, we don't want to hang around people who have made our lives miserable either." But the other side, our soul shares with the disciples this sadness: "But now we cannot see you. Would that you would stay just a little while longer, just as long as we are here below. It would be easier then to overcome temptations to doubt and all the other temptations that plague us our whole life long." (See how we can never get over it? We always have to give him our opinion, our advice!)

But as in John 16, so in his parting words Jesus anticipates our sadness. As always when he speaks to us it is with compassion, with love, with comfort so astonishing and so far above anything we could have asked for or imagined.

He says it plainly: "Surely I am with you always, to the very end of the age." Oh, wondrous grace! Oh, matchless love! We would have thought that he would be glad to be rid of us and all our foolish advice. But no; he assures us that he, our God and Savior, true God and true man, will always be with us. That's not just the sentimental thought that we have of departed loved ones—that they are sort of with us in our memory of them. No, he means just what he said. He, true God and true man, has gone to fill all things in heaven and earth. He has in his person as God *and* as man all the attributes of God, including omnipresence; that is, he miraculously and according to both his divine and human nature is wherever he chooses to be. For it is just as he said: He has all power in heaven and on earth. Nothing is impossible for him. Nothing—neither time nor space—can limit or contain him in any way.

So it is that this great festival is like everything else in Jesus' Word and work: It is *for us!* He did not ascend to leave us orphans. He did not ascend to be rid of us. He did not ascend so that in eternity, he could forget about the ingratitude of humanity and its cruelty. He did not ascend so that the noise of the world would be drowned out by the songs of the angels and the praises of the saints. No, it's all just the opposite. He ascended for us. He ascended—paradox beyond all paradox—so that he could and would always be with us.

His presence moreover is not a fractional or divided presence. His words are plain and clear: *I*, he says, *am with you always!* He who does not lie and can never deceive gives us this amazing promise. When you get up in the morning and go to bed at night and during every moment in between, Jesus is there. He is there not as a fraction, not even just in his divine nature as a spirit, but wholly and completely. For that's who this "I" is: Jesus, true God and true man, one undivided person. When you open your Bible to read it and bow your head to pray, Jesus is right there. When you enter his house to worship, it is Jesus who invites you; it is Jesus who speaks to you in the liturgy, in the readings from his Word, and in the sermon. When you kneel at his altar it is the real, the true, the living Jesus, true God and true man, who reaches out to you and feeds you with his real body and true blood.

Could there be anything more amazing, anything more comforting or joyful than all of that? His presence and his attention to you and to your need is never interrupted by a phone call. No text message takes his eyes off of you. The doorbell doesn't ring with someone more important requiring his attention. How rare such attention is among us! His love and devotion is perfect, is constant, is without interruption. Could there be a better reason than that for singing at the top of your voice on this great festival of our Lord's ascension? And so we note it now for the final time as we have noted it so often before: For us this great event is all about Jesus, and for Jesus this great event is all about us!

> Lord Jesus, even before I pray at mealtime, "Come, Lord Jesus," you are already there. Even when I sigh in sorrow over my sins and over the pain of my existence, you are there to pardon and sustain me. Even when I rejoice on good and healthy days in the company of friends and family, you are there to share in my godly joy as its giver. To be sure, I long to see you face-to-face in heaven. But for now, in your Word and Sacrament bring me to an ever more thankful and joyful trust in your presence; for you are my God and my dear Savior; you are the giver of all that is pleasant in my life; you are the sustainer of my body and soul in weakness and grief; you are the forgiver and Redeemer of my body and soul in this time of my pilgrimage on earth. Preserve me to the end of my pilgrimage, and in the hour of my death let me ascend to the home your work has prepared for me and that your Word has promised me. Amen.

II.

Matthew 28:19,20 – "Therefore go and make disciples of all nations, baptizing them in the name of the Father and of the Son and of the Holy Spirit, and teaching them to obey everything I have commanded you."

Therefore: What now is the only possible—the only logical and reasonable, indeed the only most obvious—result of Advent and Christmas, of Epiphany, Lent, and Easter? It is that we are the Father's gifts to Jesus and

Jesus' gifts to his Father; it is this that we find in him and his Word the center, the heart and core of our lives. And how do we do that? We see it as the entire business of life that disciples be made of all nations. For what could be more important than that others become like us, gifts of the Father to his Son and of his Son to the Father? What could be a more glorious goal in life than this: that others find in Jesus what we have in the Savior at the center of our lives, the reason for living?

We are so used to dividing our lives into cubbyholes and compartments. There is a time and a place for family, another for friends, another for work, another for pleasure, another for problems and challenges, another for our toys and our wealth and our health. But given the greatness of our status as the gifts of the Father and the Son to one another, that's not the way we want it to be. No, what we want is for Jesus and his Word to be the center, the unifying whole of our lives. Then all of these cubbyholes will have importance to us not in and of themselves; they will be important when they are united together under the Word of God with Christ at their center. They will be seen as equipment in a life devoted to making disciples of all nations.

Just how does that work? Jesus tells us. It works when we see everything from the vantage point of teaching all the world everything that he has commanded us. Most obviously we see that when we work in union with the church to support the pure preaching and teaching of his Word and the administration of the sacraments in accord with that Word. Notice too that it is a teaching of *all* that he has commanded. There is no room for picking and choosing. There is no place for compromising, for leaving out what isn't popular these days or what might offend some people. If we have learned nothing from our meditations, we should have at least learned this: that God doesn't need or want and isn't interested in our advice about what he should have done and taught. Quite the contrary, in all that he did and said—whether we see it at once or not—he did and he says in his Word what is best for us and for all nations. Therefore with St. Paul in our teaching all nations, we want to take every thought and make it captive to Christ (2 Corinthians 10:5).

But our work in union with the church in spreading the pure gospel is not the only way we make disciples of all nations. For have we not noticed how often Jesus taught not only by words but also by what he did and the way he did it? His life was in harmony with his words. And then his words explained and made clear to all what his life was all about. That's the way it is with us too. Not everyone can be a pastor or a teacher. But everyone can see his life and then use words that explain his life as a teaching of what Jesus has given in his Word. The way a father and a mother are with their children is a way of making disciples of those children. The way we handle life's problems and the world's temptations is a way of showing our family, friends, and neighbors how Jesus' Word is translated into life. The way we behave when Jesus is ridiculed and his Word is mocked is a way of holding up all of his Word before the world, whether it will receive it or not. The Word directs our life, and our life points back to Jesus any who will listen to his Word. For Jesus is present there with us in his Word and not apart from it.

And that's the *therefore* of Jesus' Ascension Day commission to each of us. See in your family and friends, your health and wealth, your work and pleasures, your good days and bad, your challenges, even your temptations the goal of teaching all nations who and what Jesus is to you. For your family, your friends, and your neighbors are part of all nations, and as such, they are people who can become as blessed as you are through the teaching of his Word. That teaching begins in the home. It is carried forward with the Christian example at work and among friends and neighbors. Increasingly rare are Christian examples these days. But when you are such an example, your life and behavior may provoke the question of the one who does not know Jesus: "What makes you tick? What makes you different?" Sometimes the answer may be rich and full. Sometimes it may be not much more than St. Philip's first answer: "Come and see" (John 1:46). That is often the beginning of teaching your portion of "all nations."

The peaceful and so useful life of a Christian can still be a magnet to those whose lives in this fallen world are increasingly confused and chaotic. The Lord often visits people with the painful consequences of their selfishness or vice. At such times they may look to a Christian to explain why his life isn't full of despair or anger, even when things do not go well for him. When such people see the contrast between their lives and yours, there is the opportunity to heed Jesus' call to make disciples of all nations. There is your honor—that of pointing to Jesus, the source of your redemption, your peace, your confidence in every circumstance and even to the hour of death.

Notice that Jesus connects this *therefore* with the fact that he has all power in heaven and on earth and is with us still to the very end of the age. That's what keeps our efforts to make him the center of our lives with the goal of making disciples of all nations so blessed a goal and purpose. He himself abides with us. With his almighty power he sees to it that we have opportunities to carry out his Ascension Day commission. With his Word as he continues to teach it to us, he equips us with the love and the knowledge to look for those opportunities and to take advantage of them.

It's a sad thing to notice how bold and courageous people are in defending sins and vice but how shy and almost apologetic Christians so often are in holding out the cure for sin and vice in Jesus and in his Word. The

The Ascension of our Lord

sin and vice bring ruin and chaos and misery in this life; they bring eternal separation from any peace or joy in the eternal torment of the next life. There is nothing in that to brag about! May we not fall for the devil's lie that makes us hide like the disciples before Jesus' resurrection. May we rather rejoice in his resurrection; and then, confident of his power and his presence with us, may we grow in the ambition of being in life the disciples who join in making disciples.

> Lord Jesus, you are my Savior and the center of my life. I give you heartfelt thanks this day that you have not left me an orphan; in your Word and sacraments you abide with me every day of my life. By that Word help me to grow in the ambition to show you as Savior and Lord by my life and my words to all around me. Grant that in heaven I may rejoice to see some whose lives were rescued because you gave me the honor of sharing with them your forgiving and saving grace. Amen.

Scripture Index

Matthew
2:1,2—36
2:3-8—38
2:9-12—40
2:13-15—43
2:16-18—45
3:16,17—54
4:1,2—56
4:2-4—58
4:5-7—61
4:8-10—63
4:11—65
4:18-20—70
26:26-28—151
26:47-50—157
27:3-5—163
28:18,20—218
28:19,20—220

Mark
1:40—80
1:41,42—82
1:43,44—84
1:45—86
5:9-13—88
5:14-17—91
5:18-20—94
5:32-34—97
5:33,34—99
5:35,36—101
5:40-43—104
10:32—139
12:28-31—117
12:29—119—121
12:30,31—123
12:32-34—126
12:35-37—128
15:34—171

16:6—183
16:7,8—187

Luke
2:1-3—8
2:4-7—10
2:8-12—12
2:13,14—14
2:15,16—16
2:17,18,20—17
2:19—19
2:21—21
2:22-24—24
2:25-27—28
2:27-32—29
2:33-35—31
2:35—34
2:43-46—47
2:46-50—50
2:51,52—52
4:24-30—108
6:12-16—68
7:18-23—1
7:24-27—4
7:28—6
9:28-31—131
9:32,33—134
9:34-36—136
22:23-30—153
22:39-46—155
22:59-62—159
23:34—166
23:43—169
23:46—176
24:30-32—192

John
2:1-5—73
2:5-10—75

Scripture Index

2:7-11—78
2:13-19—111
2:17,19—114
12:20-24—141
12:25,26—144
12:27,28,30-33—146
17:6,9,10—214
18:7,8—157
19:26,27—167
19:28—173
19:30—174
19:38,39—178
20:15-18—189
20:19,20—194
20:20-23—197
20:25-28—201
20:29-31—204
21:15-17—206
21:17-19—212

Romans
6:1-4—180
6:8-12—182

1 Corinthians
11:23-26—149

1 Peter
3:18-20—185